D1601660

ELGIN BAYLOR

ELGIN BAYLOR

THE MAN WHO CHANGED BASKETBALL

Bijan C. Bayne

ROWMAN & LITTLEFIELD
Lanham • Boulder • New York • London

Published by Rowman & Littlefield
A wholly owned subsidiary of The Rowman & Littlefield Publishing Group, Inc.
4501 Forbes Boulevard, Suite 200, Lanham, Maryland 20706
www.rowman.com

Unit A, Whitacre Mews, 26-34 Stannary Street, London SE11 4AB

British Library Cataloguing in Publication Information Available

Library of Congress Cataloging-in-Publication Data

Bayne, Bijan C.
Elgin Baylor : the man who changed basketball / Bijan C. Bayne.
pages cm
Includes bibliographical references and index.
ISBN 978-1-4422-4570-9 (hardcover : alk. paper) — ISBN 978-1-4422-4571-6 (ebook) 1. Baylor,
Elgin. 2. Basketball players—United States—Biography. 3. Basketball coaches—United States—
Biography. I. Title.
GV884.B39B39 20105
796.323092—dc23
[B]
2015007297

Printed in the United States of America

CONTENTS

FOREWORD

Did the people of Washington, D.C., where he played his adolescent basketball, know?

Did the people of Caldwell, Idaho, where he played for the College of Idaho, know?

Did the people of Seattle, Washington, where he played his major college basketball, know?

Did the people of Minneapolis and St. Paul, where he played his first year of professional basketball, know?

Did the people of Los Angeles, where he made his ultimate reputation, know?

At every juncture, savvy basketball fans knew that this kid, Elgin Baylor, was pretty damn good. But did they know exactly *how* good? Did they truly understand what they were seeing when they watched him play? Did they really understand that they were seeing the most influential individual offensive player of the last 60 years?

I would have to say that Emmett Watson had a pretty good idea.

Emmett Watson would become the great literary defender of his beloved Seattle. In his later years, you could call him the Mike Royko, Herb Caen, or Jimmy Breslin of the great Northwest. But in 1958, he was a 40-year-old sports columnist for the *Seattle Post-Intelligencer*, with a moonlighting assignment to write a magazine profile of a sensational basketball player at Seattle University. And in the February 1958 issue of an utterly indispensable publication, *SPORT* magazine, Watson introduced this young man to a national audience with one of the greatest attention-getting leads I have ever read:

> If you're a rabid basketball fan, you may go right up in flames. Just a few more lines now and you will rise up out of that chair and throw this magazine clear across the room. . . . So, are you a red-hot basketball fan? And do you have a favorite player? Okay.
>
> Elgin Baylor, a junior at Seattle University, is probably the best basketball player in the world today. Pro or amateur. Let that statement sink in.
>
> All right, now that you've gone and picked up the magazine, aren't you ashamed? A grown-up guy like you acting that way. And after all that *SPORT* has done for you! So you admire Wilt the Stilt or Bill Russell: You hadn't even seen Elgin Baylor play.

I don't know for sure how that proclamation affected anyone else in the United States, but it sure as hell made an impression clear across the country on 12-year-old basketball fanatic Bobby Ryan of 214 Ellis Avenue in Trenton, New Jersey. I became an Elgin Baylor fan without, as Mr. Watson presumed, ever having seen him play.

I also can't tell you when I first saw Elgin Baylor. I assume it was on a rare NBA national telecast (yes, there really were such things in the late 1950s). But when I did, I became a convert, a certified true believer in the Cult of Elgin.

There is no denying Hank Luisetti's historical impact when he elected to shoot the basketball with—gasp!—one hand. Next came the jump shot, and I won't get into the ongoing debate as to who deserves full credit for that innovation. Bob Cousy certainly influenced ballhandling. Bill Russell changed the entire concept of big-man defense.

And then came Elgin Baylor.

What Elgin Baylor did was take a game that was essentially horizontal and occasionally vertical and make it diagonal. And so it remains.

Some say Jim Pollard was an uncredited forerunner of the modern game, and I am in no position to refute that assertion. But I know that Jim Pollard was, at best, Elgin Baylor on training wheels. East Coast diehards swear that Connie Hawkins brought a certain flair to the game, and indeed he did. But his signature move was waving the ball around with one enormous hand, and with all due respect I say to Connie Hawkins and his followers: You were no Elgin Baylor.

What, therefore, did Elgin Baylor do that was so special? As you will learn in Bijan C. Bayne's splendid biography of the great Elgin Baylor, the last person on earth who can explain it is Elgin Baylor himself. He just did what came natural to him on the court. Thus, we had a 6-foot, 5-inch, 225-pound athlete stutter-stepping, swooping and up-and-undering, and double-pumping and releasing shots from decidedly unfixed release points, adding up to a style of individual offense no one had ever seen before. Period.

I mean, even athletically limited, vertically challenged teenage white kids in faraway Trenton, New Jersey, were pretending they were Elgin Baylor.

Time has not been especially kind to Baylor, who retired eight years before the advent of ESPN. Few people are aware that Elgin Baylor begat Dr. J, who begat Michael, who begat LeBron, who will beget??? (it *will* be someone). Anyone can go to BasketballReference.com and see the resume and be suitably impressed. But nothing in the numbers or listing of accomplishments—for instance, 10 consecutive first team All-League selections—will convey the essence of Elgin Baylor, who, I repeat, had more influence on how the game of basketball is played than anyone in the past 60 years.

Bijan C. Bayne has performed a magnificent and necessary service by telling the full story of a basketball innovator who lived a very full life as a coach and basketball executive after his playing days concluded and who also happens to be a very nice man.

But forgive me if I focus on those early days and how completely revolutionary Elgin Baylor was. And before anyone says, "What about Oscar Robertson?" understand that the vaunted "Big O" was the king of orthodoxy, perhaps the most fundamentally sound player ever. The Big O was the basketball equivalent of classical music.

Elgin was improvisational jazz.

Emmett Watson knew whereof he spoke.

Bob Ryan
Hingham, Massachusetts
January 2015

ACKNOWLEDGMENTS

Those who maintain that life's efforts are about the journeys, not the destinations, have never researched or written a book. Life is about closure and punctuation, from womb to tomb. I would not have been capable of leaving the world a biography worthy of Elgin Baylor's contributions to his sport without the love, guidance, and support of my parents, Richard and Sandra Bayne. I would also thank my late maternal grandmother, Armaka Carmichael, for bequeathing me, through both genetics and reading, her fondness for wordplay. And the brief but cherished life of my brother, Javan E. Bayne, was and always is a source of inspiration. My boyhood love of the game was kindled by the giant presence of a neighbor, the late coach McKinley Armstrong.

One reason I was compelled to donate this work to the library of sport was the collegial camaraderie of fellow sports historians, authors, and journalists. Many have provided encouragement or assisted with my research or both. Among that number are Howard Cole; Jim Kaplan; Bob Kuska; Association for Professional Basketball Research director Ray LeBov; the APBR's founding director, Robert Bradley; Aram Goudsouzian; Wil Haygood; Howard Manly; Dan Raley; Bob Ryan; Brad Snyder; and Dr. Richard Zamoff.

While researching and writing are primarily solitary pursuits, we are yet social beings, with obligations beyond the realm of literature. During the writing process the kindness of Coach Jay Schofield; Kenneth Carroll; Bob Fisher; Aviva Kempner; Keith President; Randall Fauteux; Ronald Faust; Troy Madoo; Glenn Marcus and his wife Missy; Patrice

McCullough; Angela Mitchell and Washington's premier literary patron Dr. E. Ethelbert Miller; Lynn Parramore; Marian Smithey; George Tankard; Ginger Thompson; Marj Valbrun; and Brian Vaughn cannot be understated.

Cindy Ladage merits a shout-out for giving me feedback on my book proposal during a pivotal period.

My discussions and interviews with Janet Hopps Adkisson, Al Attles, Ira Berkow, "Sweet" Charlie Brown, Coach John Castellani, the late R. C. "Alley Oop" Owens, and Bill Sears enriched this project beyond measure. The staffs of the Manuscript Division, Newspaper and Periodical Room, and Photographic Division of the Library of Congress deserve mention. The photographic collection of Dave Eskenazi requires special appreciation. Ginger Stone-Singer reached out to me upon learning I was working on a biography of her brother's favorite athlete and connected me with longtime Harlem Globetrotters announcer David Stone, who unfortunately died before this work went to print. She called me to tearfully share that Mr. Stone's memorial service in Los Angeles was replete with recollections of his admiration for Elgin Baylor, whom his widow called the second primary love of Stone's life. Thank you Ginger, and, having lost a brother myself, you have my deepest sympathies. Another David, David Dickerson, was the first media host to invite me to discuss the book.

I have a special appreciation for the faith and vision of my publisher, Christen Karniski, and my editor, John Grasso. Had they not come aboard for the ride, Elgin Baylor's literary legacy would still be grounded.

INTRODUCTION

What's in a name? The bard felt that names were overrated. I am not one to second-guess the insight of Shakespeare, although names create a stronger impression on the young. My first brushes with big-time basketball were television specials featuring the Harlem Globetrotters. So entertaining was that version of the game, merging sleight of hand with a race-car pace, that I enjoyed what I saw. By contrast, at the time, when I was about eight years old, the version of the game I saw teenage boys playing one-on-one at a playground near my home looked boring and lacked skill. I couldn't believe older boys would waste a perfectly good spring day in that fashion. Where was the fun in that?

I felt the same way about the game until I transferred to an all-male school for fourth grade, a school where the American Basketball Association's Washington Caps practiced in our gym. My classmates followed professional sports and to fit in, I followed suit. One of the first pro basketball players I took notice of on trading cards and in the basketball books by Zander Hollander I borrowed from the Bookmobile was Elgin Baylor. Elgin Baylor.

When I was nearly six years old, my family moved to Washington, D.C. The first little boy I met was named "Elgin." But the combination of the names "Elgin" and "Baylor," with their regal ring, attracted me to a player whom I read was capable of hanging in the air to release his "hesitation" jump shots. I had never seen him play. When I was 10, I embraced basketball, shooting around by myself in the Jelleff Boys Club gymnasium. I didn't know what a hesitation jump shot looked like, but I could imagine Baylor airborne for that extra instant, and sometimes pretended I was him. It was the summer of 1970. The power of a name.

The first National Basketball Association championship I watched on television involved the upstart New York Knicks and the gold-clad Los Angeles Lakers (on a black-and-white television set). Elgin Baylor was one of the Lakers' players. I saw the Knicks warm up for the seventh game of the NBA Finals, in their beautiful white warm-up suits, as the announcers wondered whether big Willis Reed would be able to play with a debilitating knee injury.

One of the first things I processed in reading about Elgin Baylor was that he had suffered horrible knee injuries. The man who once floated beautifully to score, and score a lot, was largely grounded. For me, much of his grace resided in his name. By then, I was head over heels in love with basketball, the sport I had dismissed two years before. I was entranced by everything, from my sanitary white Converse All-Star sneakers, to the unique "phffft" sound the basketball made when I shot jump shots through the cotton net on the courts across the street from my school, to the shimmering hardwood floor of the school's indoor court, to the jeweled glistening of the fiberglass backboards in the same gym. The game was aesthetic, in a pristine manner not possible outdoors on a baseball diamond or football field. Even the orange ball and the orange rims added to this experience.

As I became more familiar with the history of the game, I learned that Elgin Baylor was a local legend, a Washington product. He was also a prolific scorer, more dangerous than any offensive force, with the exception of goateed giant Wilt Chamberlain. As I immersed myself in the lore of the sport, Chamberlain's 100-point game took on the status of myth, a mix between the tales of Hercules and Zeus we read in school and the Superman comic books we craved during our free time. But Wilt the Stilt was a mythical giant, like Goliath, or the giant in the children's story *Jack and the Beanstalk*. As legendary as the 100-point game loomed, Baylor's season scoring averages of 38 and 34 points, including the NBA's first 70-point game, jumped out at me. Who was this force of nature whom writers described as twisting, hanging, and baffling defenders? And why was his name, in basketball-mad D.C., mentioned in hallowed tones by older Washingtonians? He seemed the perfect player for the Lakers, whose backdrop was Hollywood. But during my childhood, his skills were on the wane.

Elgin Baylor: The Man Who Changed Basketball connects the D.C. schoolboy phenom with all the dots of detail to the first pro basketball star of the West Coast. Who is the Baylor behind the numbers? Why was he the first NBA player to boycott a game because of racial discrimination? What separated his game from the game played by his peers? Did he have influences? How did he deal with his two serious knee injuries? How was he regarded by his contemporaries? What is the real story of his long tenure as general manager of the Los Angeles Clippers under notorious owner Donald Sterling? Why did Baylor sue Sterling for, here's that term again, *racial discrimination*? Elgin Baylor is 80 years old as of this writing. What is his legacy, and why do basketball fans, journalists, and announcers at times evoke Wilt Chamberlain, Bill Russell, or Oscar Robertson as stars of the 1960s but seldom cite Baylor? How did the scoring king fall between the historical cracks? What happened to his reputation as an innovator of the one-on-one, aerial style of basketball we take for granted today? Even with the ravages of time, in this society of instant media and disposable stars, one would think a former superstar who played most of his career in one of the two largest media markets would have left an indelible mark on his sport and the city where he played.

This book answers these questions, features many surprises, relives pro basketball's rise to major league status, and paints a portrait of a man among men. To understand Elgin Baylor, one must understand his origins and those of his parents. It is a colonial heritage. That story begins in Caroline County, Virginia, with the first British arrivals.

The first European to explore the area now called Caroline County was Captain John Smith, less than a year after he arrived at Jamestown. The earliest settlers were English, followed by the Scottish in the mid-18th century and French merchants at the end of the century. French Huguenots began arriving after 1685. Germans operated businesses in the county in the latter part of the 19th century, and people of Italian descent were among the first settlers in the Port Royal area even before the establishment of the county. Caroline County was established in the British Colony of Virginia in 1728, from Essex, King and Queen, and King William counties. It was named for Caroline of Ansbach, the German consort of England's King George II.

In the 1866 records of a planter named George Tyler, a freedman named "Suker Lewis" is listed. A Henry McCalley lists a James "Jim" Lewis as a freedman in his 1866 labor contracts. Planter William Thornly records both a "John Baylor" and a "Lewis Baylor" as his only laboring freedmen.

Arthur Lewis was reportedly a Native American who changed his surname from "Acesa" to make it easier to find work. In 1908, a number of Slovaks arrived from Pennsylvania and New Jersey and settled on depleted land in the upper part of Caroline County. Arthur Lewis's daughter, Uzziel Lewis, was born on May 4, 1910, in Caroline County, Virginia, two days before George V became King of England. For centuries, there had been an air of royalty and aristocracy in her birthplace.

The Uzziel name means "God is my strength" in Hebrew, and Uzziel is a minor male character in the Old Testament. Her siblings were her sisters Virginia, Ellie Mae, and Mary, who was nicknamed "Goldie," and her brother, James. The Lewis family lived in the town of Ruther Glen, about 30 miles north of the former Confederate capital of Richmond. Family lore states that John Wesley Baylor met Uzziel Lewis in what was called "Baylor Town."

In the Jackson Davis Collection of African American Photographs at the University of Virginia, there is a 1913 photograph labeled "'Uncle' Washington Baylor at Home Makers Exhibit." In the picture, a distinguished, white-haired Negro with a thick mustache, dressed in a long coat and tie, and what appear to be morning pants, stands, hands behind him. In the background, ladies in white blouses are looking at a table dressed with food. In a second photo, Baylor, a man of average height, wearing a bowler hat, appears to be joshing with at least two well-dressed white gentlemen, one of whom is smiling. "Uncle" Washington looks animated, mouth wide open and eyes smiling, and the photographer's caption reads, "'Uncle' Washington Baylor to Superintendent (illegible) 'You done turn' de kivers down and woke us up."

Jackson Davis was an educational reformer and amateur photographer who took nearly 6,000 photographs of colored schools, teachers, and students throughout the southeastern United States. His work was intended to demonstrate the poor conditions of colored schools in the South, in hopes they could be improved. In 1921, he photographed the segregated Caroline County Training School, a three-story wooden-framed house. The school was founded by the Caroline Baptist Sunday School Union in 1903, seven years before Uzziel Lewis was born, as Bowling Green Industrial Academy. It began with a teacher and five students. A man named Liston Leander Davis, pastor of Port Royal's

Shiloh Baptist Church, was the principal and vocational education teacher. In 1914, ownership transferred to the Caroline County School Board, which qualified the school to receive Slater Funds. The John F. Slater Fund for the Education of Freedmen was established in 1882 for the encouragement of industrial education among southern Negroes. In May 1882, textile mills industrialist and Congregationalist worshipper John Fox Slater of Norwich, Connecticut, transferred one million dollars to a board of trustees incorporated by the state of New York. For Caroline County Training School, the school board provided teachers and some of the maintenance, while the Sunday School Union was responsible for fuel and room and board for the students and teachers. In 1922, when Uzziel Lewis was 12, the Training School ranked second in reading and first in reading and writing among Virginia's 11 colored high schools.

By 1924, some 1,700 of Caroline County's Negroes were homeowners, and there were a thousand colored farmers. That ratio was rare in the American South, where, in the 1910 U.S. Census, most Negroes lived on farms, and nine out of 10 resided in the South. In 1924, a "James Baylor" was one of three surviving members of the 1866 founding of Bowling Green's Shiloh Baptist Church. Elgin's father's name, John Wesley Baylor, however, suggests a preference for the Methodist church. For Elgin Gay Baylor, basketball superstar, the princely name, the personal dignity, the professional pride are earmarks of the merger of the Lewis and Baylor families of Caroline County, Virginia. The other key ingredient in the recipe that formed Elgin Baylor was his being raised in Washington, D.C.

On September 16, 1934, in Caroline County, Virginia, John W. Baylor glanced at his wristwatch while awaiting the delivery of his fifth child and saw the brand name "Elgin." A true son of Caroline County, he liked the regal sound of it, and when the baby arrived (his and Uzziel Baylor's third son), he gave him that name. Three days later, Bruno Richard Hauptmann was arrested for the kidnapping of aviation hero Charles Lindbergh's baby. Little could the Baylors have known their own baby was destined for a life of fame and "flight."

Elgin entered the world the same year as the comic strip *Lil' Abner* (which fostered cynicism about government) and the American Soap Box Derby. The week he was born, director of Yale University's Clinic of Child Development, Dr. Arnold Lucius Gesell, published a book about infant development that was heavier than the newborn Elgin. The 15.5-pound compendium, in two volumes and illustrated with 3,200 action photographs, was entitled *An Atlas of Infant Behavior* and chronicles typical milestones for certain ages. The 107 babies studied were of American-born parents, mostly of North European heritage. Dr. Gesell lived until May 1961, and one wonders if, in hindsight, he would have documented the infantile progress of a colored baby named Elgin Gay Baylor, who was born the week the *Atlas* was published.

John and Uzziel Baylor took Elgin home to Washington from Virginia when he was nine days old. Elgin was not quite two weeks old when America's greatest sports hero, Babe Ruth, hit his last home run at D.C.'s Griffith Stadium on September 29, 1934. On Sunday, September 30, when Elgin was two weeks old, millions of Americans listened to their radios as President Franklin D. Roosevelt delivered the sixth of his famous fireside chats. Elgin was born the same year as three seminal athletes: Bill Russell, Henry Aaron, and Roberto Clemente.

In August 1935, just before Baylor's first birthday, the Colored Elks Club of Washington honored Joe Louis and Jesse Owens—the former not yet a heavyweight champion and the latter not yet an Olympic hero. Both were giants in their own community and the Negro press. Black Washington set a great store by the race's athletic titans. On the occasion, Owens said, "When white folks see that we . . . eat and drink the same things, and laugh and cry over the same things, they begin to realize we are human beings." More than two decades later, Elgin Baylor would protest that he was no caged circus animal. His story is one of how basketball achieved major league status, in part due to his star quality and moral stance.

I

FROM STREET BALL TO SPINGARN

The best playground basketball in the country is played in Washington.—Arnold "Red" Auerbach

On Sunday, September 30, 1934, millions of Americans listened to their radios as President Franklin D. Roosevelt delivered the sixth of his famous fireside chats, and the day before, America's greatest sports hero, Babe Ruth, hit his last home run as a Yankee at D.C.'s Griffith Stadium. That same year saw the birth of three other seminal athletes: Bill Russell, Henry Aaron, and Roberto Clemente. In August 1935, the Colored Elks Club of Washington honored Joe Louis and Jesse Owens—the former not yet a heavyweight champion, the latter not yet an Olympic hero.

A child of the 1940s, Elgin acquired the nickname "Rabbit" because he could run and jump. He grew up on big band music and was a schoolboy in wartime Washington during the period when blacks migrated there for government and defense plant jobs.

When World War II ended, President Harry S. Truman integrated U.S. troops, as well as the federal government. These changes brought about a new Washington, full of federal employees and African Americans who had left the small-town South for the first time. Washington was home to baseball's Homestead Grays, who played at Griffith Stadium and featured Josh Gibson and Buck Leonard as stars, and basketball's Washington Bears, who won the World Professional Basketball Tournament in 1943 and whose nucleus was the Harlem Rens, stationed in D.C. because of defense jobs and gas rationing.

Elgin Baylor's boyhood was one of segregated streetcars, loyal friends, and life as the baby of his family. The 1940 Census lists John Baylor, father and head of household, 37, mother "Ozzie," 29, Elgin, 5, and siblings Gladys, 12, Arthur, 11, and Columbia, 8. Baylor's cousin Alphine Jefferson, Director of Black Studies at Virginia's Randolph-Macon College, said Baylor's sister died young. He attended Brown Junior High School, not far from where RFK Stadium is located today. Elgin's mother, Uzziel, worked as a clerk at the Department of the Interior, while his father John was a school custodian.

The Baylors lived on Heckman Street Southeast (later renamed Duddington Place), on Capitol Hill, in a row house near 2nd and E Streets, S.E. The home was near a recreation center on Virginia Avenue named Garfield Park. The center had a pool, tennis courts, softball fields, and a basketball court, but it was for whites only. Baylor recounted for *SPORT* magazine,

> This was the 1950s. Most of the hotels and restaurants were segregated; we couldn't stay in them. There were two playgrounds not 500 yards from our high school. One had basketball courts, tennis courts, a baseball field, a football field, benches, and all kinds of stuff. We [blacks] were not allowed to play on that playground. It was right around the corner from our neighborhood, about a four- or five-minute walk. The police even put chain locks on the gates around the basketball court so we couldn't get in when the park was closed. The older kids would sneak in at night over the fence and play with whatever light they could get, but most of the time, we just played stickball in the streets.

Baylor added, "I didn't play until I got to high school. We didn't have basketballs. We used to play with tennis balls, believe it or not. Finally, somebody got a volleyball. Eventually, somehow, we got hold of a basketball."

Baylor played recreational basketball for the Southwest Boys Club and then joined the team at Phelps Vocational High School in 1950–1951, scoring 18.5 points a game.

Phelps's following season, 1951–1952, began with a road trip to play colored high schools in Virginia. In Newport News, Phelps thrashed Huntington, 50–33, and Carver High, 36–30. These segregated schools were no athletic patsies; in years to come, Huntington would graduate basketball and football standout Earl "Tree" Faison, who became a noted San Diego Chargers defensive lineman in the 1960s, and University of Illinois and 1960s Chicago Bears defensive back Bennie "The Bat" McRae. Carver's Leroy Keyes, a three-sport legend, finished second in 1969 Heisman Trophy balloting at Purdue.

The tour continued with the first home game for Peabody High of Petersburg. Phelps whipped them, 66–43, as Baylor thrilled spectators with 21 points. Norfolk's Booker T. Washington hosted Phelps in its season opener, with Baylor hitting 35 in a 78–53 romp. The Phelps team traveled to Richmond to face that city's traditional black powerhouse, Armstrong High School. Baylor finished with a game-high 21 points, as Phelps defeated Armstrong, 63–43, giving the home team their first loss in Binga Gymnasium since 1946.

In mid-February 1952, Elgin scored 42 as Phelps thrashed Cardozo, 110–42, in the second game of an Uline Arena doubleheader. In that game, his team broke Armstrong's city scoring record of 76 points, and Baylor topped Greeky Watson's individual scoring mark of 31. Phelps met Armstrong High for the city's African American championship, which Armstrong managed to win in a victory that locals still discuss in reverent tones. Elgin Baylor's reputation, earned in the schoolyards, grew as he excelled at Phelps. Longtime friend and eventual college teammate Lloyd Murphy told Grantland.com, "Let me try to put this modestly. Elgin was a god around here."

Yet, for the first time, Baylor turned inward. He told *SPORT* magazine, "I think the publicity put me in a shell. People would say, 'There's Elgin Baylor, he made All-City.' I didn't want people to see me. I didn't want to play anymore." Baylor enjoyed basketball, but not the adulation that came with it, especially since he had only recently learned the game.

Disillusioned, Elgin dropped out after two years at Phelps Vocational. In 1961, he told *SPORT's* Milton Gross,

> Several times I wanted to quit school, and I finally did. I stayed out a whole year and worked as a kind of checker in a furniture store. My mother and a cousin of mine kept trying to convince me that I was all wrong. My mother kept telling me that because I played ball so well I could get a chance to go to college if I went back to school.

But, he explained, "my marks were lousy; I just didn't care."

Baylor still played plenty of basketball but on Boys Club and recreation league teams. In 1952, he played with a group called the Stonewalls, a team he would return to after high school, and also on the Census Bureau team with his brother Kermit, whom the *Baltimore Afro-American* newspaper voted one of the five outstanding players in the federal basketball league. The Census team also featured former North Carolina A&T player Clyde Foster and former Howard University player Frank Booth. Baylor was playing with men, and playing well.

After the valuable experience playing with older athletes, Baylor made a school transfer to a relatively new high school called Spingarn, where he resumed his high school basketball career. While there, the *Washington Post* called him "literally unstoppable." Measuring at 6'5", he averaged almost 35 points per game. In his first year at Spingarn, Baylor scored 31 points against his former team, Phelps Vocational, in an 85–36 win for Spingarn. He was taking scoring, both individual and team, into the stratosphere.

On February 1, 1952, the *Post* named Baylor the Division II Player of the Week. The notice read, "'Rabbit,' as he's called, is as fast as he is tall. In addition, he can touch the backboard a foot above the basket on a jump." It went on to say that Baylor was considering college after graduation, but the Harlem Globetrotters were interested in his services.

On February 9, after Spingarn faced Archbishop Carroll in a rare contest between a colored city school and a Catholic team, James Clay proclaimed in the *Washington Post*,

> I have seen just about all of them, with the [Stan] Kernans, [Jack] Georges, [Jack] Sullivans, [Bob] Kesslers, etc. All are good or better than good basketball players, but before you begin your selecting [for All-Met honors] this year, go out and see Elgin Baylor of Spingarn. He is the greatest high school player of all time. Don't take anyone's word about him. See him for yourself.

Although he garnered some media attention, in Baylor's recollection, colored high schools were generally an afterthought to the city's major newspapers. Baylor later told *SPORT* magazine in a profile interview, "We'd be undefeated and ranked about 10th, and we're saying to ourselves, 'How can that be? They didn't even play us.' We wanted to play the white schools, to find out if they really were better. And we didn't feel that they would be."

The media bias was especially apparent when it came to coverage of Baylor's scoring record. When Jim Wexler, an outstanding white basketball player from Western High, scored 53 points against Charlotte Hall during the 1952–1953 season, the Washington newspapers called it the greatest performance in high school basketball history. In 1953–1954, as a senior, Baylor broke Wexler's city record by scoring 63 points against his former Phelps team in a 91–48 cakewalk, a league scoring mark that still stands. Yet, as Wexler himself recalled in a 1999 *Washington City Paper* article, Baylor didn't get the accolades he deserved. "I was reading the *Post* one morning and saw this real small article, maybe three inches, about my single-game record being broken by Elgin Baylor," said Wexler. "My headlines were bigger than that whole article. Baylor never got any coverage from the *Post*."

Elgin had played in Washington's last segregated city championship tournament in March 1954, when five of the city's high schools were for colored students. Two months later, the Supreme Court ruled in favor of desegregation in *Brown v. Board of Education*.

Later that month, Wexler and Baylor did get to have a showdown on the court, outside of the segregated circle of the D.C. public schools. Wexler was a year out of high school, but a few months younger than Baylor, when he got a call from Sam Lacy, the legendary sportswriter for the *Baltimore Afro-American*, asking if he'd play on a team of white high school ballplayers from throughout the city in a game against Stonewall A.C., an all-black club team featuring Elgin Baylor and his two older brothers. Wexler quickly agreed. "I'd never heard of any white team playing a black team in this city before that. It was pretty radical here," Wexler says in the *Washington City Paper* article. "But, I said I'd bring my sneakers, just tell me where."

Bill McCaffrey, a senior at all-white Anacostia High, was tasked with finding white players to play alongside Wexler. In an article for the *Washington City Paper* in 1999, McCaffrey recalls,

> I'd gotten a lot of the best players from the white schools to agree to play because they all wanted to say they played against Elgin Baylor. But the principals at their schools found out they were playing against blacks and threatened to suspend or expel them. So I had to use mostly guys who were already out of school.

McCaffrey, ignoring his own principal's threats, put himself in the lineup, too.

On March 12, 1954, the big game was played at Terrell Junior High School. More than 900 people bought tickets, almost all blacks. Another 500 people milled about outside after being turned away. "When I showed up, the police were there because kids were trying to climb into the gym through the windows," McCaffrey said. "Kids ran up to me asking if they could carry my bags, just so they could get in. Guys were literally hanging off the rafters. Everybody wanted to see Elgin go up against white kids."

The headline in the *Baltimore Afro-American* read, "Baylor, Wexler Point Duel." The *Post* and the other major dailies did not cover the game. Elgin made his first eight shots and scored 44 points total as the Stonewalls routed the Scholastic All-Stars by 25 points. Wexler scored 34 points but realized early in the contest that he wasn't Baylor's equal.

"Here I am guarding Elgin Baylor one-on-one," Wexler recalled to the *City Paper* journalist,

> and he showed me basketball at a totally different level—another world, heads and shoulders above anything I'd ever seen. He could do everything. He was a scorer. He could jump out of the gym. He reverse-dunked on me! You have to remember, nobody did that before Elgin Baylor. That's not how basketball was played before him.

2

SUPERSTAR OR SECRET SCHOOLBOY?

Mordecai: I'm just about done here, I never did know your name.
Stranger: Yes you do.—*High Plains Drifter*, starring Clint Eastwood
as The Stranger

In the Spingarn High School yearbook, the career goal beside Elgin Baylor's name reads, "gym teacher." In a 2012 article, Baylor told *Grantland* magazine that was the only career he really considered.

Upon graduation from high school, Baylor wasn't sure of his next step. He considered both military service and college but was ultimately uncertain. He just wanted to get away from Washington, D.C. Fellow athletes like Dunbar High's Warren Williams were playing sports on the West Coast.

"They always said I had bad grades and that was bull," Baylor told Dan Raley of the *Seattle Post-Intelligencer* in 2008. "I never got a grade below a C. None of the white scouts came to our games." Curtis Jackson, one of Baylor's coaches, personally visited the *Washington Post*'s newsroom to protest the lack of coverage being given Baylor and other talented colored schoolboys. Unfortunately, such bias was not unusual in the mid-1950s. Bob Gibson, a future big-league pitcher, was a schoolboy star in Omaha during the same years; he was named All-State by the newspapers in Lincoln, but not by his hometown *World-Herald*. "Back in those days, it was pathetic," Gibson recalled in 2005, in the Creighton University sports publication *White & Blue Review*. "Not wanting to sound like it's sour grapes, but they had a lot of problems voting for black people."

Recent profiles of Elgin Baylor imply that he was overlooked by pretty much every college and university except the historically black Virginia Union. Yet, a 1954 *Washington Post* article, under the headline "Baylor Prize: Area High School Stars Sought by Colleges," offers a different account, citing several Eastern college basketball powers that were interested in him, including Villanova, St. John's, and Indiana. "When you are six feet, six inches tall," the article begins, "can cover a basketball court from end to end in 12 bounces, and have such a variety of shots that the opposition stands and stares, you're a cinch to be popular with basketball coaches." The article goes on to describe Elgin's 39.9-point scoring pace and arms that reach the "inside, not just touch, the rim of a standard basket on a jump." According to the feature, Wyoming, Duquesne, Niagara, Seton Hall, and Fordham also coveted the player known as "Rabbit." "The Harlem Globetrotters and the Boston Celtics also want to talk to him," it continues.

Baylor was welcome in Boston. The *Post* article on recruiting said the Celtics' chief scout, Ralph "Shags" Shaughnessy, was quoted at a Maryland–George Washington University game as saying he'd like to take Baylor to the pro team's tryout camp. Boston even wanted to pick his college for him, hoping he'd choose Georgetown, Boston University, or Holy Cross, since either of the latter would ensure that the Celtics could draft Baylor with their territorial pick. In the 1950s, each NBA team was afforded an extra first-round draft choice to spend on a local college star because it helped teams at the box office. "If he isn't going to college, we want him with the Celtics now, and we'll get the tampering rule waived," Shaughnessy told the *Washington Post* in its article on the recruitment of Baylor.

Longtime Boston Celtics coach Red Auerbach later wrote in his memoir, *Seeing Red*, that he knew Elgin Baylor from his schoolboy years, but Auerbach denied that the team had been interested in Baylor's services when he was a high school star. "At that time I was the general manager, the coach, the chief scout, the guy who arranged travel things, the marketing guy, everything," Auerbach said. "So I'd know if that was going on. Shags (Shaughnessy) was a friend of mine, and he might have said that to a reporter, but he wasn't even on the payroll! As great as Baylor turned out, I didn't have any time for high school kids."

Hugh Beins, a Washington resident who had previously played against Baylor, said that when he was an assistant coach at Georgetown University while attending the university's law school, he recruited Elgin Baylor. Baylor actually worked out at the college's McDonough Gym. Beins felt Baylor wasn't interested in attending a preparatory institution to improve his grades, so he shunned Georgetown.

In his autobiography, *They Call Me Big House*, legendary Winston-Salem State coach Clarence "Big House" Gaines recalls Baylor working out at Kentucky State in the early fall, prior to the start of school, before deciding where to enroll. A profile in a national sports magazine during Baylor's junior year of high school cited Seton Hall, Michigan, LaSalle, and Notre Dame as interested schools. The article says his grades were an obstacle to admission, although, at times, Baylor would say his grades were fine. When the story ran in 1954, Baylor told the *Washington Post*, "I don't know what those grades were, but they weren't very good, I'll tell you that."

After seeing Baylor play, celebrated Seton Hall coach Honey Russell told the *Washington Post* of Baylor, "I've got the best high school basketball player in the world, a kid from Washington." In the same recruiting article, Donald "Dudey" Moore, of Duquesne, agreed, but added, "[W]ith his marks, nobody'll be able to touch him."

Dunbar High School football star Warren "W. W." Williams intended to follow Baylor to college. They visited Virginia Union together, although neither athlete was impressed. As fall approached, Williams's neighbor's brother, who played for the western touring troupe of the Harlem Globetrotters, said the football coach at the College of Idaho was looking for athletes. The college was in Caldwell, in western Idaho, near the Snake River and the Oregon border.

Williams's father took W. W. to D.C.'s Union Station for his journey west. Warren told the *Washington City Paper* in 2005, "I spent three nights and two days on a train. I remember after switching trains in Chicago, the whole ride to Idaho I was looking at all the beautiful mountains and scenery. I had never seen anything like it. I was in love with all of it."

Sam Vokes, who worked as both a football and basketball coach at the College of Idaho, expressed his admiration of Williams's game after a basketball tryout. Williams told Vokes there was a guy back home in D.C. who was not only a far better player than he, but the player doubled as a 6'4" end in football. During high school and in the summer afterward, Elgin joined his older brothers playing in a semipro basketball league, the formidable Stonewalls. The Stonewalls A.C. were headquartered in a clubhouse near the marine barracks. They also fielded a football team. Former Cardozo High School quarterback Maury "Sonny" Wills played with them between minor-league baseball seasons. The team was a Washington sports institution, especially within the confines of black society. The Stonewalls was run by a numbers, or street lottery, banker named John Jones.

In an April 1954 tournament, Elgin scored 29 to lead the Stonewalls to an 84–48 win over the Central YMCA in front of 2,000 fans at Turner's Arena, a popular dance hall at 14th and W Streets in Washington. The *Post* said Baylor never even "opened his bag of tricks." Big brother Kermit Baylor scored 11 points. The Independents, Temple Cleaners, and Musemeei Auto Body were among the other entries in the tourney. The stands were filled with black fans, and for the Stonewalls' games the referees were black, too.

Jones booked a game that was unique in D.C. at the time, placing the Stonewalls in a tournament featuring an all-white team of college players. The Stonewalls advanced through the tournament, attracting 1,500 fans to Turner's for its finals game against the white collegiate team, which was called Maryland A.C. The nucleus of the Maryland team, also called the College Park Merchants, was the Maryland University basketball team starring All-Atlantic Coast Conference guard and future NBA All-Star Gene Shue. Georgetown's Tommy O'Keefe and former LaSalle star Bud Donnelly also represented the collegians. Hugh Beins of Georgetown, who played in the game, described the crowd as "electric" and said both squads were "loaded." Shue got things rolling with a basket from midcourt, while Baylor answered with a twisting layup. When Maryland went up, 7–5, Elgin began to assert himself against the collegians. By the end of the first quarter, he had scored 16. He hit from the key and the foul circle. The teams stayed within 10 points of each other in the first half, as the Stonewalls led at intermission, 43–37. Beins said one of Elgin's larger brothers ran over him twice during the contest but, each time, offered him a hand up with a smile.

Shue, who was guarded by 6'4" former North Carolina College star Ernie "Hands" Warlick, was the only reason the contest did not become a complete joke. The first five minutes of the second half were close. The D.C. squad, however, dominated the backboards. Baylor outscored the older star, 38–34, and the Stonewalls won, 90–68. Not only did the teenaged Elgin Baylor outplay Gene Shue, but he also earned tournament honors for outstanding scorer and rebounder. The game against the collegians was so popular that a rematch was played during the same tournament. Prior to the second game, University of Maryland player Ralph Greco vowed that Baylor wasn't going to score "any 38 on [him]!" Elgin scored 47 in the second game and 116 in the tournament. Shue was named outstanding defender.

"I think about that game all the time and still shake my head," says James "Sleepy" Harrison, who played alongside Baylor with Stonewalls A.C. and against him on the playgrounds. "Here you have Shue, a college senior, and Elgin's still in high school, but he put him in his hip pocket."

The next week, in a *JET* magazine photo captioned "The Long and the Short of It," Mrs. Baylor, whose name was misspelled "Ezziel," was pictured standing between her 6'9" son Kermit and Elgin, whom the caption listed as 6'6". The sons are wearing their Stonewalls uniforms, with Elgin in kneepads.

As part of the Stonewalls, the Baylor brothers continued to face such semipro competition as Seaboard Finance, a team led by Villanova's Nick McGuire and Rhode Island University's Bob Mitchell. In August, playing the Tradesmen summer league team, Elgin scored 43 in an 86–68 win over his old Spingarn mates at D.C.'s Number Two branch of the Police Boys Club. In his next outing, his 38 led the Tradesmen over the Foxy Dodgers, 85–66, in the Boys Club quarterfinals.

That same summer, while Baylor was enjoying his time with the Stonewalls, Coach Sam Vokes called him two or three times a week, salivating about his talents and thinking about where the youngster could take the College of Idaho's tiny athletic program. Despite having played only sandlot football, Baylor accepted a football scholarship to the College of Idaho, a nearly all-white school with an enrollment of 450 students. "I thought, well, I'll play football, and maybe I can make the basketball team, too." Make the basketball team? The kid who scored 63 in a high school game—still a D.C. record—and outplayed All-ACC gun Gene Shue and his Maryland team?

* * *

The first black athlete on the Idaho campus was Raleigh C. "R. C." Owens, born in Shreveport, Louisiana, and raised in Santa Monica, California. Owens had arrived in 1952 to play football and basketball, along with four high school football teammates on a team of 28. When Owens enrolled, the only other black student was an African. "There were no black girls on the campus," Owens said. "We didn't have any segregation. I can remember myself and a group of guys my first year—we wanted to go to Garden City, 26 miles from Boise. They had slot machines there." The bus pulled up in Garden City, and the Idaho players walked into a restaurant. "The booths were all taken," recalled Owens. "Only the counter was open. I was the next to last guy." The waitress took every order until she got to R. C.

"I'm sorry," she said. "We don't serve Negroes."

"I don't eat Negroes; I want a hamburger." The teammates looked at one another. One by one they rose from their stools and left.

When Owens was a junior in his third year, Vokes brought in Elgin Baylor, Chicago guard Carl Lewis, and Larry Patterson of Little Rock. Owens roomed with Baylor for a time. Later, Owens and three others took a furnished basement apartment. Baylor, Lewis, and the other black players lived in housing across the street from the campus.

Owens was a great football end, a Little All-American player, a National Association of Intercollegiate Athletics receiving leader, and the first receiver anyone had seen wear gloves on the field. ("They told me, 'gloves are not part of football,'" said the Santa Monica native, "but it was cold, so I wore gloves with rabbit fur lining, and I did not drop any balls.") As a double-scholarship athlete, Owens would prepare for basketball during gridiron season by hitting the court after dinner. He totaled more than 600 rebounds for the 1952–1953 team, 27.6 per game, but still managed to be awed by his new teammate in 1954. "I would take a peek at the gym," said Owens,

> and I saw this guy Elgin Baylor, and I would stand and watch him play. I said, "Oh my goodness, look at this guy play! Look at the things he does!" I could hardly get myself over to football practice. I would tell the guys back in Santa Monica, "We've got this guy at the College of Idaho that is unreal. He does things I have never seen before. It's going to be a joy to play with him."

In the fall of 1954, Baylor went to see the College of Idaho Coyotes play football. Said Owens,

I had a great game. I caught 15 passes. When I came off the field, I knew he was watching. He said to me, "R, I'm going to go out for football." I said, "Hey man, don't do that. You've got such a great career ahead of you in basketball. Don't put that in your head. You could get hurt out here, and ruin your career."

Elgin told him, "I've been playing intramural, and I can catch and run." "That's not what I'm talking about," said Owens. "That's not the same thing. Please don't do that. I'm looking forward to playing with you on the basketball team."

W. W. Williams made Elgin's travel arrangements—by train. He arrived in Caldwell a couple weeks before practice began and was fitted for football gear on a Sunday. Practices were rained out for the next three days. Vokes took the players indoors to work out in the gym. Baylor grabbed a basketball and shot around. According to a 1950s *Sports Illustrated* feature on the team, Baylor told Vokes, "I'd rather play basketball than football."

"Maybe you'd better," agreed Vokes.

The College of Idaho played in the Pacific Northwest Intercollegiate Conference. Coach Vokes had what it took to run a respectable sports program at a remote school with less than 500 students. Since his basketball team generated only $2.40 in gate receipts for one game his first year, he convinced school officials to admit athletes who fell well short of admissions standards at other schools. It worked for Idaho, and other coaches would follow Vokes's model.

The Idaho Coyotes' home gym seated about 500, but fans lined the walls to see the new team at the beginning of the 1954 season. "People packed the gyms to see something different," said R. C. Owens. "They let in as many people as possible. We had a following in the Northwest and on the Pacific Coast." Baylor scored 57 and 46 points in his first two starts. The Coyotes went undefeated in its conference for the 1954–1955 season, winning 18 consecutive games from December 23 through February 25. As a freshman playing center for the varsity, Baylor averaged 31.3 points per game. Owens led the team with 532 rebounds. Baylor's 492 boards, although second for the team, still ranks third in school history. "He was a great, great player," said Owens.

He led the way in scoring, and he and I were the only two guys on the same team that had double-doubles in scoring and rebounding the whole year. We were cleaning the boards on every missed shot, and every tip-in is considered a rebound and a shot. Rabbit was way ahead of himself in a lot of areas, like tip-ins, and going toward his shot.

Baylor scored a record 53 points in his last conference game of the season, at Nyssa, Oregon, just south of Ontario, Oregon. In addition to being named small-college All-American during his first semester in Caldwell, Baylor carried another important average: an academic B.

Opponents were stymied by the agility and acrobatics of Baylor and Owens. "They were so awed," Owens said, that opposing players used no racial slurs or dirty play against them.

> Even the referees couldn't do their job. I remember we played Montana State in the NAIA district playoffs. The refs had never seen a player like Rabbit, and they called three or four infractions on him. They had never seen a guy play like that, and they said, "He took steps." We said, "How can you call that? He didn't take steps; you've never seen this stuff before." We ended up losing that game.

Owens was one of few players who could catch Baylor's look-away passes. When Coyote teammates shot free throws, they would try to aim their second shot so it would carom off the rim in Baylor's direction. When it worked, Baylor would float high and guide the ball through the net. *Sports Illustrated* reported,

> He jumped high in the air, shot his wrists over the rim before reaching the peak of his jump, and whipped the ball downward into the net with a sharp wrist snap. Then, while he completed upward motion to the peak of his jump and appeared thus to hang suspended in air, he quickly brought his hands downward in a parenthetical arc to the bottom of the net and caught the ball as it emerged from the net.

According to Owens, the *Boise Statesman*, *Portland Oregonian*, *Reno Gazette*, *Seattle Times*, and *Seattle Post-Intelligencer* all took note of the Coyotes' exploits. Baylor recommended that Coach Vokes offer a scholarship to another Washington athlete, a baseball catcher and basketball player with one arm named Gary Mays. Vokes was incredulous that a one-armed man could be a talented basketball contributor, but Baylor persisted. Mays had held Baylor to 18 points in a public school championship game. A Seattle newspaper reported that "One-Arm" Gary Mays and Baylor staged "Globetrotter-like" dribbling exhibitions during half-times. The Coyotes actually played the Globetrotters once, and Baylor tried to match the magicians trick for trick. "Listen, kid," the Globies warned him, "we put on the show around here." They proceeded to embarrass him, so he headed for their locker room after the game, too ashamed to enter his own.

"Students liked us. The community liked us," said Owens. "They saw things they had never seen before. . . . We played the University of Nevada, Gonzaga, and Montana State, and we showed these guys how to play basketball!" The basketball program that had total gate receipts of $2.40 a few years earlier was now turning away fans from sold-out games.

In 1955, Baylor was faced with a decision when the College of Idaho began deemphasizing sports and then eliminated its basketball program. "One-Arm" Mays, who had gone west to join his East Coast friends, turned down an offer from the Harlem Globetrotters, and he and Warren Williams, both homesick, returned to D.C. Owens put his leaping ability to use in the NFL from 1957 to 1964, most notably with the San Francisco 49ers, where he earned the nickname "Alley Oop" Owens when he became the target for quarterback Y. A. Tittle's "alley oop" passes into the end zone. Baylor was unsure what to do. He liked Coach Vokes and considered following him to his next coaching post if the college disbanded its athletic programs. Vokes discussed employment with a few western junior colleges and the University of Portland.

In 1955, Baylor walked into his dorm and listened to a radio broadcast of the National Collegiate Athletic Association championship game between Bill Russell's undefeated University of San Francisco Dons and All-American Tom Gola's LaSalle Explorers. In Bert Randolph Sugar's book *The Sports 100*, Baylor says, "I'd read about Bill Russell and Tom Gola in the papers, but just to listen to this game on the radio was like seeing them play. I could see them blocking the shots and rebounding and scoring. It was so exciting—it was better than any game I had ever seen." Using his vivid imagination, Baylor thought seriously for the first time about playing major college ball. He shared his thoughts with his teammates. A rumor spread on campus: "Elgin Baylor is leaving C of I!"

By the mid-1950s, black players were beginning to make their presence known in West Coast college basketball. In 1947, the University of California, Los Angeles's Don Barksdale was the first black player named consensus All-American, and he played on the 1948 U.S. Olympic team. Andy Johnson had played for Coach Mush Toron at the University of Portland from 1950 to 1953, where he scored 1,000 points and averaged 20 rebounds. In 1955, the University of San Francisco started Bill Russell, Hal Perry, and K. C. Jones, with Warren Baxter coming off the bench. The 1955 UCLA team starred Willie "The Whale" Naulls, Morrie Taft, and Johnny Moore. The Bruins just missed out on a big prize from their own backyard: Compton High School coach Ken Fagan, who also refereed Pac-8 conference games, tried to steer his star player, 6'7" Woody Sauldsberry, toward UCLA, but a scout named Al Tabor recruited "Saulds" for a historically black college called Texas Southern. With standout player Sauldsberry, UCLA coach John Wooden could have won a national championship a decade before the 1965 team that starred Gail Goodrich and Walt Hazzard. Sauldsberry would go on to win the NBA's Rookie of the Year award the year before Baylor entered the league.

Not all schools and teams were receptive to black players on the court, however. In New Orleans in 1956, basketball's Sugar Bowl tournament, which accompanied its better-known football counterpart, was to host Kentucky, Dayton, Notre Dame, and St. Louis University. The three Catholic schools—St. Louis, Notre Dame, and Dayton—withdrew from the tourney in protest of Louisiana's law forbidding interracial athletics. Coach Adolph Rupp of Kentucky—who was considered a bigot by some and a product of the times by others—was unconcerned by the prejudicial law. Rupp convinced Alabama, Virginia, and Houston to join his team in the Sugar Bowl, and while the quality of basketball was not what it would have been with the other regional powers, the show went on. Less than a decade later, Kentucky would face a Seattle University squad featuring Elgin Baylor and two other black players.

3

"I WAS SCARED TO DEATH. IT WAS MY FIRST FLIGHT."

Go West, young man, and grow up with the country.—Horace Greeley

Elgin Baylor's exploits in Idaho drew the attention of Seattle University basketball coach Al Brightman, but Brightman needed help bringing Baylor out West. Serving as middleman in the recruitment process was Westside Ford auto dealer and Seattle Chieftains booster Ralph Malone. Malone called Baylor, said his brother-in-law was traveling to nearby Boise on business, and asked the athlete to fly back with his relative and visit Seattle University. "I thought about it a day or two," Baylor recalled to the *Seattle Post-Intelligencer* in 2008. "We rode in a Piper Cub, a four-seater, and I was scared to death. It was my first flight." The man whose name would become synonymous with basketball and flight was a nervous plane passenger.

On the verge of becoming a boomtown at the time, Seattle proved an impressive city to Baylor. Boeing was then developing its 707—the world's first successful commercial jet airliner, substantially larger than the plane Baylor had to ride in to Seattle—which it would introduce in 1958. Although Seattle's black population numbered a little less than 5 percent in the mid- to late 1950s, the city seemed to offer promising opportunities. It was home to a vibrant black music scene that launched the careers of Ray Charles, Quincy Jones, and Ernestine Anderson, and it was a place where black professionals like Dr. Walter Scott Brown, a well-regarded black plastic surgeon who also helped recruit Baylor, found success.

Coach Brightman and booster Malone suggested to Baylor that he would thrive at a larger school like Seattle University, which had a better social network for black students and a stronger track record for black athletes. Seattle's 1954–1955 basketball team had featured two black forwards, Larry Giles and Larry Sanford. Emmett Watson reports in the February 1958 *SPORT* magazine article "Elgin Baylor: Too Good for College Ball" that Baylor's former Idaho coach, Sam Vokes, encouraged him to make the move: "It's a big school in a big town. You'll get more recognition there. Go ahead."

Baylor agreed to play at Seattle if they would also offer scholarships to two of his Spingarn High School teammates, Francis Saunders and Lloyd Murphy. Baylor's brother Sal accompanied him on that first trip West, just for the ride. Near summer's end, Baylor went to Saunders and asked him where he was going to college. Saunders, whom Baylor nick-named "Pockets," told Baylor he was considering joining the military. Baylor convinced Saunders to go along with him to Seattle, saying he would arrange everything. Saunders went into his kitchen and told his mother everything was set. Baylor had gotten him a scholarship to Seattle U.

Although the Chieftains had an impressive 21–4 record for the 1954–1955 season, after the season Coach Brightman was enthusiastic about what Baylor would bring to the team when he announced the ath-lete's transfer to local media on May 26, 1955: "Just think about what a team he will make for us. I think Baylor is going to be pretty good."

Dr. Llewellyn Berry remembers Baylor as a summer parks employee in those years. "He was working recreation at Banneker Rec Center at the pool," said Berry, a D.C. public school administrator.

> I was a camper at the 12th Street YMCA Summer Day Camp and went to Banneker pool daily. This day I didn't go in swimming, so I and a few other campers went to the rec center. We played basketball and immediately recognized Elgin. That was a fun day. He was great as probably an older guy was then. He was probably in his early 20s maybe, or at the end of high school. I just remember him being fun and very nice.

Baylor was initially ineligible for varsity ball during his transfer year at Seattle, but he was able to get into some three-on-three games with his future teammates. "I knew right off I was better than them," he said. One of his teammates, Jim Harney, also noted his promise. "The first time I saw Baylor play," Harney told the author, "I said to myself, 'You are actually going to be playing on a NCAA championship team.'"

While he awaited eligibility with the Chieftains, Baylor played on Westside Ford's Amateur Athletic Union team. As opposed to today's AAU basketball, essentially known as a youth league, the AAU teams in Elgin's day were company-owned units that placed several players on Olympic teams and—in the cases of the Buchan Bakers, Phillips 66ers, Peoria Caterpillars, and Akron Winged Foot Goodyears—often beat, or even featured, past and future NBA stars. Johnny O'Brien, the former Seattle University star who, along with his twin, Eddie, had led the Chieftains to a victory over the Harlem Globetrotters in 1952, served as the player-coach. In the nine months he played with Westside, Baylor averaged 33 points and 19 rebounds. Meanwhile, Westside Ford owner Ralph Malone found his new recruit a job and loaned him an old blue Ford to drive.

In March 1956, before Baylor had a chance to play with the Chieftains, Al Brightman suddenly resigned the Seattle coaching job. Some attribute his unexpected departure to university officials' negative reaction after he picked a fight with UCLA coach John Wooden upon losing the NCAA Tournament to UCLA. According to Dave Eskenazi in his February 7, 2012, article in *SportsPress Northwest*, "Wayback Machine," Brightman said at the time, "I am leaving the school with what I believe are the makings of a fine team. I hope that my successor will have a fine record."

Seattle hired a new basketball coach named John Castellani, a 29-year-old bachelor who had been the freshman team's coach and assistant coach at Notre Dame for five years. When the young new coach arrived in Seattle, sportswriters asked if he knew about transfer Elgin Baylor. "He said, 'Oh, I've heard of him,'" former Chieftains publicist Bill Sears recalled. "'What's his name? L. G. Bailey?'" "They didn't want me to take the job just because of Baylor," Castellani explains.

Castellani first saw Baylor play in pickup games that spring. By October, on just the second day of practice, he knew Baylor was "point-blank the greatest ballplayer I had ever seen," adding,

The way he rebounded, the way he put the ball back up after a rebound. You see guys rebound today, and it's not the same. Elgin
would squeeze that ball, and no one could get the ball away from him.
He could run the court, dribble, and he had a jump shot from today's
three-point range.

In Seattle's 1956–1957 preseason scrimmage against the national
AAU champs, the Buchan Bakers, some of the best AAU players in the
Northwest ganged up on Baylor, sometimes quadruple-teaming him. He
spun free, outjumped them, faked them out, and sank free throws in a 33-
point effort, helping the Seattle collegians win, 76–73. A Universal-Inter-
national newsreel of the game shows a fluid, lanky Baylor pitching outlet
passes, tapping a defensive rebound up the court to his teammates, and
moving smoothly on the wing without the basketball.

When the Chieftains met the Bakers for a rematch, Royal Brougham
of the *Seattle Post-Intelligencer* wrote, "They were playing the full-
grown men, with hair on their chests. Baylor almost blew them off the
court." Brougham added that newcomer Baylor "blocks shots in the air,
rebounds like a big cat, and passes with such speed and quickness that he
often befuddles his own team, as well as the defense."

For the 1956–1957 season, Seattle would feature four black players:
Elgin Baylor; his two former teammates from Spingarn, Lloyd Murphy
and Francis Saunders; and 6'7" Thornton Humphries of Apalachicola,
Florida. Humphries had averaged more than 25 points in AAU ball in
1954, a record later broken by Baylor.

Baylor lived on the Seattle University campus in room 331 of Xavier
Hall with cousin and teammate Francis Saunders. For social diversion,
the guys sometimes hung out at the off-campus apartment shared by R. C.
Owens and former Westside Ford AAU teammate and Seattle native Bill
Wright, who introduced the group to the scene in his hometown. Owens
never played college basketball for Seattle U, but he was a local AAU
star. Baylor enjoyed his new city. He seemed to settle in well to his new
home in Seattle, and his career with the Seattle Chieftains was looking
bright.

4

HOW THE WEST WAS WON

Butch Cassidy: Who are those guys?
Sundance Kid: Hey, Butch?
Butch Cassidy: What?
Sundance Kid: They're very good.—*Butch Cassidy and the Sundance Kid*

Elgin Baylor made his mark on college basketball during his time at Seattle University, where he led his team to history-making games and winning seasons. Seattle's first opponent for the regular 1956–1957 season was Denver University on November 30, 1956, in the opening round of the Idaho State Invitational in Pocatello. Baylor started off the season strong, finishing with 40 points and 18 rebounds in a 67–60 victory.

At the All-College Tournament in Oklahoma City, on December 30, 1956, Baylor led all scorers with 76 points, made the all-tourney team, and was named MVP. Seattle ended up with a 70–69 win in a nail-biter with the host school. As noted Oklahoma City coach Abe Lemons told the Associated Press in 1957, "We fouled out everybody on their team, Baylor, all of them. Then they put in a couple of priests and beat us in the last second."

Thereafter, Baylor quickly began to rack up big points and gain national recognition. On January 5 and 6, 1957, at the University of Portland, in back-to-back games pitting Seattle against the Pilots, Baylor scored 33 points and snared 21 rebounds in the first game and 41 points and 23 rebounds in the second, giving him a two-day total of 74 points and 44 rebounds. On January 20 at Gonzaga, he tallied 44 points with 17 rebounds, even scoring a basket for the opponent on an errant tap-in.

By late January, Seattle boasted a 12–2 record, and Elgin was averaging 27.7 points a game, among the nation's top 10 scorers. He was also ranked among the collegiate rebounding leaders, and Emmett Watson writes in *SPORT* magazine in "Elgin Baylor: Too Good for College Ball" that his "slick pass-offs [enhanced] his overall team value." Coach John Castellani told Watson, "Baylor gets as much a kick out of a slick assist as he does out of scoring two points. Records don't seem to bother him." Although one teammate made a comment about "never getting to shoot on a one-man team," forward Bill Wall felt differently: "The best thing about Elgin is he's no hog."

On February 18, again against Gonzaga, Baylor scored 26 of his total 40 points in the second half, despite facing double- and triple-teaming defenses. That output raised his scoring average to 29.1 and placed him fourth in the nation. On February 26, he exploded for 51 points and 20 rebounds against Portland. At season's end, he had scored 826 points, a national record for a sophomore, and broken the university record for field goals, his 300 exceeding Johnny O'Brien's 1951 standard of 275.

After beating the University of Portland on consecutive nights—January 30 and 31, 1957—in Puget Sound Arena, Seattle finished the season 24–2 and was invited to play in New York's prestigious National Invitation Tournament. Seattle took its victory streak into the NIT quarterfinals at New York's Madison Square Garden in a game against St. Bonaventure University. "It was his first exposure in the East on a major level," said Seattle guard Charlie Brown of Baylor's big trip to New York. A huge crowd of 10,469 fans came to see the Western phenom in person. Among the spectators were Elgin's parents, John and Uzziel Baylor, who traveled from Washington, D.C., for the tournament. With Mrs. Baylor wearing a topcoat with a V-shaped lapel and her husband in a stylish double-breasted striped suit with a hand-painted tie, the proud parents watched their son play college basketball for the first time.

The game proved a disappointment for the Seattle Chieftains, whose players appeared nervous in the Garden. "We had never seen a trapping press like that," said Coach Castellani of the way the Bonnies successfully trapped the Chieftains at midcourt.

Seattle managed only seven first-half baskets, while Baylor, shadowed by the Bonnies' Brendan McCann, committed three offensive fouls within the first nine minutes. Eventually fouling out with five minutes left to play, Baylor came away having scored 23 points, with 25 rebounds, but he had passed poorly and committed uncharacteristic turnovers. Stymied by the Bonnies' full-court pressure, Seattle fell, 85–68. Afterward, Baylor was tough on himself. He told *SPORT* magazine's Emmett Watson in a February 1958 cover story, "It was the worst game I ever played. I just couldn't catch my breath. Everything I did was wrong." Overall, however, he was happy with the trip. "My parents and a lot of friends came up," he said. "It was fun. I enjoyed it."

The Seattle Chieftains finished their 1956–1957 season with a record of 24–3. In its final college basketball poll, the Associated Press ranked them number five in the country. Baylor finished third in the nation in scoring and led the National Collegiate Athletic Association in rebounding. Sportswriters were calling the school "Baylor Tech." In a 1957 *SPORT* magazine profile of Baylor by Watson, the experts weighed in on his talents. The Globetrotters' West Coast representative, Leo Leavitt, said, "Nobody in the last 20 years compares to Baylor. When Russell and Chamberlain are forgotten, Baylor will be discussed." In the same article, Santa Clara coach Bob Feerick, whose team had faced Baylor's four times, agreed. "I've seen Chamberlain and . . . most of the other hotshots," Feerick said. "Wrap 'em all up in one and I'll still take Baylor. Chamberlain's big, sure. But did you know Baylor can jump 22 inches over the rim?"

Not every basketball leader was fond of the athletic trend Baylor was helping to set. At the annual Basketball Writers Luncheon in Boston, Celtics All-Star Bill Sharman, himself a long-distance set shooter, advocated for raising the rims. "Raising the basket a foot or two would do away with layups and tip-in shots," said Sharman, "and make shooters like [Bob] Cousy, who rely more on skill than brawn, a premium." Accompanying Sharman's remarks in the *Boston Globe* was an action shot of Baylor in the NIT—his feet far above the floor, dunking in a shot—with the caption, "See What Sharman Means?"

Off the court, Baylor generally preferred to avoid the limelight, although he still managed to have some fun. Teammate Charlie Brown remembers Baylor occasionally being "a ham, a joker." Coach Castellani's secretary, Janet Hopps, who went on to become world-class tennis ace Janet Hopps Adkisson, also remembers some lighthearted times with Baylor and his teammates:

I used to play H-O-R-S-E with Elgin and his cousins. It wasn't serious. . . . Elgin would shoot from the stands, which meant he had to
shoot in a straight line, with no arc. None of the rest of us could make
that shot; we didn't have the strength. It was fun. Not even Fran
[Saunders] could make the shots Elgin made.

But, for the most part, the basketball star remained quiet and private in
everyday life. "He was a very withdrawn guy," said Chieftains publicist
Bill Sears. "He responded to media guys after practice, or if we needed to
take pictures he got along with the media fine, but you had to kind of pull
it out of him. He was quiet and kept to himself." Around this time, Baylor
developed a facial tic that both teammates and reporters began to notice,
especially during the NIT games. "He had that built-in head fake, that
twitch," remembers Charlie Brown, "and in competition, his head moved
faster." "Everyone would make comments on it," Baylor said, "and I
wasn't aware of it until I looked at film. I didn't know why I was doing
it." After undergoing tests at Georgetown, a physician diagnosed it as
ataxia and explained that it was likely an unconscious nervous habit
common among athletes in high-pressure situations. For all his coolness
on the court, Baylor evidently felt the stress of playing to his full potential.

In the classroom, Elgin was a history major, carrying a 2.4 GPA. In
1957, the society column of *JET* magazine reported he was engaged to
Howard University student Ruby Saunders, a development some thought
might affect his decision to return to Seattle for his final year of eligibility. The two had met at a holiday party in D.C. The Harlem Globetrotters
had tendered him their customary offer to the best black players in the
United States, but Baylor didn't bite. The offer stood.

In the summer of 1957, Baylor returned home to D.C., where he spent
time coaching the Stonewalls, the club team that continued to reign,
having won 19 of the 20 tournaments they competed in. That same summer, Wilt Chamberlain, a rising sophomore at Kansas University, came to
Washington, D.C., in a brand-new red-and-white Oldsmobile convertible,
on the promise he'd get to play Elgin Baylor on the playground. Baylor
and Chamberlain played a series of games, first at Kelly Miller Junior
High playground at 49th Street Northeast and then on courts at Brown
Junior High, adjacent to the Spingarn High School campus in Northeast
D.C.; Randall Playground in Southeast D.C.; and Lincoln Recreation

Center in the southwest part of the city. Baylor was nonchalant about playing the college basketball star who would also become his friend.

Baylor may not have thought of these street games as anything too significant, but he didn't discount the importance of winning. He told journalist Dave McKenna that his pickup teams won most of the games. Although there was no social media in 1957, there was word of mouth, and on a few occasions as many as 2,000 onlookers saw Baylor play against Chamberlain in a playground or park. One interesting aspect of the games was that Baylor generally picked average players for his four- or five-man teams, while Wilt selected the best guys in the park that day. Longtime Washington sports radio host Butch McAdams feels Elgin wanted to demonstrate he was carrying his teams, defeating Chamberlain's more balanced squads.

As Seattle University's 1957–1958 season approached, the cover of the campus basketball media guide exemplified the Chieftains' big-time status. It featured a stereotypical, barely clad Native American pecking on a typewriter with one hand, holding a standup microphone in the other and facing a TV camera to his right. Two tall strips of film, wound in the shape of the letters "SU," showed a photo of Baylor inside one frame of the "S" and a picture of Coach Castellani in an upper part of the "U."

The new Chieftains roster had some strong players. These included 6'5" sophomore Don Ogorek, who had averaged 25.9 points a game for the freshman team; newcomer Don Piasecki; and Charlie Brown, expected to quarterback the Chieftains' fast-breaking offense. Depending on the size of the opposing center, either Baylor or Francis Humphries would defend the post. "We played a man-to-man, switching defense," said Castellani. "If Elgin's man got away from him, he could tail him and block his shot without fouling him. You couldn't get a rebound away from him." The 1957–1958 season would be more challenging but still feature the home-and-home contests against Portland and Gonzaga.

In December 1957, the Chieftains faced the previous season's NIT champ, Bradley University, in Peoria. In an 82–76 triumph for Seattle, Baylor scored 28 points, while his opposing guard, All-American honorable mention Barney Cable, scored only nine.

Seattle was invited back to one of college basketball's premier showcases, Madison Square Garden, for its Holiday Festival. Castellani's Chieftains drew a match against the University of Connecticut Huskies, a team with enough talent to go on to win the Orange Bowl Classic later in the year, including Negro stars Al Cooper, Wayne Davis, and Ed Martin. The 6'7" Cooper was an All-District One player from New Brunswick, New Jersey, who had turned down a scholarship to Rutgers. Davis was All–New York City in high school and a high jumper on the Huskies' track team. In his *Hartford Courant* column on December 15, sportswriter Bill Lee predicted that Seattle could be had, pointing out, "Oregon State had them the other night, 63 to 55. Elgin Baylor, Seattle's hot shot, was 5–7–17."

According to the *Hartford Courant*, as many as 12,852 fans gathered for the 7:15 p.m. game on December 22. Connecticut led early, 10–8, and then 35–32 after 15 minutes. Yet, against Coach Hugh Greer's varied zones, man-to-man defenses, and half-court presses, Baylor dominated the backboards against the tall Huskies' front line. Jim Harney and "Sweet" Charlie Brown scored before intermission to put Seattle up, 44–41. The first five minutes after the break were close, but then Connecticut went cold. Baylor warmed up, scoring 12 points in the second five minutes of the half. His team led, 71–60.

Energized, UConn fought back, led by the offensive surge of Jack Rose, Jim O'Connor, and Ed Martin. With the game tied at 83, Seattle's Ogorek was fouled at the 30-second mark and made both free throws for a two-point edge. After Baylor was also fouled, he converted both free tosses to seal an 87–83 win. He had scored 25 points since halftime and finished with 22 rebounds.

In the semifinals on December 28, against highly rated Temple, led by ballhandling whiz Guy Rodgers, Baylor suffered a cut above his eye and had to leave the game for a while. He scored only 18 points, and Seattle lost, 91–73. Seattle played Dayton in the third-place consolation game and ended up falling, 81–75, in part because their ace, Baylor, fouled out with five minutes to go.

Temple won the tournament, and Rodgers took home the MVP trophy. *Hartford* sportswriter Bill Newell took a potshot at Baylor in his "Grist for the Sports Mill" column on January 4, 1958: "Seattle's much publicized Elgin Baylor lived fully up to expectations against Connecticut, but Temple's Elmer C. "Tink" Van Patten did a job on him on the second night, and nobody had Tink on his All-American team."

Baylor returned to form on January 12, in time to gain 48 points and 17 boards against the University of Portland. Writes Dave Eskenazi in a May 10, 2011, *SportsPress Northwest* feature entitled "Wayback Machine: The Two Lives of Elgin Baylor," the performance prompted Portland coach Al Negratti to declare, "It's the best I've ever seen Baylor play. He'll be a great pro player. He's strong as an ox, too."

Three days later, Seattle was scheduled to play Montana State, a good team with a 10–4 record. Baylor was running a fever and not feeling well. Even though he told teammates he thought he might have the flu, he managed to play, going on a tear to score 20 before halftime. The 4,156 fans roared their approval as Seattle topped Montana State, 108–83, with a sick Baylor contributing 22 rebounds and 53 points, breaking Johnny O'Brien's school scoring record of 51. Opposing coach Keith "Dobbie" Lambert gushed, "Baylor's just fantastic. He certainly has a variety of shots—some I've never seen before."

At the end of the month, the Chieftains met Portland two more times at Seattle Civic Auditorium before a standing-room-only crowd the first day and a record crowd of 6,100 the next. Seattle won both games, with Baylor snagging 60 points on day one and 43 points on the second. The 60 points in one game remains the Seattle record in 2015.

A week later, Seattle faced Gonzaga and its much ballyhooed 280-pound, 7'3" French freshman center, Jean Claude Lefebvre. When Lefebvre and Baylor went up for a jump ball, the 6'5" Baylor outjumped Lefebvre and swatted the ball into the stands for good measure. Baylor netted 42 points to Lefebvre's 26. Of the Gonzaga giant, Baylor said Lefebvre was the toughest player he faced all season. Yet, when the teams played again the next day, Baylor managed to collect 30 rebounds and score double Lefebvre's output, for a total of 46 points, taking over the national scoring lead at 33.7 points per game from Cincinnati's Oscar Robertson (32.9) and Kansas's Wilt Chamberlain (32.7). His 23.5 rebounds per game also led the nation—including Chamberlain.

After a matchup against Regis University on February 13, which Baylor ended with 48 points, United Press International reported that in the annals of college basketball only Furman University's Frank Selvy (1954) and Darrell Floyd (1955) had averaged more points per game as far into a season as Baylor's 34.4 clip through 19 games. In fact, he had averaged 47.6 in his most recent five performances.

That same month, famed Seattle sportswriter and newspaper columnist Emmett Watson wrote a feature on Baylor for *SPORT* magazine in which he poses the question, "Elgin Baylor, Too Good for College Ball?" "Elgin Baylor, a junior at Seattle University," Watson writes, "is probably the best basketball player in the world today. Pro or amateur." Indeed, Baylor's point totals were astounding: During the Chieftains' 1956–1957 and 1957–1958 seasons, he scored 40-plus points on nine occasions, 50 or more in four other performances, and 60 in one game. "The University of Washington had a player named Bruno Boin," said Seattle tennis star Janet Hopps Adkisson, "and they tried to compare him with Baylor, but there was no comparison." Boin, a Seattle boy, was a 17-point-per-game scorer who was named second-team All-Pacific Coast Conference in 1959.

In 1957–1958, Baylor's 32.5 points a game was second in the country, behind only Oscar Robertson and one spot ahead of Wilt Chamberlain. Castellani told the Associated Press, "If Baylor were point-conscious, there's just no question in my mind he'd be the highest scorer in the nation."

By the spring of 1958, Seattle University was ranked number 18 in the final regular-season poll and invited to play in the NCAA Tournament. In their first-round game on March 12, 1958, Seattle faced the University of Wyoming. They were winning, 51–25, at halftime, before coasting to an 88–51 win. Baylor scored 26 points and had 18 rebounds before Coach Castellani took him out with eight minutes to play. While local media sang the praises of the Chieftains, national fans and sportswriters were less optimistic about their chances in the NCAA Tourney.

The 1958 NCAA Western Regionals were played at a former San Francisco agricultural auditorium called the Cow Palace. There, the University of San Francisco enjoyed home-team status, along with much greater experience. USF had played in three consecutive Final Fours, and Dons followers hoped for a return to the NCAA glory of the Bill Russell era, which had ended two years before. The Bay Area's largest basketball crowd ever was expected. Dismissing upstart coach Castellani, the *San Francisco Examiner* pretournament headline read, "Bears and Dons Favored," shining the spotlight on both the University of California and the University of San Francisco.

The March 14 match between Seattle and San Francisco turned out to be closer than predicted. USF led Seattle at halftime, but by a close margin of 33–31. The teams traded leads in the second half. After Baylor was fouled with 1:35 left on the clock, he sank his 12th and 13th free throws, giving Seattle a 67–66 lead. Castellani took a time-out with 10 seconds left and then, according to Charlie Brown, called his favorite

play, "Give It to Elgin." When play resumed, Chieftain Jim Harney inbounded to Charlie Brown, who dribbled a few times before giving it up
to Baylor. After receiving the ball, Baylor stopped midway between half
court and the top of the key, still dribbling. "I was watching the clock,
and I started counting down in my head," Baylor told the Seattle U.
athletic website a half-century later. "They set up their defense not to let
me drive." Suddenly, Baylor rose up and, from 30 feet out, beyond the
top of the key, let a shot fly. The 16,382 fans were stunned to see the ball
sail through the net.

"The crowd went pretty wild," remembered Bill Sears. Although USF
would make a free throw at the end of the game, the game remained with
Seattle. Even the Cow Palace announcer was shaken up as he gave the
score: "Baylor 69, USF 67." Baylor alone had scored 35 points. San
Francisco's coach, Phil Woolpert, called his performance the best indi-
vidual effort he'd ever seen, telling the *Idaho State Journal* on March 16,
"I don't know how anyone could see a better show than Baylor put on."
Decades later, author Tobias Wolff from Concrete, Washington, would
memorialize Baylor's key play in his 1989 memoir *This Boy's Life*: "I
couldn't feature myself sinking a last-second clincher from the key, as
Elgin Baylor did for Seattle that year in the NCAA playoffs against San
Francisco."

The next night, Seattle played Coach Pete Newell's University of
California team. Against Seattle, Cal employed Newell's deliberate style
of play to lead, 37–29, at intermission, punctuating the half with a tap-in
by Don McIntosh as the buzzer sounded. Seattle trailed most of the second half by seven points. Near the end, the Chieftain known as "Sweet"
Charlie Brown saw an opening when he noticed the attention his opponents were giving to Baylor. "Nobody was guarding me," said Brown.
"He had three guys guarding him like flies go to sugar. 'This is it,'" he
thought. "I knew, everybody else knew Elgin was supposed to get the
ball. I had an opportunity to score without being closely guarded." Brown
faked the ball to Baylor and then sank an acrobatic 15-footer to send the
contest into overtime at 60–all. Two minutes into overtime, Cal's Al
Buch and Seattle's Baylor had scored the only points for each side. Castellani borrowed a page from Pete Newell's book and called a stall, allowing Seattle to hold possession for a minute and a half. After a time-out,
everyone in the gym assumed the next play was designed for Baylor to
score. They assumed wrong. Instead, Brown made a long jump shot from

the very spot where Baylor had dashed USF hopes the night before. Baylor's roomie, Francis Saunders, was fouled as the final horn sounded and hit both free throws to seal a 66–62 victory and send Seattle to the NCAA Final Four in Louisville. When the victorious Chieftains flew home, 6,000 supporters greeted them at Sea-Tac Airport.

Although Baylor aroused some local controversy when he asked for permission to play for the Buchan Bakers in the national AAU tournament in Denver the week between the Western Regionals and the NCAA semifinals—a request that Castellani denied—the Chieftains stayed focused on the big NCAA contest ahead. In Louisville, the University of Kentucky would have a decided advantage, packing Freedom Hall with thousands of Wildcat faithfuls from Lexington and beyond. Chieftain fans couldn't wait for Seattle to face national number-two team Kansas State in the semifinals on March 21, 1958. Priests at Assumption Catholic Church in Seattle even moved Friday Mass from 7:45 p.m. to 7 p.m. so parishioners could be home to watch the game on TV. "And if a miracle happens," read their announcement, "Saturday's service will be held at 3."

There were 400 coaches in Freedom Hall that night, and none gave Seattle a prayer. K-State's frontcourt was imposing, all measuring in at 6'8": Jack Parr, Wally Frank, and the star, All-American black player Bob Boozer. Boozer and company had beaten Wilt Chamberlain's University of Kansas team to advance out of the Big 8 and then knocked Oscar Robertson's University of Cincinnati team out of the Midwest Regional. But K-State's coach, Tex Winter, unwittingly gave Castellani a strategic weapon when he openly opposed the proposed 24-second shot clock, because it denied smaller or underdog teams a way to counter taller opponents by freezing the basketball. Castellani took the information to heart, given the skyscraper Wildcat front line. "We had our guards fall back and double on their forwards," Castellani said of the height disadvantage. "We had never played that way before in our lives, but it was obvious the only teams to beat Kansas State used ball possession strategy, so we decided to chance it."

In what *Sports Illustrated* called "Harlem Globetrotter" dribbling and passing, big-city boys Sweet Charlie Brown and Elgin Baylor played keep away from the taller, slower Wildcats. When Ogorek got into foul trouble, Baylor took over defending Boozer, who'd scored 14 in the first half but managed only two points after the break. Baylor ended up scoring 23 points and snaring 22 rebounds as Seattle dispatched Kansas State by a lopsided 73–51. Kentucky assistant coach Harry Lancaster told *Sports Illustrated*, "Seattle made monkeys out of Kansas State. Elgin blocked shots in their faces, made behind-the-back passes, and just took charge of the game." But Baylor suffered a broken rib in a collision with Boozer, which Kentucky could use to its advantage in the championship game.

Coach Adolph Rupp called his 1957–1958 Kentucky Wildcats his "Fiddlin' Five" beause they fiddled around with the lead during games before winning. But with no scouting report on Seattle, they weren't sure how to beat them. In an unexpected turn of events, Coach Harry Grayson of Idaho State came to Kentucky's rescue, bringing some game film that would show them how to stop Baylor. According to Jeremiah Tax's *Sports Illustrated* article "The Fiddlin' Five Make Sweet Music," Grayson told them, "Baylor has trouble staying with a man who drives on him. The key to beating Seattle is to get him in foul trouble."

According to *Sports Illustrated*, after watching the film with their players, Rupp and Lancaster laid out the strategy. Baylor would guard Ed Beck, who would then screen for Vern Hatton, forcing Baylor to switch men. Beck was told to roll to the inside for easy baskets.

A record 18,803 fans gathered for the game, but only 500 of them were Seattle rooters; in addition, Castellani felt that the only black people in the gym were his three ballplayers. With Baylor struggling with his rib injury from the Kansas State game, Kentucky seemed to have the upper hand.

Yet, at the start, the Wildcats' game plan ran into an obstacle. To preserve Baylor's energy, Castellani had him guard John Crigler, who hadn't scored a basket against Temple. In response, Rupp signaled for a time-out to set up fast-moving patterns to force Seattle into a continuous switching of defensive assignments. Rupp instructed Crigler to screen for Hatton and then drive to the hoop, as he had told Beck the night before. Ten minutes into the game, Baylor had committed three quick fouls, trying to stay with the hard-driving Crigler as his torso ached. "It was one of those games that we didn't play well and I wasn't 100 percent," Baylor told Bob Condotta of the *Seattle Times* on November 18, 2009. "I couldn't breathe or anything. I could barely lift my arm." Still, the Chieftains appeared to dodge the proverbial bullet in the first half. At intermission, they led, 39–36.

In the second half, Castellani put Seattle into a zone defense, with four men out front to cover the Wildcats, and Baylor posted under the basket to avoid further foul trouble. When Baylor picked up his fourth foul only four minutes into the half, Seattle led, 44–38, but the momentum then shifted to Kentucky. The Chieftains went up, 60–58, but the foul-plagued Baylor could no longer play aggressively. As the clock ticked, Seattle play was marked by careless passing and poor offensive rebounding, and Kentucky's by deliberate offense and accurate free-throw shooting (some of it the underhand variety still in favor then).

Baylor managed 25 points, but he shot only 9-for-32 from the floor. He gathered 19 rebounds, but Kentucky won, 84–72. Rupp went into the Seattle locker room to shake Baylor's hand. Castellani was so upset by the defeat that Bill Sears had to go onto the floor to accept the second-place trophy. Castellani later admitted Baylor's rib injuries made breathing difficult for him, but he told *Sports Illustrated*'s Jeremiah Tax in March 1958, "We have no alibis, and we were outplayed." Of the win, Rupp told *Sports Illustrated*, "Against Seattle, we threw everything against Baylor to get him out of there. He is a great boy." Years later, in 1990, Rupp would still remember Baylor as one of his Wildcats' most formidable opponents and named him to his all-time team of opponents.

Although Seattle lost the national championship, Baylor was named the NCAA Tournament's Most Outstanding Player, earning 18 votes to Johnny Cox's 15 and Vern Hatton's 13, both Kentucky players. He was a unanimous choice as All-Tournament, an honor in which Charlie Brown joined him. And later that month, the National Association of Basketball Coaches selected an All-American team that included Elgin Baylor, Wilt Chamberlain, Guy Rodgers, Oscar Robertson, and Bob Boozer—the first time five black players had been so honored.

Without a doubt, Elgin Baylor's skills were helping him build a legendary reputation in the game of basketball. "He was 50 years ahead of himself," Chieftains point guard Jim Harney told the *Seattle Post-Intelligencer*'s Dan Raley for a February 12, 2008, article. For all the credit Baylor has since received for paving the stylistic path for Connie Hawkins, Julius Erving, and Michael Jordan, he was a thoroughly unique player. Unlike his aerial descendants, Baylor was a novelty because of his many unpredictable moves from the wing. His ballhandling ability at 6'5", 220 pounds made him a one-man revolution. He had all the fakes and a sure handle, and some of his spectacular plays culminated in twisting, hanging, or gliding near or past the basket. Yet, it was the combination of those elements—the yo-yo dribbling, the subtle feints, the knifing reserve layups between taller defenders—that set Baylor apart from his predecessors and peers. Where such players as Hawkins, Erving, and, of course, Jordan became known for their trademark dunks, Baylor scored on one-hand push shots, banks, floaters, and fallaways. While he would influence future players, expanding their ideas concerning one-on-one moves, Baylor seldom receives sufficient credit as an offensive rebounder, passer, or ball handler. Seattle sportswriter Emmett Watson famously quipped, "He has never really broken the law of gravity, but he is awfully slow about obeying it."

George "Bird" Yardley led the National Basketball Association in scoring in 1957–1958, the first player in the league to score 2,000 points in a season. Yardley, a balding, 6'5", 30-year-old Stanford grad from Hollywood, often hung at the peak of his jump shot with his legs tucked under him. His nickname stemmed not from that practice, but was an abbreviation of "Yardbird"—a name given him by his frat brothers because of the chores he was given on the college's yard. Although Yardley fired shots from the air, he did not knife between big men, twist his body in flight, or float from one side of the basket to the other as Baylor did. He also lacked Baylor's assortment of spins, feints, and ballhandling jukes. Yardley, who ran an engineering business in the off-season, topped out at an impressive 27.8 points a game. Baylor exceeded that by 10 points in 1961–1962, while mainly playing NBA games during weekend leave from reserve duty. In his 1968 book chronicling the NBA's history, *24 Seconds to Shoot*, Leonard Koppett reflects on the young Baylor as the "vanguard of a new generation of college stars."

Recognizing Baylor's talent and skill, professional basketball recruiters began to take notice. Minneapolis Lakers coach John Kundla had scouted him at the Final Four and, while there, tried to gauge his interest in turning pro. According to John Taylor's 2006 book *The Rivalry: Bill Russell, Wilt Chamberlain, and the Golden Age of Basketball*, Kundla's scouting report read, "By far the best player in the draft. Could we use him!" Baylor began to consider the possibility of going pro for himself, too.

Two days after the NCAA Tournament, the Terre Haute (IN) *Star* and the Abiline (KS) *Reporter* related on March 24, 1958, that Baylor said, "I would like to play pro ball." But, in the local *Spokane Spokesman-Re-*

view, Baylor and Coach Castellani insisted that the player—who had a remaining season of college eligibility, although his entering class had graduated because of his transfer from Idaho to Seattle—would stay in school. According to *Sports Illustrated*, when Minneapolis Lakers owner Bob Short consulted Harlem Globetrotters owner Abe Saperstein about Baylor, Saperstein said, "He won't turn pro," because Baylor had turned down a $20,000 offer to sign with the Trotters.

At the time, Baylor seemed unsure of his options. He told author Terry Pluto in the 2000 book *Tall Tales: The Glory Years of the NBA*, "Everyone said I'd be a high pick in the NBA Draft, but the only GM I talked to was Fuzzy Levane from New York."

Meanwhile, Baylor's Seattle University coach, John Castellani, would soon leave the school. A month after taking his team to the NCAA championship, he got caught improperly paying for an airplane ticket for Phelps High School star Ben Warley, who'd played with Baylor on the playground for years, including during Wilt Chamberlain's visit in the summer of 1957. (Admitting he broke the NCAA's rules all those years ago, Castellani has since come to terms with his zealous recruitment, which largely focused on players from Baylor's old D.C. stomping grounds. "We would have won at least two NCAA titles had we got [Warley]," says Castellani.) As a result of Castellani's actions, the NCAA placed Seattle on probation for two years for recruiting infractions, and the school became ineligible to participate in postseason tournaments.

On April 21, 1958, the *Spokane Statesman-Review* reported that Baylor said Castellani's dismissal, while it saddened him, had not changed his mind about returning to school. He told the newspaper he did not know what type of professional basketball offer "would make [him] change [his] mind." He went home to D.C. for spring break.

The Minneapolis Lakers were distinctly interested in Baylor, even though they were struggling as a team. At that point, the Lakers had the worst record in the league, with 19 wins and 53 losses. The team drew an average of only 2,000 fans for home games. The team's owner, 40-year-old Robert Earl Short, a Minnesota hotelier and trucking executive and a graduate of Georgetown University Law School, had put together a group that purchased the Lakers in 1957 for $200,000. Short's personal investment was $100,000, one he made largely out of civic pride. The businessman, who had formerly served as a World War II naval commander and was currently playing a major role in the Minnesota Democratic Party, would not be content to settle for a subpar franchise. He worked to build a stronger Lakers basketball team, starting with actively participating in the recruiting process.

Short had first considered selecting 6'8" Indiana All-American forward Archie Dees, who had been named Big Ten MVP in both 1957 and 1958; however, his attention turned to Baylor. Short flew to D.C. to meet with the player and his family. Elgin was there visiting family on a Friday, two days before he was to appear on the *Steve Allen Show* with the college All-American basketball team. "Everybody was there," Short told *SPORT* magazine, "his mother, his father, and his fiancée Ruby Saunders, to whom he was engaged after the NCAA Tournament." Relying on his skills as a Washington attorney, Short tried to determine how important the money was to the family. He told *SPORT* magazine he detected a "twinkle in the father's eye and in the mother's eye." But on the popular *Allen* show that Sunday, when the host asked Baylor if he was going to play pro ball, Baylor answered he was going back to school. He loved Seattle, he explained. And his feelings for the Chieftains were genuine.

The determined Short didn't give up. He sought the family's confidence, telling Baylor if he joined the Lakers, the team would ensure he would complete his degree at St. Thomas College, the alma mater of Short, Lakers GM Louis B. Mohs, and Lakers coach John Kundla. Curtis Jackson, the high school coach who had lobbied Washington, D.C., newspapers to cover Baylor and other Negro high school basketball players, served as an advisor to Elgin. Short, referring to Jackson as Baylor's uncle, found him a "pretty sharp fellow."

The Lakers owner polled his fellow owners about Baylor's ambition, and they were divided as to whether they thought he would leave Seattle. Time was running out for the NBA Draft. Short needed an answer. He told Jackson to catch a flight to Seattle, where they would continue to discuss the prospects of his "nephew." Jackson finally accepted that Baylor was in a prime position as a top college player and that he could finish his studies in Minnesota. According to *SPORT* magazine, Jackson told Baylor, "There's no reason to turn the money down." He told Short, "Draft him."

Short flew to the league meetings in Detroit and announced his intention of selecting Baylor, even though he was still unsure Baylor would leave college or that he could sign him. According to Pluto's *Tall Tales*, the day before the draft, Bob Short called Baylor and said, "We may draft you."

The New York Knicks offered the Lakers $100,000 for the rights to draft Baylor, a move that reminded NBA owners why they held Knicks owner Ned Irish in such low regard. Irish saw a class attraction in Baylor, who had lit up Madison Square Garden during the 1957 Holiday Festival. As cash-strapped as Minneapolis was, owner Bob Short rebuffed the team in the largest U.S. media market. When the 1958 NBA Draft was held in New York City on April 22, 1958, Elgin Baylor was selected first overall.

Baylor signed for more than $20,000 a year. Bill Russell had signed for $22,500 as the second overall pick two years earlier, but the Celtics subtracted $3,000 for the months Russell missed due to the 1956 Olympics. "He's pretty close to Russell in salary," Short told the press of Baylor. For the West Coast's first pro basketball star, Elgin Baylor was quite the bargain. Archie Dees, whom Short had considered selecting, went on to play with four NBA clubs, none with distinction. His best year was 1959–1960, when he averaged 9.7 points per game for the Detroit Pistons. The third player taken in the 1958 draft, the University of San Francisco's Mike Farmer, would play with four teams through 1965–1966, averaging 6.7 points and 4.6 rebounds. Curtis Jackson was right: Baylor was the cream of the crop. Had he gone back to Seattle University and waited for the 1959 draft, he would have left school the same year as Chamberlain, who would forego his senior year to play with the Trotters (although the Philadelphia Warriors had snatched up Wilt as a 1955 territorial draft pick when he was a high school senior).

Baylor seemed to be prospering in his personal life as well. He was developing friendships with several of his fellow basketball powerhouses, including the man he dueled on the playgrounds of D.C., Wilt Chamberlain. In his autobiography, *Wilt*, Chamberlain recalls one experience he had with Baylor and Oscar Robertson in New York City. The three All-Americans decided to have a footrace in street clothes, right down Broadway in the midst of Times Square. "Elgin started riding me and Oscar about being 'the slowest guys I've ever seen,'" Chamberlain writes. "Elg always loved to needle guys, so we didn't let it get to us for a while, but finally I suggested we all have a race. . . . Well, Elg was a great basketball player, but he was no track star, and he knew it. When he said, 'Go,' me and Oscar took off." Meanwhile, Baylor stood laughing at Chamberlain and Robertson sprinting down the middle of Seventh Avenue in their coats and neckties.

JET magazine published a photo of Baylor and his fiancée, Ruby Saunders, with the label "Engaged." In the photo, taken while he was visiting D.C. that spring break to mull over his career options, Baylor is smiling shyly, gently holding Ruby's hand as she beams. The caption captured the moment just before Baylor revealed his career move, saying he was "considering turning professional, although he has another year of eligibility at Seattle." It also announced he was marrying Miss Saunders that summer. Baylor and Ruby were wed in a ceremony at Mount Olive Baptist Church on Sixth Street in Northeast Washington. Fellow All-American Wilt Chamberlain served as best man, after the original best man, celebrated Washington basketball star and Stonewalls player Wil Jones, a small college All-American at American University, said he could not perform the honor because he'd gotten drunk.

Back at Seattle University, the promotional priority for the 1958–1959 season shifted to Sweet Charlie Brown, whose picture now graced the athletic department's stationery. Yet, even after he was gone, Seattle University still capitalized on Elgin Baylor's acclaim. The cover of the Chieftains' 1958–1959 basketball media guide, under the heading "NCAA 1957–1958 Western Champions," featured the words "SU's All-Americans," above a publicity shot of a dribbling Sweet Charlie Brown and a smiling headshot, at Brown's feet, of Baylor.

5

"I'M NOT AN ANIMAL PUT IN A CAGE . . ."

The ultimate measure of a man is not where he stands in moments of comfort and convenience, but where he stands at times of challenge and controversy.—Rev. Dr. Martin Luther King Jr.

When Baylor made the move from Seattle to Minneapolis, the Lakers team was a struggling franchise. Although they had won five Basketball Association of America and National Basketball Association championship titles between 1949 and 1954, much had changed in the few years since. Power players like George Mikan and Jim Pollard, who had led the team to one winning season after another, had retired from the court. Only burly Vern Mikkelsen remained from the team's salad days.

After the franchise lost $100,000 in 1957–1958, Bob Short had shown interest in selling the team, once calling his Lakers a "lousy risk." Reports say he would have accepted $250,000 for his stake during that time. Controversial, dynamic baseball owner Bill Veeck came to Minneapolis to express his interest but without his checkbook. Another generous offer for Baylor's services came from New York owner Ned Irish. That proposal involved sending the Lakers two top Knicks players and $75,000. When the Knicks offered a much-needed $100,000 in return for the option to draft Baylor in the spring of 1958, Short turned it down. Swimming in financial losses, the team owner made the bold decision to tie his future to Baylor.

The Lakers management knew they needed an appealing player to attract fans, a player who could bring back the past glory of the dominant teams starring Mikan and Pollard. Short and his team pinned their hopes on Baylor. *SPORT* magazine's Murray Olderman would later write, "Never before had a major sport franchise depended so much on the individual effort of one player."

Even though Coach John Kundla had briefly moved to the position of general manager and convinced legendary former Laker George Mikan to coach, Mikan's leadership was short-lived. Kundla reassumed his coaching duties and, looking ahead to 1958–1959, prepared to regain the winning record he had become known for during the past decade.

The 1958–1959 Lakers were a collection of characters. There was Bob Leonard, the former Indiana University guard who answered to the nickname "Slick." According to Terry Pluto's *Tall Tales: The Glory Years of the NBA*, flashy Rod Hundley, known to his fans as "Hot Rod," once showed up late for a game and pleaded, "The traffic, baby." In their downtime, Leonard, Hundley, and Dick Garmaker enjoyed going out at night and playing poker. When Mikan had coached the team the previous year, he wanted to go out on the town with these night owls. "We told him that having the coach along just wouldn't be fun," recalls Hundley in *Tall Tales*. But they did allow the bespectacled giant to join their poker games, where he always lost.

As Baylor settled into his new home and career, he was unsure how he would fit in with the team dynamic and meet the expectations of his teammates and coaches. "Baylor came in with a lot of hoopla," said former University of Kentucky All-American Cliff Hagan, who then played for the St. Louis Hawks.

Elgin and Ruby Baylor moved into a duplex on Fuller Avenue in the Twin City of St. Paul. Ruby enrolled as a junior education major at the University of Minnesota, where she pledged with the black sorority Alpha Kappa Alpha. Her husband—who would eventually take up fishing as a hobby during his free time—kept his focus on basketball during those early days in Minnesota.

Baylor had concerns about making the grade as a player. "Seattle was a small school, and I knew the NBA would be a big step," he told *SPORT*'s Milton Gross in 1961, adding,

> I figured I'd make the league, but I had doubts. Was I good enough to start? How would my moves work? On offense, I had to learn all over again how to play the frontcourt after being a middle man [center] in college. I had to learn to push and shove in rebounding. In pro ball, you have to learn to fight your way through to the basket.

Teammate "Hot Rod" Hundley figured Baylor would average about 15 points as a rookie. But Baylor had been hired to score, the only black player to be given such a starring role at the time. In a 1966 *SPORT* magazine cover feature on whether the NBA had too many Negro players, Wilt Chamberlain said, "The first black player with a white-collar job as far as scoring points was Elgin Baylor." In fact, when Baylor joined the Lakers, there were only 20 black players in the league. During the 1958–1959 NBA season, no team employed more than four black players; the St. Louis Hawks, the league's southernmost franchise, had only one. The previous year, 1957–1958, no NBA team had more than two black players on their roster at the same time.

Boston's Bill Russell was then the league's premier black player and the only superstar of his race. Yet, as brilliant and revolutionary a talent as Russell was, he had been drafted—like other early black NBA stand-outs Chuck Cooper and Earl Lloyd—to rebound and play defense, and as a result, he didn't receive the recognition that some of his fellow white players enjoyed. Although Russell was named MVP in 1958, sportswriters had not voted him first team All-NBA—in fact, no centers were named among the top five players. The Hawks' strong forward, Bob Pettit, fourth in the MVP voting, was among those selected ahead of Russell.

But Baylor, one of the first players selected early in the NBA Draft as a scorer and star, would stand out from his peers. "The early black player had all the skills, except the shooting skills," says Celtics legend Bob Cousy in *Tall Tales*. "The first good black shooter was Elgin Baylor."

It didn't take long for Baylor to hit his stride on the court. "After a couple weeks of practice, I knew I could play," Baylor told *SPORT* in 1961. At the time, several recent developments in professional basketball helped pave the way for Baylor's success. In 1951, as a reaction to George Mikan's dominance in the low post, the free-throw lane had been widened from six feet to 12 to move the giant Laker center away from the basket. The now-wider lane meant more operating space for Baylor and facilitated his penetration into the lane. The institution of the 24-second clock, devised by Syracuse Nationals owner Danny Biasone in 1954, to eliminate stalling tactics would also prove beneficial to Baylor. Opposing defenses could not hold the basketball to limit a forward's possessions, and as a result, more points could be scored. During the first season of this new rule, average NBA scores had jumped from 79.5 to 93.1 points per game, and for the first time ever, one team, the Boston Celtics, had averaged more than 100 points per game. The faster-paced game was tailor-made for Baylor's scoring prowess.

Baylor made his NBA debut on October 22 against Cincinnati. On the opening center jump, Lakers center Jim Krebs tapped the ball to Baylor. The rookie glided down court with a dribble, raced past Royals forward Jack Twyman, and laid the basketball in uncontested. In 1958, *Sports Illustrated* ran a feature on the impressive rookie and reported that Bob Short, who was sitting behind the Lakers' bench, gave Coach Kundla the "okay" signal with thumb and forefinger and exclaimed, "This is it!" Baylor scored the Lakers' next two buckets. "After my first shot, I considered it as easy as college or school ball," Baylor explained. Baylor's experience playing older boys in rec leagues, his schoolyard training, his battles with his older brothers, and his time with the semipro Stonewalls and the seasoned Amateur Athletic Union Buchan Bakers had paid off. "Right then I knew I could go in this league," Baylor told Gross in *SPORT* magazine. "I thought to myself, 'I can make it.'" Baylor scored 25 points in his first game.

On November 8, despite hype about the University of Minnesota's homecoming football game against defending Big Ten champion Iowa, the Lakers sold out the Armory for a game with the Knicks. Baylor sparked the interest. Kundla told *Sports Illustrated* that Baylor was a "real pro," continuing, "I knew he was good, but I didn't know he could catch on this fast."

On November 11, the Lakers hosted the Boston Celtics before a sell-out crowd, although most of the fans had come not to see the NBA teams, but rather a preliminary game featuring Wilt Chamberlain and the Harlem Globetrotters. Trotters owner Abe Saperstein still had pull in NBA arenas, and his prize signee "The Big Dipper"—Wilt Chamberlain—was having the time of his life cavorting with basketball's most celebrated team.

Later that month, Minneapolis and Boston played a neutral-court game in Charlotte, North Carolina. The Negro players stayed at a Jim Crow hotel under what Baylor termed "decrepit" accommodations. The team owners, Bob Short and Walter Brown, vowed to do better by their colored players.

By late November, Baylor was averaging 23.8 points per game, with his total of 285 points in 12 games coming in second to George Yardley.

He had averaged 27 a game in his most recent four outings, and his 50 assists ranked third in the NBA. His 193 rebounds led the league. Just a few weeks later, Baylor was leading the league in scoring, his 500 points only 27 more than St. Louis's Bob Pettit. He was also the league's third leading rebounder.

On December 27, the Lakers lost to Boston, 112–94. Guarded variously by Frank Ramsey, "Jungle Jim" Loscutoff, and former Kentucky star Lou Tsioropoulos, Baylor made only one basket in 14 attempts and 6 free throws for a season low of 8 points (his previous low was 12). On the other side, Celtic Bob Cousy tallied 34 points for the winners. "He was tired," allowed Celtics coach Red Auerbach in a *Boston Globe* article. "We played him well." Only three times in his first 34 games as a pro had Baylor scored less than 15 points.

In the late 1950s, few nationally prominent Negro athletes—with the notable exception of trailblazer Jackie Robinson—spoke out about racial inequality in the United States, but they were all facing it. In big-league baseball, players were assigned Jim Crow spring training accommodations, and players of most sports endured segregated lodging on the road. The Syracuse Nationals once asked black player Earl Lloyd not to accompany his team to a game they were playing in segregated Greenville, South Carolina. When he did go along to other destinations, Lloyd remembers not feeling welcome. "The fans were vicious," he says in his autobiography, *Moonfixer: The Basketball Journey of Earl Lloyd*, recalling that they "spit a lot of racial venom at you." He adds, "St. Louis was tough. Baltimore was tough. You heard it. . . . Boston was a big Eastern city, and you didn't expect it there at first, but then you got there and you heard it and you knew. You knew fast." Lloyd remembers a road trip to St. Louis in which his 1956–1958 teammate Bob Hopkins was along. When they walked inside Kiel Auditorium, a young fan shouted, "Look at that. They got n----s on the team!"

One of Baylor's most unforgettable experiences with racial discrimination happened in Charleston, West Virginia, where the Lakers were scheduled to play the Cincinnati Royals on January 16, 1959. The Lakers arrived that day at 4 p.m. and went straight to their Charleston hotel to get ready for the 8 p.m. game. When captain Vern Mikkelsen went to the hotel's front desk to register the team, with Baylor standing about 10 feet from him, the desk clerk told the blonde Mikkelsen, "You can stay here, but the colored fellas can't." When Mikkelsen tried to argue, Baylor heard the clerk say, "Then take the team somewhere else."

Baylor walked over and asked, "Did I hear you right? Did you say we can't stay here?" but the clerk ignored him.

Coach Kundla got involved, and then Short, via phone, but the hotel wouldn't budge. Hot Rod Hundley made matters worse by telling the desk clerk, "This man is more successful than you, and makes a lot more money than you ever will!"

After Hundley, a Charleston native, called two other hotels and learned that neither would house Negroes, the team checked into Edna's Retirement Hotel (also called "Edna's Tourist Court"), an establishment for Negroes. Baylor could tell most of the guys weren't thrilled about this change, but it was a show of solidarity.

At that time, with the support of his team, Baylor still intended to play against Cincinnati, but when he and the only other black Lakers, Boo Ellis and Ed Fleming, went out to grab a bite, the only place that would serve them was the concession stand in the Greyhound station. For Baylor, it was the last straw. According to *Tall Tales*, after being turned away by hotels and restaurants, Baylor vowed, "I'm no dog." He decided to boycott the game rather than support the hypocrisy. That would show the city of Charleston, the NBA organization, and the press how ridiculous the double standard was. "I was torn up inside," he said of the decision.

Although Hundley pleaded with Baylor and he listened, Baylor's stance was not a betrayal of friendship, but an opportunity to expose a double standard. "Rod," he said, "you are right; you are my friend. But I'm a human being. All I want to do is be treated like a human being. I'm not an animal put in a cage and let out for the show. They won't treat me like an animal." For the first time, Hundley, the flashy white kid from Charleston, understood the great pride that defines Elgin Baylor. "It was then," Hundley says in *Tall Tales*, "that I could begin to feel his pain."

The Lakers' leaders were in a tough spot. Baylor had been advertised by local sponsors as one of the top attractions of the game. But Coach Kundla believed it was Baylor's choice, and he refused to comment on Baylor's stance or discuss the events in public.

Most of the 2,300 West Virginians who braved the icy Charleston streets and near-zero temperature that night to come to the game thought that Lakers star Elgin Baylor was in street clothes because he was either ill or injured. As Baylor watched from the bench, the Lakers lost the game to Cincinnati, 95–91. Only after the game was it revealed that he had refused to play in protest. Baylor later said he wouldn't have played even if it cost him his entire year's salary. Not only was Baylor's style of play revolutionary, but by refusing to suit up, he showed a spirit that was years ahead of his time. Los Angeles's black newspaper, the *Sentinel*, applauded his decision: "Baylor's refusal to compromise with all the evil segregation stands for is a tribute to his character and should give the faint-hearted something to think about. He has shown the way."

Not all reaction was positive, however, when the protest made national news. Charleston sportswriter A. L. "Shorty" Hardman denounced the city's segregation ordinances but called Baylor's actions "inexcusable." The city's mayor initially refused to apologize for the incident, while the mayor of another town wrote the Lakers and said Baylor should apologize to Charleston.

The American Businessman's Club of Charleston filed a protest with the NBA and the Lakers. Both the NBA and the Lakers refused to discipline Baylor, although Commissioner Maurice Podoloff considered suspending him. Podoloff said no decision would be made until the league investigated the facts of the protest. Bob Short supported Baylor and told the *Minneapolis Tribune*, "I know his failure to play cost us the ball game, but he was under great emotional strain because of his attitude towards segregation."

A few days later, the mayor of Charleston called Baylor to apologize. Two years later, Baylor was invited to an All-Star Game in Charleston. He stayed in the establishment that had refused to host him in 1959. "I knew they were trying to make changes." he told Terry Pluto in *Tall Tales*. "The people apologized to me, and I thought that was real swell. The luncheon, too, was very nice. They really had the welcome mat out."

On that return visit, local African American leaders told him they had been able to parlay his boycott into some changes in the city. "[T]hat made me feel very good. But the indignity of a hotel clerk acting as if you aren't there, or people who won't sell you a sandwich because you're black . . . these are things you never forget."

Several years later, at the height of the Civil Rights Movement in 1963, Baylor reflected on his boycott in Charleston to Myron Cope of *SPORT* magazine in the March 1963 profile "Life with Elgin Baylor":

Certainly I don't regret having done it. I'm no pioneer or anything like that, but I'm interested in my people and I'm interested in progress. I'm Elgin Baylor, and I don't want anything more than I'm entitled to or anything less.

When you do something you hope something good will come out of it, that people will recognize it and be conscious of what's going on in the country. If it serves its purpose, great. At the time when you're being embarrassed or humiliated, you're not thinking, "I have to do this for everybody else." You're just thinking about what's happening to you.

Baylor told *Sports Illustrated*'s Frank Deford for a 1966 feature, "When you are a black man lucky enough to be in my position, how you show yourself is important to all blacks. I think that every day I serve by showing that I can conduct myself as well as anyone."

The first game the Lakers played after the Charleston sit-out, against the Philadelphia Warriors, drew 7,156 fans, three times the average attendance for Minneapolis. The hometown fans rallied around the courageous player. The Lakers broke a five-game losing streak by beating Philly, 119–98. Baylor scored 30 points, 22 of them in the second half.

On January 19, 10 months after leading Seattle University to the NCAA Final Four, Baylor returned to Seattle with the Minneapolis Lakers for the first NBA exhibition game in Seattle history. A publicity image of Baylor in a Chieftains uniform, dribbling a ball, graced the cover of the game program, and 11,500 fans paid to see their hero come home to Hec Edmundson Pavilion. He scored 30 points in a loss to the Boston Celtics.

In February, NBA team owners met in Detroit with Commissioner Podoloff and adopted a policy that insisted on nondiscrimination policies in team accommodations as an assurance to book future games. Baylor's stance had influenced the decision.

On February 25, Baylor scorched the Cincinnati Royals for 55 points. Lakers captain Vern Mikkelsen told *Sports Illustrated*, "We've been starving for a guy that can do things with the ball like he can. This town is hungry for a winner." The team improved from 19 wins the previous season to 33 with Baylor. Baylor broke Bob Pettit's NBA scoring record for rookies, averaged 15 rebounds for third best in the league, and led the Lakers with 287 assists. He led the team in minutes, points, field goals made, field goals attempted, free throws made, free throws attempted, rebounds, and assists. Baylor proved he was worthy of Bob Short's investment in him.

Despite their losing record, the Lakers made the playoffs. On March 14, they faced the Detroit Pistons, whom they defeated in the opening game in Minneapolis, 92–89. The series shifted to Detroit, where the home team won, 117–103. Minneapolis advanced by routing the Pistons at home, 129–102, on March 18, the day Hawaii became a U.S. state. They would play the St. Louis Hawks, a team that had posted the best record in the Western Division and won three straight games over Boston, whose fans bombarded the Hawks with eggs. Baylor looked forward to proving his mettle against the Hawks, who were perennial finalists.

As the division finals started, St. Louis won the playoff opener at home in a 124–90 cakewalk. In game two, played on March 22 in Minneapolis, the Hawks squandered a 19-point lead and lost, 106–98, tying the series. The teams returned to St. Louis, where the Hawks ran the Lakers out of Kiel Auditorium, 127–97. Back home, the Lakers won game four, 108–98, tying the series at two games apiece. Minneapolis went on to take the fifth game in a 98–97 nail-biter in overtime in St. Louis and then clinched the series back home, 106–104. Baylor scored 33 in the deciding game, to Pettit's 24. He had made 13 of 23 shots and seven of his eight free throws. In the series, Baylor not only scored 170 points in the first six games, but on defense, he held Pettit and then Hagan to some of their lowest scoring outputs of the season.

Baylor has called that series upset against the Hawks the greatest highlight of his career. Hawks coach Ed Macauley couldn't help but praise him. Macauley told *Sports Illustrated*,

> Put a small, fast man on him, and Baylor will overpower him. He'll get five or six points quickly, and you're out of business. Put a bigger man on him and maybe he won't score that quickly, but he'll beat you some other way. He handles the ball better than Pettit and dribbles better than Hagan, and he kills you on the boards. He has no area of weakness. We can't put two men on him, but we sort of one-and-a-half him.

In the 1959 NBA Finals, the Lakers met the champion Celtics. Fans throughout the United States were surprised and disappointed because they expected to see the NBA's biggest rivals at the time: Boston and St. Louis. Saturday and Sunday TV audiences had grown fond of the clashes between Bill Russell and Bob Pettit, Tommy Heinsohn and Cliff Hagan, and little men Bob Cousy and Slater Martin.

Boston arrived at the Finals spent, having been extended to seven games by a Syracuse club that had added George Yardley to its cast. But that didn't help the Lakers' luck. The Minneapolis team lost in Boston, 118–115, and then 128–108. They dropped the next two games in Minneapolis by scores of 123–110 and 118–113. Coach Red Auerbach was carried off the Minneapolis Armory court by his giddy Celtics. Baylor, who averaged 22.8 points in the series, told the Celtics' radioman, Johnny Most, in his postgame interview, "We tried everything we could think of. We had no one to match up with Russell and no one to stop Cousy on the break."

It was the first sweep in NBA Finals history, partly because Elgin Baylor needed a stronger supporting cast. Baylor averaged 25.5 points and 12 rebounds for the Detroit, St. Louis, and Boston playoff series. No other Laker averaged more than 15 points. After the playoffs, sportswriter Murray Olderman titled his *SPORT* profile "Elgin Baylor: One-Man Franchise." Baylor was proving he was a sound financial investment as Bob Short had hoped he would be. With Baylor aboard, the Lakers' team revenue nearly doubled, from a gross of $174,000 the previous year to $306,724 in 1958–1959. The Lakers had even sold out some games at the Minneapolis Armory. Sensing a turn in his team's fortunes, Short raised ticket prices from $2.50 to $4. He hired a local publicist named Phil Jasen, who had worked with Cinerama and the blockbuster movie *Around the World in Eighty Days*, to promote the team.

Short also increased Baylor's salary from $22,000 to $50,000 per year, which placed Baylor in an echelon with Bob Cousy, Bill Russell, Bob Pettit, Bill Sharman, and Clyde Lovellette—the league's best-paid players.

With Elgin Baylor, the NBA's offensive production was up, and the sky seemed to be no limit. In an era when players at all positions were bigger and stronger, Baylor was a rare 6'5" forward. Prior to Baylor, the league's premier forwards, Pettit and Dolph Schayes, were 6'9" players the size of the average center. Schayes was a master of the long-range set shot, a gritty product of the Bronx who entered the NBA in 1950. Louisianan Pettit was a smooth jump shooter who was also proficient on tapins and an instinctive rebounder. Baylor brought new elements to the position of forward. He had the ballhandling dexterity associated with guards, indeed superior to many NBA backcourt men of the era.

"He was the first guy in the league, as a forward," explained Cliff Hagan, "who could handle the ball, hang in the air, and get his shot off. He didn't need screens; he didn't have a one-hand push shot. The Lakers guards were not scorers. . . . So they needed Baylor to score. Baylor had the ball in his hands every time down the floor." Other opponents agreed that Baylor had the green light to score. Celtics hatchet man "Jungle" Jim Loscutoff said in an April 1959 *Sports Illustrated* article by Jeremiah Tax, "What makes him so effective is that the Lakers work all their patterns around him." Loscutoff commended Baylor's physical toughness, an important quality because of the body contact offensive stars must absorb. Baylor endured the blows without complaint, unlike Wilt Chamberlain, whom Loscutoff called a "prima donna" who bellyached about rough tactics.

"Elgin Baylor was the premier quick forward in NBA history," states Boston's Tommy Heinsohn in *Tall Tales*. "I'm sure you would get an argument about Dr. J, Larry Bird, and other players. But not only was he a great offensive player, rebounder, passer—which is evident in the record books—but . . . he was by far the best defender."

Sports Illustrated's Jeremiah Tax describes Baylor's game in his April 1959 feature "Bunyan Strides Again":

> He turns his back to his defensive man and begins a series of rhythmic dribbling feints from side to side, all the while sliding steps closer to the basket, protecting the ball with elbows and shoulders. . . . If the defensive man gets no help, Baylor nearly always drives him with continuous feints to distraction and error, and slips in for a twisting layup. In this climactic move he hangs in mid-air, seemingly for seconds, while he makes up his mind whether to shoot or pass off, so that to the very end the defense is mystified.

"I don't know why I played like I did," Baylor told *Sports Illustrated*'s Frank Deford. "I had never seen anyone else do my moves. . . . The things I did were spontaneous." Baylor's astonishing repertoire of one-on-one moves, body control, playmaking ability, and change of pace were facets of his boyhood game on the schoolyard. Changes on the dribble, changing hands in midair, and changing body position were keys to his effectiveness. Baylor was no one-dimensional star, and the NBA was taking notice.

Baylor became only the third rookie in NBA history named to the 1959 All-NBA Team. He was named the league's Rookie of the Year, the second straight year a black player had won the honor. Woody Sauldsberry was the 1958 winner, and Bill Russell would have won in 1957 had he not missed the first few months of the season preparing for and playing in the 1956 Olympics in Melbourne. Baylor also finished third in the voting for MVP, trailing veterans Pettit and Russell.

After the season was over, Coach John Kundla was fired, and the Lakers were seeking a new head coach. Although Kundla had coached the team to the NBA Finals after winning the West Division playoffs in an upset of the Pistons, the team had finished with a losing record for the 1958–1959 season. Short asked Baylor if his college coach, John Castellani, who was back in his native Connecticut, would make a good professional coach. Baylor allowed only that Castellani was a good man, predicting neither his NBA success nor failure. The Cincinnati Royals' Jack Twyman, who was an insurance man during the off-season, was working with Aetna in Hartford when he ran into Castellani. He encouraged a reluctant but unemployed Castellani to take an insurance course: "It lasted a week or two. Jack and I had dinner at the Manero's Steak House on the Berlin Turnpike. I told him I'd applied for the Lakers' job but hadn't heard back from Bob Short."

"How long has it been? "Twyman asked.

"Two weeks."

"Do you have Short's number?"

"Sure."

Twyman said, "Call Bob now."

Castellani took him up on it. Short asked the coach if he was still interested in the position. "He thought I was only using my application with the Lakers to get colleges interested in hiring me," said Castellani. Short told him he would call him back in an hour, during which time he ran Castellani's name by the team board.

The return call came, and Short said, "I've got you on a flight to Minneapolis, arriving at 2 p.m." The men met the next day in Short's office, where Elgin's college coach signed a one-year contract for $10,000.

Castellani replaced John Kundla. His former assistant, Vince Cazetta, replaced Castellani at Seattle, before going on to coach Baylor's stylistic heir, Connie Hawkins, with Pittsburgh in the American Basketball Association.

"When I first got the job, Short and I went to a bar for martinis. There were a couple nice-looking blondes there, and I was flirting." said Castellani, who never did marry.

Short said, "Easy John, there are too many women in this town. You have to be careful when you get here, I know."

Castellani assured Short, "Bob, I'm a good Catholic bachelor."

"There's no such thing," quipped Short, "as a good Catholic bachelor."

In pro basketball, Castellani was admittedly out of his element. "Pro ball was different," he said. "You have practices, but then the guys are gone, you never really get to know them." He even once asked Dartmouth rookie Rudy LaRusso, "You got any good plays from college?" The team only drew 2,000 to 2,500 fans to the Armory, which Castellani says "wasn't a NBA floor."

One of Castellani's regrets was turning down the Lakers' assistant job in 1958, when Baylor left Seattle. "We'd have had a good team, with young guys like Rudy LaRusso and Tom Hawkins. We'd have won a few more games, and they never would have drafted Jerry West," he speculated.

When Castellani won a game, he would celebrate by entering the locker room and slowly loosen his tie, which he would then place around a player's neck. The players came to infer that the gesture meant the recipient of the tie was player of the game, but they could hardly stifle their laughter at the routine.

Cincinnati drafted Baylor's buddy, All-American "Sweet" Charlie Brown, in the fifth round. The Royals mailed Brown a $5,000 contract, the league minimum for a rookie. When owner Pepper Martin asked Brown when he was coming to camp, Brown balked at the contract. "We don't pay colored boys no more than that." Martin told him. Brown found rewarding work with a YMCA pilot program for kids involved in gangs on Chicago's West Side instead.

Baylor proved worthy of his salary increase when he opened the Lakers' 1959 season by scoring 52 points against Detroit, despite having spent the preseason at basic training as a member of the U.S. Army

Reserve in Fort Sam Houston near San Antonio. On November 8, he scored 64 points against Boston in a 136–115 victory that broke a 22-game Laker losing streak against the Celtics. For that game, Coach Auerbach had put four defenders on Baylor, with orders to prevent him from shooting. Laker teammate Steve Hamilton told *Sports Illustrated,* "Boston put on a freeze with 24 seconds to go to stop Elgin. Sam Jones had the ball. My job was to foul him so we could get the ball after the toss and pass it to Elgin." When Jones broke to dribble, Hamilton went to foul him, and their knees collided. Hamilton suffered torn cartilage. After the 1959–1960 season, Hamilton left the NBA to focus on a career in Major League Baseball.

Baylor caught a pass near the end of the game, was fouled, and hit his free throws to break Joe Fulks's NBA record of 63 points in a game. "I had no choice," he told *Ebony* magazine in February 1965. "They kept throwing the ball to me, and I had to shoot."

By late November, his 328 points led all scorers—even Wilt Chamberlain. In a four-game stretch, he had scored 174, an average of 43.5 points. For a time, he was even second to Bill Russell in rebounds, until Chamberlain moved ahead of him.

A couple of weeks before Christmas 1959, the Lakers lost 10 of 12 games. Ahead, they would face Cincinnati and St. Louis, and they would play Detroit twice, with only one of those games at home. "I should think we would win at least three, and we have a chance to win four if we play well at St. Louis," said Short in a *Sports Illustrated* article. "If we don't play well against that opposition, a lot of people may be looking for jobs."

One person whose job was in jeopardy was Coach John Castellani. At midseason, Short entered the team dressing room, his arms full of pencils and slips of paper. "We're gonna vote right now," he told his players, "on who should coach this team. Rank the guys, one to five, that you think should coach. You can vote for John," he said of Castellani, who was in the room. A couple of players who disliked Castellani yelled, "Gimme that paper!" Only guard Frank Selvy voted for Castellani. "He played me," Selvy later explained. "He's the only coach who's played me in five years." Castellani, who did not last half a season in pro basketball, was officially fired on January 2.

Short replaced Castellani with former Lakers star forward Jim Pollard. As a player, the 6'4" Pollard, called "The Kangaroo Kid" for his aerial style of play, had been something of a forerunner of Baylor. But, as with George Mikan a few years earlier, Pollard's history with the club would not benefit him as a coach.

Around the same time, while the national political scene was heating up with the beginnings of the 1960 presidential race—with Massachusetts senator John F. Kennedy announcing his candidacy on January 2, followed by Republican candidate Richard Nixon a week later—the Lakers team and the professional basketball world were beset by their own internal politics. Associated Press news reports that Los Angeles would be granted a NBA franchise set pro basketball abuzz with rumors, speculations, and negotiations, many of them involving Bob Short and his Lakers.

Sports Illustrated reported that although Short said at the NBA annual league meetings, "I'm not here to move my franchise. I'm not bankrupt, and I want to stay in Minneapolis," he also admitted, "but if I can't make a go of it then I'll have to consider a move." Some L.A. sportswriters believed Short was a prime candidate to do so because the Lakers weren't drawing well.

Despite a losing season in terms of finances and games, the Lakers made the 1960 playoffs. Under Castellani they were 11–25, and 14–25 under Pollard, for a 25–50 record overall.

In the Western Division semifinals, the Lakers upset the Pistons, beating them two games to none, and then met the 46–29 Hawks in the Western finals. The Lakers took a 3–2 lead in the series. Meanwhile, Hawks owner Ben Kerner interrupted a trip back to Minneapolis to stop in Chicago, where he met with, and secretly hired, a new coach for the Hawks' 1960–1961 season: former NBA guard Paul Seymour, who was then coaching the Syracuse Nats. The Hawks responded by shellacking the Lakers, and Bob Pettit and Cliff Hagan told their dismissed coach, Ed Macauley, "Ed, that one was for you." The Lakers lost the seventh and deciding game on national TV before an audience unaware that the victors had two coaches.

Despite the Lakers' standing in the season and the playoffs, by 1960 there was widespread sentiment that Elgin Baylor was the game's premier player. According to sportswriter Bill Reynolds, Baylor was "bigger than Cousy, more skilled than Chamberlain or Russell, more athletic than Pettit." And when Baylor was compared to fellow star Wilt Chamberlain, many thought Baylor came out ahead. Bob Cousy told the *Boston Globe*,

"I was much more impressed with Elgin than I was with Wilt." Coach Jim Pollard told *SPORT* magazine, "If I had my choice the way I'd like to see basketball played, I'd have to go with Elgin. He's the greatest all-around player in the game."

Yet, even while jockeying for status and stats on the court, Elgin and Wilt remained friends outside of the game, in part because they shared some common ground, with a few significant contrasts. Both were custodians' sons from the big city. When they were unleashed on the college basketball scene in the late 1950s, their arrival signaled the dawn of a new game, where size was no hindrance to agility. But where Wilt had been a high school phenom profiled in *LIFE* magazine and the *Saturday Evening Post*, Baylor was more of a secret weapon who sneaked onto the national scene from the fringes of Idaho and Seattle. Wilt grew up with six sisters and a little brother, Elgin in an athletic household dominated by males. Both were recruited by college coaches who did not end up coaching them. Baylor married before his rookie professional season, while The Big Dipper remained a bachelor to his grave. The two basketball greats bonded during an era when black athletes stuck together out of both social solidarity and mutual respect.

Among the few black NBA players of the 1950s and 1960s, a support system naturally developed. Philadelphia Warriors radio announcer Bill Campbell found it odd that opponents Wilt Chamberlain and Willie Naulls rode back to New York City together in Chamberlain's new Caddie after Chamberlain exploded for 100 points against the Knicks in Hershey, Pennsylvania, in March 1962, but such sights were common among African American athletes in the racially segregated United States. When the Lakers played at Syracuse, for instance, Baylor dined at Earl Lloyd's home in the city's black residential section, the 15th Ward. "[T]hat's how we did it for one another in those times, the way we took care of each other when a guy came to your town," recalled Lloyd. "You didn't want those guys just sitting in their hotel rooms."

Even though Baylor's old Seattle teammate Sweet Charlie Brown turned down a draft offer from the Cincinnati Royals and decided against the NBA, he remained tied to his old basketball friends, including Wilt Chamberlain: "When Wilt was in Chicago he'd call me. I'd walk him out the back door of the Chicago Sheraton," he said, explaining that otherwise he would have been mobbed by fans. "My wife cooked for him; he wanted to be comfortable when he was in town."

This network of black athletes and friends also helped pave the way for others who would follow. As a testament to the college game Baylor had helped revolutionize, the 1960 NCAA All-Tournament Team included three African Americans: Oscar Robertson, New York University's Tom Sanders, and champion Ohio State's Mel Nowell. In the National Invitation Tournament, where Baylor had also played, four of the top five young men were black: Lenny Wilkins of Providence, Bradley's Mack Herndon, and St. Bonaventure stars Tom and Sam Stith. These athletes of tomorrow would continue to help build the sport of professional basketball—although they might also take some of the limelight from the current stars. As one *Los Angeles Sentinel* columnist put it, "The Big O and Elgin Baylor will be the big men of the game next year, if some dark horse from Tugaloo or Tennessee State doesn't come forth to make everybody forget the Stilt."

6

NEW FRONTIERS: THE NBA'S FIRST MODERN PLAYER

I've found you've got to look back at the old things and see them in a new light.—John Coltrane

In 1959, a Gallup Poll of Americans showed that basketball was the third most popular spectator sport. Of the people polled, 18 percent selected basketball as their favorite sport, with baseball winning 28 percent of the voting and football 23 percent. Although attendance at National Basketball Association games was on the rise—jumping 23 percent during the 1959–1960 season, partly due to rookie Wilt Chamberlain's and sophomore Elgin Baylor's appeal as popular road attractions—pro basketball had to fight an uphill battle against what many sportswriters and fans deemed its minor-league pedigree. Other sports, from baseball to hockey, enjoyed a bigger fan base, especially in the big cities. Even though both New York and Boston supported basketball, the National Hockey League remained far more popular. In 1961, *Sports Illustrated* reported that Madison Square Garden owner Ned Irish said, "The Knicks are nothing but a tax write off anyway." The Celtics' original owner, Walter Brown, told broadcaster Curt Gowdy in 1951, "This isn't a basketball town. It's a hockey town." And Hawks star Cliff Hagan's recollection of game one of the 1957 NBA Finals supports that view; when the Celtics hosted the Hawks in Boston Garden, the venue was only half full.

There were a number of reasons why the NBA had trouble achieving big-league status. One major obstacle to basketball's financial progress was the fact that NBA home teams kept all gate receipts. As a result, a number of teams—including the Lakers—struggled to turn a profit. St. Louis staged postgame concerts by Tommy Dorsey, the Four Freshmen, Count Basie, and Guy Lombardo to boost Hawks' ticket sales.

The league also lacked consistent officiating, and referees were underpaid and not respected by the players and coaches. As a result, veteran coaches verbally rode the refs in a manner that offended many TV viewers. And at games that weren't televised, the refs had no accountability. Former Pistons and Bullets guard Rod Thorn says in *Tall Tales: The Glory Years of the NBA* that the lack of televised games meant the "officials could do almost anything they wanted." Players called referee Sid Borgia, who had called games in the 1940s and would become chief of officials in 1961, "The King of the Makeup Call." Some refs would peek at the scoreboard late in a quarter and, if one team had committed all the fouls, suddenly call three fouls in succession on the other squad. In 1957, due to inconsistent officiating, home teams won 71 percent of NBA games. As things began to improve, the advantage decreased to 60 percent by 1961. That same year, the league ruled that coaches must remain at their benches, which would calm the atmosphere of pro games.

Rumors and assumptions about refs' loyalties ran rampant, as no one tended to believe the officials were objective. At the 1960 NBA Finals, Commissioner Maurice Podoloff found himself in the midst of a controversy about the officials deciding the games between St. Louis and Boston. Hawks owner Ben Kerner criticized ref Jim Duffy, from New England, for a potential bias toward Boston but then later felt so guilty he held a "Jim Duffy Night" to honor him at an exhibition game before the next season. According to Laker forward Rudy LaRusso, however, Duffy showed special favoritism toward St. Louis. "We called Duffy 'Pettit's guardian angel,'" relates LaRusso in *Tall Tales*. "You would just look at Pettit hard and Duffy would blow the whistle."

Even when they tried, the refs didn't seem able to control the unruliness of NBA games, which had some of the elements of arena wrestling. Fans were so unruly at the home arena of the 1950s Fort Wayne Pistons it was nicknamed "The Tub of Blood." Syracuse fans spat on opposing players, and a fan called "The Strangler" heckled visiting players from behind their bench. Spectators jiggled the guy wire under the basket to thwart opposition shots. In 1962, a Philadelphia fan was ejected for grabbing a referee. Another tried to attack Red Auerbach at halftime, and a third raised a stool in a threatening manner. At Philly 76er games, Mike Farmer of the Royals learned to stand near rookies during the national anthem to avoid being pelted with garbage. Another 76er fan swung at Red Auerbach during the 1965 playoffs, and others rained eggs and drinks on his players; in Aram Goudsouzian's book *King of the Court: Bill Russell and the Basketball Revolution*, Auerbach calls Philadelphia a "bush town." The phrase was so rampant in NBA circles that, as stated in John Taylor's book *The Rivalry: Bill Russell, Wilt Chamberlain, and the Golden Age of Basketball*, Commissioner Podoloff's wife asked a sportswriter, "What do they mean by the term *bush* I keep reading?"

Things were rough on the court as well. Veteran players the likes of Celtic Bob Cousy criticized the physical nature of play, and Cousy annually considered calling it quits. In 1953, Cousy and the Warriors' Neil Johnston got into a fight, which police officers had to break up. During the 1954 playoffs, a melee interrupted a Boston–Syracuse game for 30 minutes. In a late October 1961 *Sports Illustrated* article about whether new Warriors coach Frank McGuire would be able to handle Wilt Chamberlain, author Ray Cave writes, "[H]is eventual effect may be to measurably change the character of professional basketball from the brawling, hustling, cigar-in-the-face and eye-on-the-till game it has been for decades to the major-league sport which it longs and deserves to be."

Elgin Baylor took the considerable contact in stride. "I've got no kicks to make about opposing players," he told Milton Gross of *SPORT* in 1961. "They've got a job to do just like I have." He attributed the physical style of play, in part, to an influx of younger players who were "bigger and better every year." But his friend Wilt Chamberlain was among the most vocal about the roughness of the sport and even threatened to retire after his first season. In a March 1960 *Look* magazine article entitled "Pro Basketball Has Ganged Up on Me," Chamberlain complains about teammates, officiating, and dirty tactics used by opponents. Yet, few took the gentle giant seriously, since he was earning $65,000 a year—more than Pettit, Cousy, or Baylor. "My main reason for leaving the NBA," Chamberlain later told *Sports Illustrated*, "is that I don't think I could uphold the same status I had in the league last year. That is mainly keeping my self-respect as an individual and a ballplayer." This was Wilt's code language for saying that the way his opponents were roughing him up, he would be hard-pressed not to belt a Clyde Lovellette or George Dempsey here or there. But The Big Dipper was young, gifted, and had a passion for the game and its fans, and he would end up staying.

Chamberlain's objections to the brutal and somewhat archaic schedules of late 1950s and early 1960s NBA games were well founded. Teams sometimes played five games in six days. Philadelphia owner Eddie Gottlieb still created the entire league's schedule, and back-to-back playing nights meant players had to wash their own sweaty uniforms in hotel sinks. Others took their uniforms into the locker room showers to wash them and then dried them on radiators in their hotel rooms. When he was with the Celtics, Bill Russell would have rookies tote his foul-smelling gym bag, which he nicknamed "Old Yella."

"Seems like you travel all the time," Baylor told *Sports Illustrated* his rookie year. "But I like being with the fellows." There was plenty of road time. The Minneapolis Lakers of the late 1950s played half a dozen games in such towns as Hibbing, Minnesota; Minot, South Dakota; and La Crosse, Wisconsin. Chamberlain's famous 100-point game in 1962 was played in one of these remote locations, in front of only 4,124 fans in a hockey arena in Hershey, Pennsylvania.

Travel conditions were also substandard, the elongated players crammed into coach airplane seats or train seats, knees in their own faces. Train rides were long, made tolerable only by marathon card games. "We'd take a train up to Minneapolis from Syracuse," recalls Earl Lloyd in his autobiography *Moonfixer: The Basketball Journey of Earl Lloyd*, "and we'd start with a night train to Chicago. We'd ride all day, your legs pushed up in those seats. . . . We'd arrive at three, three-thirty in the afternoon. You'd barely have time to eat and take a nap, and it would be game time. You had more or less been up all night." Because there were no train routes between Rochester and Fort Wayne, NBA players used to walk from the railroad terminal closest to Fort Wayne, through a cornfield, to an establishment called the Green Parrot Inn in South Whitley, Indiana, where they would pay high school boys $15 or so to drive them to Fort Wayne.

On one of the infrequent plane flights, the entire Lakers team nearly died. In an effort to save money, Bob Short bought an old World War II DC-3 to charter the team's flights. On Sunday, January 17, 1960, after a 135–119 loss at St. Louis, the Lakers boarded the DC-3 for a three-hour flight to Minneapolis, not knowing the plane's generator had conked out. The guys took up their customary poker game, putting blankets on the floor to catch the cards. When the plane's lights went out, they made little of it, but the game stopped. They were flying into a snowstorm. While the copilot busied himself scraping snow off the window, the players shuddered under G.I. blankets. Forward Tommy Hawkins asked Bob Leonard if he thought the team was going to die. The pilot, a World War II fighter vet, told the team he only had about 30 minutes worth of gas left, so he could either try to land in a cornfield or look for another airport. The Lakers ordered him to land the plane.

The plane was so close to the ground, the players could see red lights from an ambulance and a fire truck, as well as people turning lights on in their homes because the engine noise had awakened them.

According to *Tall Tales*, Baylor rose out of his seat to his full 6'5" frame. "Not me," he said. "I don't want to be any part of sitting there like a duck when this happens." With that, the basketball player everyone associated with being airborne—a man who seemed to flirt with the laws of Newtonian gravity—made his way to the rear of the aircraft. He spread out a blanket, folded his $250 alpaca topcoat into a pillow, and made his own announcement: "If I'm gonna go, boys, I am gonna go in style."

The crew made several risky passes at landing, only to bring the plane level again. They finally shut off the engines and drifted onto a snow-covered cornfield in Carroll, Iowa, at 2 a.m. Baylor compared the sensation to landing on a blanket. A man with a hatchet knocked at the plane's door, and when it opened the first thing Baylor saw was a hearse. It was the town mortician, who had seen the stuttering craft out his window. The relieved players rushed out of the jet's rear, snow up to their backsides. "I'm positive I detected a slightly disappointed look when the driver found out everyone was all right," Jim Krebs said of the mortician, in a June 23, 1964, *Sports Illustrated* firsthand account of the landing called "The Night Their Luck Turned."

Rudy LaRusso explained Baylor's unusual demeanor to Frank Deford for a 1966 *Sports Illustrated* cover profile of Baylor, saying,

> Elgin is one of those people who might feel panicky inside but who has a personal code that makes it impossible for him to show it. He's full of pride. He absolutely won't show weakness, to anyone. . . . If the lights were going out for him that night, then by golly, it was going to be under his own terms.

Cash was tight, for both players and their management. In 1961–1962, Warriors owner Eddie Gottlieb surprised a few of his rookie players when they checked out of a hotel, telling them how much cash each man owed for phone calls made from their rooms. Most were charged 20¢ or a little more. Players scrimped on meal money to save for upscale restaurants, often eating at greasy spoons in between. In the Midwest and St. Louis, some of the dives refused to serve African American players. And the giants of the league slept in hotel beds too short for their lengthy frames.

The facilities where players did their job left much to be desired. When the Pistons moved to Detroit, the dressing rooms in Olympia Auditorium featured nails on the walls for the players' clothing rather than lockers. The benches in the hockey arena were so cold, heat lamps were placed beneath them for basketball games. Lenny Wilkens called his Hawks home arena, Kiel Auditorium, a "pit," where players were lucky if the showers ran warm. His only positive memories of the place were that the gym was separated from an opera hall by only a curtain, and the music was soothing.

The home of the 1958–1959 Lakers—the stone, hangar-shaped Minneapolis Armory built as a public works project in 1935—was no better than the pro basketball facilities in other cities. The arena's basketball floor could not have been good for the players' knees. Former Laker Tommy Hawkins told Dennis Brackin of the *Minneapolis Star-Tribune* in 2010, "The place, I think the floor was like concrete. And it was cold. Oh my gosh, I don't know if there was a big difference between the temperature outside and inside the armory." Vern Mikkelsen said, "It didn't play very well, let's just put it that way. The thing wasn't in very good shape, but we won a lot of the times we played in there." Teammate Dick Garmaker told Brackin for the *Star-Tribune* that his memories of the Armory were so negative, he "probably shouldn't even comment." (Before Baylor's second season, Bob Short put in a new basketball floor, but by then it would be "California, here we come.")

For most NBA management teams, front-office staffs were almost nonexistent. In his history of the league, *24 Seconds to Shoot*, Leonard Koppett describes the budding league: "It was an era in the pro game when a man's office was his hatband, except when he had to hock the hat." Speaking about Philadelphia Warriors owner Eddie Gottlieb, fellow owners joshed that "Gotty carries the office around in his hat." The old-school owner, who became known as "The Mogul," still organized the entire NBA schedule by himself. Marty Blake served as the St. Louis Hawks' staff from the 1950s to early 1960s, handling everything from public relations to P.A. announcing to scheduling and scouting. Red Auerbach kept a home in Washington, D.C., and his Boston existence was confined to the Lenox Hotel, where he lived amid boxes of Chinese food, his jacket pockets stuffed with notepaper bearing scribbled information about his team and others. Rumor had it Rochester Royals owner Lester Harrison and his brother scalped tickets outside their arena.

St. Louis Hawks owner Ben Kerner, for whom his team was his primary source of income, encouraged his fellow owners to emulate the exemplars in big-league baseball and the National Football League. The Celtics' Walter Brown agreed, while New York's Ned Irish, who earned his bones promoting the college game, was not fixated on major-league status. A master of promotion, Kerner staged 18 special attractions at no extra charge after his basketball games in 1960–1961, including such bands as Harry James, Sammy Kaye, Duke Ellington, and Count Basie.

Of course, the main avenue for promoting professional basketball was TV, but the NBA had a tenuous relationship with television networks at the time. In 1952–1953, the upstart DuMont Network, which manufactured its own TV sets, carried only 14 league games. On March 20, 1954, in one of the few nationally televised games that season, New York and Boston fouled and shot so many free throws that the fourth quarter took 45 minutes to play; network executives pulled the plug on the broadcast to spare their viewers. The Sports Broadcasting Act of 1961 allowed major sports leagues to negotiate for TV contracts without violating antitrust law, but NBC's ratings for NBA games were so low they dropped their league package. From 1962 to 1964, pro basketball would go without a television contract. There was so little videotaped national coverage of the league that perhaps the most famous announcer's call in American basketball memory comes from radio. Because the deciding game of the 1965 Eastern Division playoff final between the Celtics and the 76ers was not televised, Johnny Most's raspy "Havlicek steals it. Over to Sam Jones. Havlicek stole the ball!" comes from his broadcast on Boston's local WHDH radio.

In 1962, the NBA moved its weekly television broadcasts from Saturday afternoon to Sunday. The telecasts meant that teams who played on Saturday night sometimes had to play again on Sunday afternoon. These games attracted 15 million viewers, with the Celtics and the Hawks being the most popular matchup. In 1959–1960, the Hawks' "Big Three"—Bob Pettit, Clyde Lovellette, and Cliff Hagan—averaged 71.7 points a game between them, and they averaged 72.0 points a game between them in 1960–1961.

With the challenges facing NBA franchises, investors, and players, it is no wonder that management teams constantly weighed their options and considered new ones. One potential change coming to the NBA that had the potential of impacting teams throughout the league was westward expansion. Although NBA league officials denied the rumor, in the early days of 1960, reports said that Los Angeles was in the market for a pro basketball team, either by receiving an expansion team or having an existing ball club move there. Los Angeles had begun to see itself in a different light after gaining the Dodgers in 1958. City fathers understood the potential, and in 1959 they built a 14,000-seat arena (more seating capacity than any arena then in the NBA) adjacent to Los Angeles Memorial Coliseum, home of University of Southern California football, the L.A. Rams, and the relocated Dodgers.

Lakers owner Bob Short noted the enthusiasm on the West Coast. In 1959, his Lakers had played to 11,000 in Baylor's college town of Seattle, and 13,000 attended a Lakers–Celtics contest staged as a Bill Russell homecoming to San Francisco. These games earned much-needed revenue for his cash-strapped Lakers franchise. And so, as talk continued about a new team for L.A. and where it might come from, Short devised a western experiment for his Lakers.

On February 1, 1960, the same day that four black students from North Carolina Agricultural and Technical State University began a sit-in at a segregated Woolworth lunch counter in downtown Greensboro, North Carolina, Elgin Baylor and Wilt Chamberlain played in the first pro basketball game at the Los Angeles Sports Arena 3,000 miles away. The contest pitted the 1959 NBA Rookie of the Year against the highly publicized giant favored to walk away with those honors in 1960, and it reunited Baylor with the best man from his wedding. Proceeds from the game, called "Cagers for Kids," went to the Salesian Boys Club in East L.A. Tickets went on sale throughout L.A., ranging in price from $1.75 to $4.

On that rainy Monday, 10,202 fans showed up to see Elgin's Lakers and Wilt's Warriors. A preliminary exhibition was played by former Negro League baseball star Ziggy Marcelle's Vagabonds, a showy Globetrotter-style outfit that played against a team from Los Alamitos Naval

Station. The Negro paper, the *Los Angeles Sentinel*, noted that there were "so many Negroes in key roles" that night and read the high attendance as a good sign for integration.

During the headline game, Lakers pivot man Ray Felix did his best guarding Chamberlain, but the agile rookie scored with ease. Even though Baylor outscored the pass-happy Chamberlain with an arena record of 36 points, the Lakers lost to Philly, 103–96. The *Sentinel*'s L. I. Brockenbury alludes to ongoing rumors of a westward move for the Lakers, noting, "If the Minneapolis Lakers and Elgin Baylor take over a Los Angeles franchise, they would find themselves very popular here within a few weeks."

On February 21 and 22, Bob Short continued his western experiment, showcasing Baylor against the great St. Louis Hawks. In the first game, Baylor's 35 points helped lift them over the former league champs, 112–98, before 6,781 onlookers. The second-leading Lakers scorer was Frank "Pops" Selvy, with 18, while Bob Pettit scored 31 for the Hawks. In the rematch, Baylor hit only 20, and St. Louis won, 113–103. Whereas the Lakers had drawn only 1,500 home fans to their last game versus the Hawks, in Los Angeles more than 12,000 fans attended the games.

Two other NBA games in the city drew about 5,000. A game at the Shrine Auditorium was actually played on a stage, which his teammates said was the perfect platform for the showy "Hot Rod" Hundley. Meanwhile, Bob Short did the math. Although his fellow owners and Commissioner Podoloff were curious whether the first pro game at the Sports Arena had drawn well specifically because Chamberlain played in it, Short believed otherwise.

The Los Angeles newspapers fed the NBA rumor mill with their own speculations. Mort Moss of the *Los Angeles Examiner* writes that Chamberlain and the Warriors could be moving to L.A. The *Sentinel*'s Brad Pye opines, "For my money, the Minneapolis Lakers with Elgin Baylor would be equally appealing. Let's not lose the Lakers trying to land the Stilt." A week later, the African American paper's sports headline asked, "Will L.A. Get an NBA Ballclub?" The author writes that both the Lakers and the Warriors clubs were up for grabs and that, before the NBA moved to L.A., San Francisco would also acquire a franchise. The article cites the possibility of acquiring the Warriors, whose Philly arena was too small for the throngs interested in seeing Chamberlain. But an accompanying photo shows Baylor in a Laker uniform, curiously sporting the uniform number 14. The *Sentinel* remarks, "Should the Lakers decide to move West, four of the top Negro stars in the game will be coming too," citing Baylor, Ray Felix, Tom Hawkins, and former Niagara star Boo Ellis.

Just after the games in L.A., on February 24, 1960, Short petitioned his fellow owners and the commissioner for permission to move. His team had earned $32,000 for two games in L.A. against St. Louis, compared to $3,700 for a game against the Hawks in Minneapolis. Short had toughed it out three seasons in his hometown to no avail. He hoped his partner investors would remain onboard so they could finally earn a return on their investment. He characterized the three years of ownership as "miserable failure the first year," followed by mediocre success and dismal failure the current season. Had it not been for the money the Lakers made in their games in Los Angeles, they would have lost money in 1959–1960. Short's timing couldn't have been better; rumor was that Minnesota would soon be home to a Major League Baseball team, baseball being a much more popular sport. The coming of the national pastime could lessen the blow of a Lakers move, as had happened a few years earlier when Milwaukee lost the Hawks but gained the Boston Braves.

Short's initial request was delayed by the NBA owners, who urged the Lakers to consider Baltimore and Pittsburgh probably because it was less expensive for eastern teams to travel there. He was told to explore such options in the interim until the April 11 NBA Draft when they would meet again. The owners also agreed there would be no Chicago franchise the next season because the pro game had never done very well in the Midwest's largest city.

By early March, Short doubted he would gain league approval for his move because it appeared that other NBA owners wanted to keep the L.A. market open for future possibilities, perhaps even for their own franchises, or a new one. With Jim Pollard now as coach and his Lakers headed into the playoffs, Short began devising plans to play 1960–1961 in Minneapolis and St. Paul. Maybe basketball doubleheaders with the University of Minnesota at their Williams Arena could take advantage of the city's Big Ten fan base.

At the NBA league meeting in 1960, Short initially encountered resistance to his proposed move west. Knicks owner Ned Irish and others balked about the extra expense of flying teams to the West Coast. (Irish actually hoped the cash-strapped Lakers might sell Baylor to the Knicks and had offered Short $250,000 for Baylor in January 1960.) After fellow owners voted Short down on the first ballot, he proposed a compromise on the travel expenses, offering to pay his opponents the difference between a flight to Minneapolis and L.A. If it cost the Knicks $300 to get to Minneapolis but $500 to fly to the West Coast, Short would pick up the extra $200. The owners ultimately voted to approve the Lakers' move.

Short benefited from timing in 1960, since the Lakers owned the second pick in the NBA Draft. Everyone knew Cincinnati would select hometown hero Oscar Robertson with the first choice. Minneapolis–Los Angeles took Jerry West, a spindly, 6'3" jumping-jack forward at West Virginia, with the second. West signed for $16,500—almost $6,000 less than Baylor had in 1958.

On April 26, Short met with members of the Los Angeles Memorial Coliseum Commission about the possibility of having his franchise play in the 14,000-seat Los Angeles Sports Arena. He knew the team could draw there and that city officials tied their status as a major-league town to their ability to attract professional sports clubs. "Elgin Baylor is the greatest all-around basketball player in the world," he said of his product in the *Los Angeles Times* September 21, 1960 article "Lakers Sign Jerry West." "Jerry West, our top draft choice, is going to be a fine pro." Short believed that with Hundley, Selvy, and Slick Leonard, the addition of West gave them the best backcourt in their division. A city council resolution presented by Councilwoman Rosalind Wyman officially welcomed Los Angeles's tallest new tenants.

In early May, the Lakers fired Coach Jim Pollard. Pollard had asked Short for a long-term contract but was told there were no such guarantees forthcoming. Pollard explained to the media that he had "no interest in coaching pro basketball" without job security. This change gave Short the freedom to consider such candidates as Celtics great Bill Sharman, although league rules prohibited the Lakers from contacting the veteran guard and former USC star, still under contract to Boston.

The same week, the Hawks offered the cash-strapped Short $200,000 for Baylor—twice the amount Short had paid three years prior for his controlling interest in the team and double his current debt. The offer was more than the going rate for the average NBA franchise, yet Short didn't even consider taking the cash. He needed Baylor as a L.A. drawing card and likened the sale of his star player to a "going out of business sale." "We have confidence that with Baylor as a nucleus," says Short in the

Ogden, Utah Standard-Examiner of August 8, 1960, "the Los Angeles entry in the NBA will unquestionably bring to Los Angeles the world championship of professional basketball." Baylor was his future. In addition, the fate of the NBA on the West Coast rested on Baylor's broad shoulders. This burden grew more significant as talk loomed of Harlem Globetrotters owner Abe Saperstein helping bankroll a new enterprise called the American Basketball League, which would include a franchise in L.A. Baylor had better pan out in Southern California, because Saperstein could always book the Trotters to draw fans to preliminary games. And if Chamberlain, who had displayed no loyalty to the NBA, jumped leagues, the senior circuit would be in jeopardy.

Lakers general manager Lou Mohs preserved the team during the transition to Southern California, since Short and his co-owner, attorney Frank Ryan, preferred to run the franchise long-distance from Minnesota. The 65-year-old Mohs was a former newspaper circulation director for the Hearst syndicate and a former pro football player with the Minneapolis Marines of the NFL from 1922 to 1924. The team needed Mohs's mind for management. He was known as the tightest GM in the league, which was saying something in those days. "Ask anybody around here; they'll tell you how tight I am," he admitted to *Sports Illustrated* in the February 8, 1965, feature "A Smashing Hurrah for the Lakers." Owner Short was frugal as well. According to Roland Lazenby's book *Jerry West: The Life and Legend of a Basketball Icon*, when Mohs called Short for funds, the owner would protest, "Call me for anything, but don't call me for money." Their frugality had a purpose, however: to make the Lakers the first team to earn $1 million in a season. Money was tight within the Laker organization. "Mohs watched every paper clip," Rod Hundley remembers in *Tall Tales*.

As the management team prepared for a new season in a new home, they needed to find a new coach. While still in Minneapolis, Mohs had approached West Virginia coach Fred Schaus about coaching the Lakers. Frederick Appleton Schaus had been an All-State center at Newark High School near Columbus, Ohio, and the president of his 1949 college class. Now in L.A., Mohs and Short offered Schaus $18,500 a year and an opportunity to coach his former college star, Jerry West, along with star Elgin Baylor, in the West Coast media capital. Schaus bit. The new hire would become somewhat concerned, however, when supplies delivered to the ball club arrived C.O.D.

Before the move, Short convinced his Lakers to sell everything—their homes, furniture, and clothing—and suggested they hold auctions. He told them the style of furniture in Southern California was different, and they could buy everything new when they arrived. Some of the players bought new cars with their money from the sales and drove them west.

Once in L.A., Elgin and Ruby Baylor settled into the city's Palm Vue Motel on South Western. Ruby had not missed a home game in Minneapolis until the arrival of baby Alan in 1959. She told the press she wanted two more children, one of each gender, while Elgin preferred two more boys. A modern woman by 1960s standards, Ruby planned to attend USC and add an additional degree to her education. (In one media report, Elgin calls her a "professional student," a label Ruby denied he used.) They adapted well to the role of All-American family. They owned a six-week-old German Shepherd they dubbed "Bozo." Ruby was more of a seafood lover than her meat-eating husband, who often cooked steaks himself. She described her busy, celebrated husband as "perfect," and they both loved to bowl, fish, and attend auto races. They even shared a fondness for thoroughbred racing, although neither gambled. They were guests on Groucho Marx's popular game show *You Bet Your Life*.

That summer in 1960, Elgin worked as a basketball instructor at Snow Valley Basketball Camp, where University of California, Los Angeles, coach John Wooden was a fellow mentor. The weeklong children's camp, which ran from June through August, cost $87.50, a hefty price when many Southern Californians were earning only $100 a week at the time. Coach Fred Schaus also assigned Baylor, Tommy Hawkins, Frank Selvy, Rudy LaRusso, and others to give free basketball clinics at such urban community centers as South Park, Manchester, Ross Snyder, and the celebrated Denker Recreation Center at West 35th Place, from July 11 to August 23. Baylor worked at the Snyder Rec Center on July 27, as excited youngsters in T-shirts listened with rapt attention to basketball's most celebrated player.

As they geared up for the coming season, the Lakers still had to earn their right to be Angelenos. Where the Dodgers had recently been welcomed from Brooklyn by 10,000 fans at the L.A. airport and received an official welcome at City Hall, the pro basketball team had arrived to no such fanfare. To build the gate receipts, players mounted sound trucks and visited local areas like Beverly Hills and South Central L.A., armed with megaphones and scripts. "Hello, I'm Tommy Hawkins of the Los

Angeles Lakers," Hawkins recalls his script reading in Bill Dwyre's February 5, 2009, *Los Angeles Times* article entitled "Elgin Baylor and Jerry West Are Back Together Again." "We're back in town after a two-week trip to the East Coast. We're going to be at the Sports Arena the next 10 days. First up, the New York Knicks. Please come and see us." Along with his teammates, the 6'5" jumping jack Tommy Hawkins—the greatest player in Notre Dame history and a potential star for the Lakers in his second year with them—found himself peddling his team on the streets of L.A., something that is inconceivable for eventual stars like Wilt Chamberlain, Magic Johnson, or any Lakers of later years.

The Lakers began their 1960 preseason training at Pepperdine University on September 11. In early workouts, the *Sentinel* observed, "People watching . . . say Elgin Baylor has to be considered the very best player in basketball, including Wilt the Stilt." On September 27, the Lakers played in an exhibition at Compton High School, their debut in South L.A. Proceeds went to six junior high schools and three high schools in the district. Two local Negro players joined the Lakers: former Pepperdine star Sterling Forbes and Bobby Sims. According to the *Sentinel*, "What Stan Musial is to the Cardinals, what Ted Williams is to the Red Sox [Baylor is to the Lakers] . . . and then some!"

In early October, the Lakers and Celtics met for a *Los Angeles Examiner* charity game, part of a preseason series between the two clubs. The Lakers closed their exhibition season against the Celtics on October 16 in Anaheim.

The Lakers' new home, the Los Angeles Sports Arena, was part of the new frontier in basketball, and it had hit the national map on July 15, 1960, when the Democratic Party nominated young Massachusetts senator John F. Kennedy as their presidential candidate there. The Sports Arena featured a space-age motif, along with elevators and escalators to take people to upper levels and an electronic ticker system to tally attendance and post figures on the scoreboard. At games, the Lakers would even use fans to make the American flag wave during the national anthem. This was, after all, Hollywood.

The first Lakers home game at the Sports Arena was against the New York Knicks. Only 4,008 bothered to attend, and L.A. lost, 111–101. Baylor scored 25, besting former UCLA star Willie Naulls's 18 for the visitors. The following night the teams met in a rematch, which the Lakers won, 120–118. A few weeks later, in an early November game, Lakers center Jim Krebs was elbowing Bill Russell. Russell warned Krebs, who drew back to punch, but Russell beat him to it. Krebs was out cold for 20 minutes. He received eight stitches for his trouble, Russell a $100 fine.

One difficulty for the Lakers was something fellow NBA owners had anticipated: travel. Since there were no other West Coast teams, visiting clubs would often play Los Angeles on a back-to-back nights, which meant little rest for the visitors and their hosts. Then the Lakers would head east for two to three weeks. The closest franchise was in St. Louis, so they were usually traveling long distances. "Travel does bug me," Baylor admitted to Milton Gross in *SPORT* in 1961. "Worst of all, to me, is getting up at dawn to catch an airplane. I need eight hours of sleep a night to be any good, and you just can't get it in this league."

Teammate Cliff Hagan remembered the coach flights:

> We'd ride in these prop planes. You'd try to get some sleep in the economy section. There'd be these folksy pilots, who would say, "We're now passing over the Grand Canyon. . . ," when you'd be trying to sleep. I sent one pilot a nasty little note: "This is the red-eye; let us sleep. We don't give a damn what we're flying over." Any time I wasn't playing, I was sleeping!

One trip to New York would pay off handsomely for Baylor and his team, however. In mid-November, Baylor and the Lakers headed to New York City to play the Knicks. Milton Gross reports in *SPORT* that on the way to Madison Square Garden, Baylor shared a cab with Tommy Hawkins. Gross relates that the cabbie asked the tall black men, "You two guys athletes?" Baylor smiled, stole a glance at Hawkins, and answered, "Yeah, we're boxers. And I'm going to give you a tip. We're fighting at the Garden tonight, and it's his turn to lose." The driver wasn't buying it. "There's no boxing at the Garden tonight; you guys are basketball players. You're Elgin Baylor, aren't you?" Elgin owned up. "How many points you gonna score tonight?" came the usual question. "About 70," said Baylor.

Baylor's answer was practically right on target. On November 15, 1960, the same date as the Polaris missile test launch, he propelled the NBA into the atomic age by scoring 71 points against the New York Knicks. Baylor scored 15 points in the first quarter, 19 in the second, and 13 in the third, giving him 47. Knicks fans, bored by their own hapless team, began chanting, "Give it to Elgin! Give it to Elgin!" This demonstration embarrassed Baylor, for whom basketball was a team game. In Lew Freedman's book *Dynasty: The Rise of the Boston Celtics*, Coach Schaus says when Baylor hit 59 points, "I told the team to feed Baylor." Baylor added 24 points in the final period. A gathering of 10,132 fans witnessed history in the making, as Baylor picked up his fifth foul in the fourth quarter and played matador defense the rest of the way. The Knicks would not double-team Baylor, who eclipsed his own record of 64 points with five minutes to play. He ended with 28-for-48 shooting and 25 rebounds. He also sank 15 of his 19 free throws. His point total for the night was a record-setting 71, as was his 28 field goals.

According to *Dynasty*, Hot Rod Hundley said, "We were determined he'd get the record. He's a wonderful guy and the greatest player ever."

Leonard Koppett, who covered the record-shattering game for the *New York Post*, agreed, as he writes of Baylor, "He is merely the best basketball player in the world because he does everything so well." Knicks All-Star Richie Guerin would say that Baylor's performance was even better than Wilt Chamberlain's 100-point game a few years later, because Baylor's explosion came within the natural flow of the game, while Wilt's Warriors set him up and fed him the ball. Koppett agreed with Guerin, stating in *Tall Tales*, "It was steady, basket-after-basket, one good solid play after another. Every point he scored came within the framework of the game."

Rod Hundley writes in his memoir *Hot Rod Hundley: You Gotta Love It Baby*, after the milestone game, as Baylor and Hundley shared a cab back to their hotel, Baylor threw his arm around his friend and beamed, "Wow, 78 points. I want to tell you there's a lot of points between us sitting in this cab." Hundley could only laugh along, having chipped in just seven of those points. When Bob Short uncharacteristically sprang for cuff links for the players in the form of the number "71," Hundley joked that next year the team would strike a bunch of cuff links bearing the number "7," to honor his contribution that night.

Sports Illustrated ignored the event, and NBA coverage was so rare at the time that no footage of the performance exists. *SPORT* magazine took notice in April 1961. Milton Gross's feature bears the headline, "Elgin Baylor and Basketball's Big Explosion," with the subhead, "Where will the sharpshooting end? Baylor insists we haven't seen anything yet. Soon, he says, a player will score 100 points in a game."

Managing to catch up with Baylor in his room at the Hotel Manhattan in New York City, Gross later wrote, "They are a new race of men. They have swiftness, grace, strength, and accuracy unmatched in our heritage. They have made basketball a new game." Gross declared that pro basketball had "reached its atomic, most explosive stage. Individual skills have been perfected, scores are hovering in a special stratosphere." Baylor told him there was no limit to individual scoring potential, because so many players had mastered the jump shot, which was almost impossible to defend off a screen. When Gross asked Baylor if he was capable of 100 points, Baylor rose from his seat, paced the hotel room, and pondered the idea. "I can't see myself scoring 100. The only difference between Wilt and me is his height. I just don't have it. The games are won and the points are scored off the board." He felt the man capable of scoring 100 was Chamberlain. Wilt was much taller, with the agility to score 40 or more points on offensive rebounds and tip-ins. "When it happens, when a player scores 100 points," Baylor projected, "it will be more the logical conclusion of a trend than a freak. . . . We play defense in this league," he insisted. "It's just that the shooting is so good."

The *SPORT* feature demonstrates Baylor's appreciation and understanding of the scoring trend, his awareness of the tempo and pace of a game, and the value he placed on points scored off rebounds. Gross had gone to the right man.

Others tried to nab an interview. The *SPORT* article reported that when Baylor's phone rang off the hook, he asked his roommate, "What will it be like when I score 72 points?" The *Los Angeles Sentinel*'s Brad Pye thought Baylor capable of a 100-point performance, saying he could accomplish the feat "if he were not such a great team man." Pye adds, "It's a tribute to him and to good sportsmanship that his mates fed him the ball so much in New York."

As much as Baylor played down the performance, it was historically significant. In the 1953 NBA All-Star Game, played in Fort Wayne, Indiana, the final score was only 79–75. Now Baylor had scored more than 70 points in a regular-season game in basketball's most storied arena. The 1952–1953 league scoring champion, center Neil Johnston, averaged just 22.3 points per game, and only three players averaged 20 points that season. In the next season, Johnston, at 24.4, was the only player to exceed 20 points per game. The following season, 1954–1955, the first with the 24-second clock, Johnston led with 22.7 a game and was one of only four players to barely exceed a 20-point average. In 1960–1961, Baylor was on his way to scoring 34.8 a game and would average 38.3 in 1961–1962 and 34 again in 1962–1963.

Baylor continued to play well, scoring 52 in one game against Detroit on November 20 and 51 five days later. The first of those games took place in San Francisco, a second California market testing the NBA waters. In the lobby of the Palace Hotel, Hot Rod Hundley told the *Los Angeles Times'* Bill Dwyre of Baylor, "He's got to be the toughest human that ever walked on a court." Seated nearby, Pistons assistant coach Earl Lloyd, later to be the first African American to occupy such a post, echoed, "You won't get much argument from anybody in this league on that." Even at a time when Bill Russell had world championships, Oscar Robertson was three-time College Player of the Year, and Wilt Chamberlain earned the highest salary, it was Baylor of whom many rivals spoke the highest. The *New York Post*'s Milton Gross agreed, writing, "He's just the greatest there ever was." The Helms Foundation, a L.A. association made up of a panel of experts whose college sports All-American teams had been well regarded since the mid-1930s, named Baylor its Athlete of the Month. No Negro performer had ever won the award.

On December 3, boxing took over the Sports Arena, as Sugar Ray Robinson, a stylist who had redefined his sport, fought to a draw with bullish Gene Fullmer. To hype the bout, newspapers ran a photo of middleweight Fullmer raising Baylor's lofty hand as the world's greatest scorer, in a pose generally reserved for a boxing ref lifting a victorious fighter's arm. Baylor is wearing a warm-up suit and a posed facial expression, while Fullmer sports a cardigan and appears to spot him a foot in height.

On December 4 and 5, the Celtics were in town. Baylor had 83 combined points in Sunday and Monday games against the world champions. Early in his career against Boston, Celtics hatchet man "Jungle" Jim Loscutoff had discouraged Baylor's drives by elbowing him. That practice ceased when the 225-pound Baylor began to assert his own physical style. L.A. dropped the first contest, 113–103, as Sam Jones sank five of his five fourth-quarter shots. Boston also won on Monday, 123–101, a game in which Baylor scored 31 by halftime and 43 total. His were all-around efforts. The *Los Angeles Sentinel* praises his rebounding on both ends of the floor, writing that he "often [made] the fabulous Bill Russell look silly." "He still found time to be the team's playmaker," the sportswriter continues. "[W]henever a teammate was in position for a shot, Baylor fed him the ball." The Negro paper estimated 30 percent of the turnout to have been colored fans.

* * *

The Lakers spent the holiday season traveling and playing basketball but seldom winning. The day after Christmas, they found themselves in New York, getting ready to play the Knicks. That night, the Lakers gathered in Dressing Room 34 at Madison Square Garden—a dingy, bare place with peeling plaster walls, a row of coat hooks above a line of splintery benches, and a bath and shower room that afforded no privacy.

According to *Sports Illustrated*, as they awaited their game, the players heard a roar. "Who they cheering up there?" Baylor asked. Tom Hawkins went to look inside, where the Harlem Globetrotters were warming up. "Willie Mays; they were cheering Willie," Hawk told his teammates. "He's still something around here, New York, I guess," Baylor said nonchalantly. "He's nothing at all in San Francisco," said Krebs. "They don't dig him up there."

When they took to the court, Baylor and the Lakers lacked spirit throughout the first half. The Knicks, the worst team in the NBA, led at halftime, 66–36. The *Sports Illustrated* account says one fan practically chased the Lakers into the tunnel at intermission, yelling, "Hey, Baylor, stay down there! Whyn't ya stay inna dressing room? Stay there, ya hear!"

During the break, Coach Schaus harangued the players, who hung their heads. "I never heard him name names before," Krebs said later. Jerry West commented, "We deserved it."

At the start of the second half, Baylor drove for repeated scores. He finished with 44 points, and the Lakers outscored the Knicks, 76–53. In addition to his scoring, Baylor, outnumbered by taller Knicks under the basket, grabbed offensive rebounds with abandon. Despite the comeback, New York won, 119–112.

A *Sports Illustrated* feature that followed the Lakers on their road trip recounts the Lakers' postgame. The Lakers dressed in silence after the game. Then the door flew open, and the first autograph hounds bounded in. They held their programs to Baylor first. "Hey, Jimmy," Baylor leered wickedly at Krebs. "How do you spell Khrushchev?" "K-R-U-S-C-H-E-

V," innocently advised Krebs. Baylor was overjoyed. "Naw, it's K-H-R-U-S-H-C-H-E-V. How come, here's a man, his name is in the papers every day, and you don't know how to spell it?" Happily he scribbled "Khrushchev" on a boy's program, and then, because he was one up on Krebs, he scrawled "Elgin Baylor" under it. After the game the Lakers and the Knicks scrambled aboard the same charter bus for a trip to Newark and then ultimately to Syracuse by chartered plane. Frost festooned the windows as the players settled in for the ride under the Hudson.

In Newark, at 1 a.m. on December 27, wind whipped through the city while the Lakers straggled through the airport. A porter's mop spewed wisps of steam. A cute stewardess emerged from among the tall athletes. *Sports Illustrated* assigned the *Los Angeles Times'* Jim Murray to traveling to cover the team for a feature called "A Trip for Tall Men." Murray reported that from the Lakers, a low whistle emerged, and one yelled to the stewardess, a complete stranger, "I love you very much," while the guys doubled over in laughter. "Was that you, Rudy? That was you, I heard you," insisted Baylor. Rudy LaRusso, a former Dartmouth All-American and one of the few Ivy Leaguers in professional sports, looked hurt. "It was somebody else," he said.

When their plane landed in Syracuse at 2 that same morning, Jim Murray reported it was five degrees and snowing steadily. The next day, snow flurries hit downtown Syracuse, and the temperature sign of a savings and loan building read 19 degrees.

When the Lakers took on Syracuse the next day, the game was tied, 113–113, near the end of the contest, with 37 seconds to play. Syracuse missed a layup. Krebs and Hundley both grabbed for the ball but lost it. The Nats' Hal Greer picked it up, shot, and missed. Baylor rebounded. With 23 seconds to go and 16 to shoot, he passed to West, who fired and missed. With four seconds left, Nats center Johnny Kerr threw in a 25-footer for the win.

Various Lakers complained in their dressing room about the officiating. The Lakers arrived in Philly from Syracuse on a short hop that was not allowed to land in Wilkes-Barre. In Philly, the shoeshine boys greeted the visitors with more enthusiasm than they'd seen in previous stops.

In the Murray article, one boy said, "There's ol' Tom Hawkins."

"Hawk, give 'em your autograph," encouraged Krebs.

Baylor joked, "They don't want his autograph; they want Ivy Baker Priest's. They're not basketball fans; they're money fans."

In the cigar-stenched lobby of the Bellevue-Stratford Hotel, a man asked the Lakers' Ray Felix, "Are you Wilt the Stilt? I'd like to tell my kids."

"No, I'm not," Felix said, according to Murray's account of the road trip the final week of December 1961. "But if you're looking to give Wilt some money, I'll take it for him."

A lady huffed her disapproval. "You'd think this was a gymnasium."

They beat the Knicks in Philly, 111–95, for their second win of the trip, which had started 10 days earlier in Portland, Oregon.

The next day, against St. Louis, Elgin scored five quick buckets on Cliff Hagan in the first quarter. Then the Hawks put in burly Woody Sauldsberry at forward. Sauldsberry held Baylor to only 1-for-12 shooting in the second half, for a total of 23 points, 11 below his average. L.A. lost, 107–99. In the locker room, the guys again blamed the refs, this time for allowing "Saulds" to manhandle Baylor.

The team then flew to Detroit, where a new record label called Motown had just signed the Primettes, who would become the Supremes. While the Caprice Room of the Sheraton-Cadillac Hotel prepared for rowdy New Year's Eve revelers, the Lakers lounged in sweat suits and watched college basketball on their hotel TV sets. Schaus broke out some champagne and a platter of sandwiches; the sandwiches disappeared first. The team toasted the New Year. "Happy New Ye-e-e-a-r" could be heard in the hallways outside.

Baylor lived up to his recent notices, with 39 points against the Pistons in a 116–105 loss on New Year's Day. The two teams traveled to Philadelphia, where they again met the following day. This time the Lakers won, 123–113, with Baylor scoring 46.

Baylor was a team player on and off the court, as several of his fellow black players have attested. He was a significant influence on rookie Jerry West early on. West mentions Baylor in the acknowledgments of his 2011 memoir, *West by West*, crediting Baylor with taking him under his wing and demonstrating what it meant to be a professional basketball player. West struggled during his first year with the Lakers, in part because Schaus did not start him until the 20th game of the season and also moved him to the backcourt—which required more ballhandling and passing skills than he had developed as a college forward. The lessons West learned from Baylor became invaluable, although Baylor was also known to tease his teammate about his accent and preference for tweed jackets. The combination earned West the nickname "Tweety." "Nice jacket," Baylor would reportedly say. "Does it come in men's sizes, too?"

Fellow forward Tommy Hawkins, when asked about Baylor in the August 8, 1960, *Ogden, Utah Standard-Examiner* article "Lakers Emphasize, Baylor Is Not for Sale at Any Price," said, "I count Elgin as one of my very best friends and undoubtedly the greatest player in the game." As with "Sweet" Charlie Brown at Seattle University, Baylor bonded with the talented Hawkins from Chicago. Of Baylor's game, Hawkins, a great leaper himself, admiringly said, "Elg can do everything and do it a little better than anybody else."

Coach Fred Schaus encouraged bonding among his players by asking them to rotate their roommate pairings when they traveled so that by season's end each team member would have traveled as a tandem with every other. Frank Selvy expressed only a minor objection to the system: "[W]hen a fellow gets used to one roommate, he has to change. As for the race angle, it makes absolutely no difference to me . . . and I can say . . . that I have heard no complaints on that sense from any other member of the team." Selvy told the *Sentinel* the Lakers never thought about race.

Later that January, two leaders of the new school of basketball improvisation—Elgin Baylor and Oscar Robertson—met on January 14, 1961, at the Los Angeles Sports Arena. Fans on hand were treated to 45-point performances by both Cincinnati rookie Robertson and hometown hero Baylor. Each man broke the arena scoring record during the 123–114 game, which was nationally televised. A few weeks after John F. Kennedy's presidential inauguration, Robertson and Baylor played in another game at the University of Maryland's Cole Field House. Baylor's mother attended, as did Stewart Udall, new president JFK's secretary of the interior, the government branch where Mrs. Baylor worked. Udall's brother Morris, a former professional basketball player in Denver in 1948–1949, won a special election to replace Stewart in Congress and would remain in office for the next 30 years. In 1962, as interior secretary, Stew Udall would order Baylor's hometown Washington Redskins to sign a black football player or risk being evicted from the newly constructed D.C. Stadium, which sat on federal land. It was reluctant Redskins owner George Preston Marshall who drafted offensive end Ron Hatcher from Michigan State. The city Baylor had left seven years earlier was the last in the NFL to integrate its roster.

Before another game pitting the Lakers against Cincinnati, Royals coach Charley Wolf sat in the locker room, wondering how his team should defend Baylor. Jack Twyman, a great jump shooter who NBA opponents called "Pitchin' Jack," volunteered for the unenviable duty of guarding him. Twyman stood 6'6" and weighed 210 pounds, and he had perfected his shooting touch by practicing 200 jumpers, 100 free throws, and 100 to 150 set shots a day, four days a week. Still, Baylor scorched Twyman for 28 in the first half alone. After the game, reporters asked Twyman why he, a scorer himself, had taken on the difficult defensive task. "I thought I did a heck of a job on him," said Twyman in all seriousness.

Baylor was modest under the circumstances. He told Milton Gross in *SPORT*'s April 1961 article "Elgin Baylor and Basketball's Big Explosion,"

> It's not just me. I don't think there's anybody in this league who can stop any one of 75 to 80 percent of the players on any night, playing him one-on-one. A defensive man might do it one night when the fellow is having a bad game, which all of us have. But other nights he couldn't shut the other man out.

It was a basketball truth: When a hot man is on, an all-league defender can't thwart him. In "Elgin Baylor and Basketball's Big Explosion," 76ers forward Dave Gambee says, "Actually, there's no way for one ballplayer to stop another one who's a great shot, like Bob Pettit or Elgin Baylor. You just can't stop such guys. They have too many moves. What you're doing is trying to aggravate the guy, make him give up his best shots." Gambee explains that the tactic was to force players to their weaker hand or get inside scorers to take outside shots. Wilt Chamberlain averaged nearly as many points against Russell as he did against the rest of the league. Pete Maravich once exploded for 68 against stellar defender Walt Frazier of the Knicks. Hakeem Olajuwon made some of his most famous moves ("dream shakes") against David Robinson. When such defenders as Gerald Wilkins or Paul Pressey guarded Michael Jordan, it's not as if Jordan would score only 16 points. Baylor recognized that early on and used the knowledge to his advantage—his 61 points in the NBA Finals were against Satch Sanders and the NBA greatest all-time defender, Bill Russell.

"Jack Twyman, Elgin Baylor, Tommy Heinsohn, these guys were unstoppable," St. Louis' Cliff Hagan told the author. "I thought I was unstoppable."

Warriors player Al Attles also told the author of Baylor,

> Nobody has stopped him, so you try to limit what he's doing. . . . Don't
> let him leave the locker room. You try to keep him from getting the
> basketball. He knows where he's going, and on defense, you don't
> know where you're going. He had so many other things going for him.
> He knew how to get open to get the ball. He could steal the ball, he
> could rebound, he could pass.

Knicks' coach and former All-Star Carl Braun explained to *Time* magazine for the February 17, 1961, cover article "The Graceful Giants" that Baylor was the cream of a talented NBA crop: "For doing everything, Elgin's got to be the best. He can take the big man or the small one. Put a press on against the Lakers and it won't be Hot Rod Hundley or Jerry West who'll handle the ball; it'll be Baylor." And then came the highest praise: "Not even Bob Cousy can dribble the ball as forcefully as he and control it better." At the time, Hundley and Cousy were widely considered two of the premier ball handlers in basketball. A Lakers media guide raves about Baylor's gifts as a passer: "[H]is passes from one side to the other from impossible angles and out of impossible tangles were spectacular too."

In *24 Seconds to Shoot*, Koppett says, "If anyone could match Oscar [Robertson] on the versatility scale—it was Baylor." Hawks guard Slater Martin told Jeremiah Tax for the *Sports Illustrated* profile of Baylor "Bunyan Strides Again," which appeared on April 6, 1959, "Throw a press on the Lakers, and Baylor will bring it [the ball] up. He's a great dribbler, with good control of the ball. You're not going to take it away from him."

On January 17, 1961, the NBA All-Star Game was played at Onondaga County War Memorial coliseum in Syracuse, New York. The West's starting five were Gene Shue, Oscar Robertson, Clyde Lovellette, Bob Pettit, and Elgin Baylor. With the rookie Robertson feeding Pettit and Baylor, the West raced to a 47–19 first-quarter lead before winning, 153–131.

Baylor played 27 minutes, during which he scored 15 points, including 9 of 10 foul shooting. He collected 10 rebounds and handed out four assists. Lakers teammate Hot Rod Hundley scored 14, and their rookie, Jerry West, scored 9 points in 25 minutes. The paid attendance was 8,016.

Back in L.A., where he was hospitalized for gall bladder complications, Lou Mohs told Roger Kahn for his March 27, 1961, *Sports Illustrated* article "Success and Ned Irish," "Moneywise? We are better than 2–1 over last year." Several local groups had approached Bob Short regarding the sale of the franchise, but management was satisfied at the moment.

The *Los Angeles Times* opined, "Probably the biggest reason the Lakers have been a success at the gate is Elgin Baylor, the basketball player who defies a nickname. . . . Baylor is such a complete player that no eager sportswriter has been able to coin a nickname for him," according to the *Times* article headlined "Baylor Faces Army Call in Month," from November 11, 1961.

* * *

The 1961 All-NBA Team featured old warhorses Cousy and Pettit and three dynamic young black stars, Baylor, Chamberlain, and Robertson. Baylor led all 1961 playoff performers in points per game (38.1, one more than Chamberlain), minutes played, free throws, and field goals. He was also fifth in assists, with 4.6 a game. As a rebounder, few could match his 19.8 average for the 1960–1961 season, fourth best in the league. He was still the most versatile player in the game. Jim Murray writes that Baylor's nickname in the league was "The Big Hurt" and that opposing players stocked up on liniment and aspirin before guarding him. The witty sportswriter believed the Hawks' penny-pinching owner, Ben Kerner, had spent $15,000 and a player to acquire Woody Sauldsberry for the sole purpose of containing Baylor. "It's a measure of the effectiveness of Baylor," Murray contended, "that NBA teams . . . have to have one magnetic anti-Baylor device in their arsenal at all times just to keep him from running away with the game."

On January 24, Baylor scored 56 points against Syracuse. On February 16, he totaled 57 points against the Detroit Pistons. The next day, *Time* magazine devoted its cover, featuring a painting of young Oscar Robertson, to the new-age NBA. The article celebrates not only the game's increasing popularity and soaring league scoring averages, but also a futuristic level of player: "Gone is the glandular goon of yesteryear

who could do little more than stand beneath the basket and stuff in rebounds."

Not many years earlier, 6'9" Bob Pettit had written an article in the *Saturday Evening Post* titled "Don't Call Us Freaks." But as *Time*, Milton Gross, and others chronicled basketball's stylistic evolution, early 1960s NBA team owners struggled to bring their league national acceptance. Broadcast quality of games was poor, and the biggest stars—Chamberlain, Russell, Robertson, and Baylor—were African Americans. Such major media markets as Chicago and New York featured some of the league's worst teams.

Boxer Cassius Clay declares in the October 16, 1961 *Sports Illustrated* feature "Cassius Comes of Age," that it was an era of records: "This is an age of records and record-breaking," he said. "If you don't break some records you're a no one." And 1961 was a year of big numbers in sports: In baseball, New York Yankees outfielders Roger Maris and Mickey Mantle chased Babe Ruth's single-season home run record, which Maris would break. In basketball, Wilt Chamberlain began his record-breaking average of 50 points a game. Baylor would go on to average 34.8 points and 19.8 rebounds a game for the 1960–1961 season. For the NBA, it was the first season three players—Chamberlain, Baylor, and Robertson—averaged more than 30 points a game. In the racial climate, it was difficult to ignore that all three were Negroes.

Not all sportswriters welcomed the offensive bonanza or the new type of basketball star. The *New York Times'* Red Smith and the *Washington Post*'s Shirley Povich, no fans of basketball in any case, cited the astronomical scores as another of the game's shortcomings. One headline about Chamberlain read, "The More He Scores, the More He Bores." Jimmy Powers, an influential sportswriter with the *New York Daily News*, declared basketball players "freakish" and "praying mantis types." Red Smith's boss, Stanley Woodward, who stood 6'4", said, "I have strong reservations about the masculinity of any men who play the game in short pants." Bud Collins of the *Boston Globe* suggested the Celtics hire a giraffe, saying, "His presence would be no more of a travesty than Chamberlain's."

In a 1964 Associated Press column titled "Are Court Giants Ruining Basketball?" Charles J. Livingston relates that players like Chamberlain, Russell, "and their Jack-the-Beanstalk ilk . . . have made the game an exclusive club for tall men only. . . . Many fans don't especially like this.

They think the human giraffe [*sic*] are making the game too mechanical, and thus lack-lustre." Livingston quotes a fan who barked at him that basketball had "lost its glamor." The fan protested, "All you see is a bunch of tall guys who run and shoot and dunk all night. There is no color and excitement . . . little ballhandling. . . . If someone misses a shot, one of those tall gooks tips it in anyhow." Livingston defends the larger players, citing their agility and style: "Just watch . . . Chamberlain sinking his favorite fadeaway shot, or Elgin Baylor or Bob Pettit maneuvering in for a basket." The columnist believed such stars had "brought so much color to the game." Perhaps for the spectator Livingston had quoted, that color—black—was the source of the turnoff.

This negative coverage was the polar opposite of the folk-hero status accorded such white basket-fillers as 6'9" Bevo Francis of Ohio's tiny Rio Grande College in the mid-1950s; Furman University's Frank Selvy, who scored 100 points in a college game in February 1954; or late 1960s Louisiana State University ace "Pistol" Pete Maravich. Francis became so popular in print and newsreels that Rio Grande eventually scheduled games against schools the likes of Villanova, Wake Forest, and North Carolina State. Songs were written about the mop-topped Maravich. By the mid-1960s, Baylor's own teammate, Jerry West, was promoting Jantzen sportswear in leading magazines, the kind of opportunity not afforded Elgin Baylor and virtually unheard-of for any black sports stars. Baylor and West were subject to the same racial dynamics seen with such black–white star tandems as Bill Russell and Bob Cousy, and Oscar Robertson and Jerry Lucas. "I was the darling of the media," Cousy admits in Goudsouzian's *King of the Court.* "There might have been an unspoken rivalry [with Russell]." After Cousy retired in 1963, a fan sniped at Russell, "You'd better hustle now that you don't have Cousy to carry you."

In Cincinnati, Robertson believed the front office favored Lucas, a local product of nearby Middletown High School, where he was a nationally renowned schoolboy sensation and an Ohio State All-American. Lucas was a Phi Beta Kappa who married a barber's daughter when he was 20. When his Ohio State team played on a barnstorming tour of the Buckeye State, Lucas reminded promoters that he was the cause of 50 percent of the attendance and that the rest of the players should divide the remaining gate receipts among themselves.

Although there were exceptions, for instance, the *New York Post*'s Milton Gross, Baylor was not as celebrated as he deserved to be. He tended to be the Willie Mays or Gale Sayers of his sport: Mr. Excitement. Unlike Frank Selvy, Bevo Francis, or ballyhooed Hot Rod Hundley, Baylor was a savvy all-around player. In a league that defined itself by the Russell–Chamberlain wars under the basket, Baylor explored new ways to attack the lane from the wing. For him, each play was a progression from thought to defensive reaction to counteroffensive. Here, in one athlete, were the smarts of Pettit, the creativity of Cousy, and the scoring punch of "Jumpin' Joe" Fulks, combined with the rebounding ability of the NBA's better big men. Baylor could also pass the basketball in traffic and on the fast break—the rare unselfish scorer. Longtime NBA referee Earl Strom states in Thomas J. Whalen's book *Dynasty's End: Bill Russell and the 1968–69 World Champion Boston Celtics*, "He was an excellent passer and made some mediocre teammates successful as a result. He was often double- and triple-teamed and still managed to get the job done."

"He literally became the first guy that you couldn't guard," says Bob Cousy in *Tall Tales*. Lou Mohs told *Sports Illustrated* in the April 6, 1959, profile of Baylor, "Finesse usually happens in small people, about 5 foot 9. But Elgin is so quick of mind and hand he gets his shots off no matter how good the defense is. . . . He comes up with the second and third try on the same ball."

It wasn't until years later that such players were commonplace in the professional ranks. In the late 1960s, when Detroit's Dave Bing, San Francisco's Rick Barry, and Philadelphia's Billy Cunningham floated to the hoop, they were following Baylor's flight patterns. The urban moves of Cazzie Russell, Earl Monroe, and Jimmy Walker bore traces of Baylor's game—all spins, dips, and feints. Speaking of the high flyer, Coach Fred Schaus said to Myron Cope for *SPORT* magazine's March 1963 piece "Life with Elgin Baylor," Baylor "shows me something new every game I see him play."

SLAM magazine editor Scoop Jackson said, "Elgin Baylor was the originator of the fly game. What Bob Cousy did on the ground, Baylor did in the air. Before Hawkins, Erving, David Thompson, or Jordan, there was Elgin. Relying on nothing but 'instincts,' he created moves previously unseen."

In their final regular-season game on March 12, the Lakers jumped out to a big lead in their game with the Royals. Cincinnati fought back, but L.A. withstood a late surge by their opponents. West scored with seven seconds left to put the Lakers ahead, 120–119. Then Baylor stole the inbound pass, was fouled, and hit both free throws. He finished with 49 points and L.A. won, 123–122. Oscar Robertson had scored 38; Twyman 28; and Wayne Embry 25, with 25 rebounds. Although Los Angeles' record was only 36–43, they still finished in second place in the NBA Western Division and qualified for the postseason playoffs. The first round, against the Detroit Pistons, was next.

As the Western Division playoffs kicked off, Los Angeles downed Detroit, three games to two. Baylor set the tone in the opening game by scoring 40 points in 39 minutes. The Lakers advanced to meet the more experienced St. Louis Hawks. Jim Murray speculated that Woody Sauldsberry might prepare for his confrontations with Baylor by running into the sides of garage doors with his eyes closed and beating his own ribs with a sledgehammer.

After the Lakers won the first game in St. Louis, the Hawks tied the series, 1–1, with a home victory, 121–106, although the game was marred by technical foul calls against Len Wilkens and Fred Schaus, and a verbal attack by Hawks owner Ben Kerner on ref Sid Borgia. Kerner had to be physically restrained by his associates. Lou Mohs said to the AP on March 24, 1961, that the Hawks fans were "uncivilized, crude, and vicious," and that Kerner "permits fans to get away with unwarranted abuses by condoning rowdyism," adding that "the problem existing in St. Louis is not present anywhere else." Mohs vowed to appeal to Commissioner Podoloff for protection for his squad during their next visit to Kiel Auditorium, insisting, "Our team is entitled to protection from egg throwers and other jerks at St. Louis." St. Louis native and Lakers center Jim Krebs, the target of a thrown beer during game two, said, "I'm ashamed I come from here."

This playoff series helped pull in Lakers fans in a big way. Longtime Lakers announcer Chick Hearn, who worked the Lakers radio broadcasts, believed the team caught on for good during the 1961 postseason. The Hawks and Lakers were tied at two games apiece when Bob Short called him at 2 a.m., asking him to go to St. Louis to broadcast the next playoff game on TV. Hearn informed Short he couldn't get to a TV station by the next night but suggested an alternative: He could do the game for his employer, KNX radio. The station boasted a 50,000-watt signal, and during game time its clear channel would be enhanced, as many AM stations signed off at dark. Short agreed. In those days, Los Angeles sportswriters did not accompany the team on road trips, so fans depended on radio for coverage.

When the Lakers met the Hawks for game five on March 27, Hearn was on hand for what became a tense battle, which the Lakers won, 121–112.

Game six was played on March 30, in front of 14,844 throaty fans in the Sports Arena. Tom Hawkins gave the Lakers their first lead, 96–95, with 1:58 left. The Lakers led the Hawks, 100–98, with only six seconds to play. St. Louis would pass the ball inbounds from half-court. Schaus instructed his players to foul the Hawks for a one-shot backcourt foul. Baylor practically tackled a Hawks player, but the refs missed it. An instant later, Lenny Wilkens drew a two-shot foul. He sank them both, and the teams were deadlocked at 100 at the buzzer. The teams were tied at the end of regulation. KMOX announcer Jerry Gross, Hearn's St. Louis counterpart, called his trademark plug: "Grab a bottle of Busch, we're goin' into overtime." It was the Lakers' first overtime at home all season. L.A. went up, 107–104, with 2:12 remaining, when Baylor fouled out guarding Pettit. With the home team's catalyst absent, St. Louis went on to a 114–113 victory.

In the locker room, Fred Schaus told the press that one man beat his ball club: "I don't mean Pettit. The Hawks had a guy on their side; I'm speaking of Jim Duffy, the referee that we couldn't beat along with Pettit, Hagan, and Sauldsberry." He called it his toughest loss in 17 years of playing and seven as a coach. Schaus insisted Baylor fouled Wilkens twice where he would have been awarded only one free throw, fouls Duffy ignored.

Someone asked, "Do you want us to print that, Fred?" "Go ahead. This is going to cost me anyway," he said of the inevitable fine from the league commissioner's office for criticizing an official. "I can tell you this: Duffy is not going to officiate the final game of this series in St. Louis."

Duffy, a crew-cut Irish Rhode Islander with a paunch, told media, "What Schaus says doesn't bother me a bit." He added, "He got 17 more fouls than St. Louis" in the Lakers' most recent series win.

Southern California fans were hooked by the excitement. On April Fools' Day, the Lakers succumbed, 105–103, at St. Louis's Kiel Auditorium, but Hearn considered the seven-game series against Bob Pettit's former champion Hawks a "turning point" for Lakers basketball support.

It was the beginning of a strong fan base and a bright future for the new Los Angeles team.

While he had a few obstacles to overcome—as an African American, a staunch union man, and someone toiling in a sport still struggling for respectability and coverage—Elgin Baylor would prove the perfect marketing entity for the Lakers and the NBA. He was a witty interviewee with an opinion about everything and a colorful team leader. He was a snazzy dresser, and he played in the league's second-largest market. He showcased his skills in the NBA Finals every year. As talented and appealing as Pettit and Cousy were, neither personified the NBA's move to Hollywood. While many fans and media felt Wilt Chamberlain made scoring appear too easy, Baylor's degree of difficulty warranted admiration.

Coaches abandoned the college ranks to steer the Lakers ship: Fred Schaus, Joe Mullaney, Butch van Breda Kolff. While Oscar Robertson languished in unappreciative Cincinnati, barely abiding star teammate Jerry Lucas, Baylor played for the most popular NBA franchise and teamed with West to take them to the Finals each season. Russell and Cousy combined to draw only an average of 8,000 fans during the height of their dynasty. Wilt, the statistical dynamo, floundered from city to city. But Baylor was a Laker to the painful end of his career. Had the NBA's first Western expansion fizzled, as did Cincinnati, Baltimore, and San Diego, America's basketball narrative would be absent Los Angeles's record 33 consecutive game-winning streak of 1971–1972, Kareem Abdul-Jabbar's return to the city of his collegiate glory, "Showtime," and the pairing of Shaq and Kobe. Since 1975, the Golden State (formerly San Francisco) Warriors have been an afterthought. Robertson's former team bides its time in Sacramento. Seattle lost its SuperSonics. Yet, the Lakers remain a legacy, and Baylor, with his ability to attract celebrity and pedestrian fans, laid the foundation.

7

THE FIRST SUPERSTAR

It eluded us then, but that's no matter—tomorrow we will run faster, stretch out our arms farther.—F. Scott Fitzgerald, *The Great Gatsby*

On May 5, 1961, Alan Shepard flew on *Freedom 7* as part of Project Mercury, a suborbital mission that lasted only 15 minutes and 28 seconds. On May 25, President John F. Kennedy announced his support for the Apollo program in a special address to a joint session of Congress.

The space race was largely driven by the Cold War. On June 4, Soviet premier Nikita Khrushchev threatened to sign a separate peace treaty with East Germany, effectively ending American, French, and British access rights to West Berlin. In a nationally televised address on July 25, President Kennedy requested an increase in the U.S. Army's total strength, from 875,000 to 1 million troops, along with an increase of 29,000 and 63,000 soldiers in the active-duty strength of the U.S. Navy and U.S. Air Force, respectively. He also ordered that draft calls be doubled and asked Congress for authority to order to active duty certain ready reserve units and individual reservists. The conflict concerning Berlin led to the construction of the Berlin Wall in the summer of 1961.

That summer, after his third year with the Lakers, Elgin Baylor signed a five-year pro basketball contract for an undisclosed figure. Lakers owner Bob Short hinted that the deal was worth about $250,000, making Baylor the second-highest-paid man in the game. His general popularity and All-American, family man image were literally paying off, and the city's African American community was particularly proud. In a January 1961 *Los Angeles Sentinel* poll, he and University of California, Los

Angeles's track idol and Olympic decathlon king Rafer Johnson tied as L.A.'s most popular Negro athletes. The *Sentinel* reported that at a sports banquet, teammate Rudy LaRusso told Baylor, "We honor you, Elgin, not only because you have a mountain of talent, but because you have a mountain of humility, too. I am honored to be on your side."

Jerry West told *Sports Illustrated* that Baylor was so popular, if he ran for president, "he'd be president until 1984."

In the off-season, Baylor worked as a customer relations representative in the escrow department of Great Western Savings & Loan. In August, the Lakers' 36-year-old coach, Fred Schaus, worked out with his club every Wednesday at Pepperdine University. "I'm mighty glad I hung up my uniform before I had to guard guys like Elgin Baylor," Schaus told the *Los Angeles Times*. The Lakers invited four rookies, including two Negro players from Pepperdine, Bobby Sims and Sterling Forbes, to join them. The public was barred from the team's two-a-day practices during their preseason camp at Pepperdine.

The first preseason game was scheduled against the repeating champion Boston Celtics in San Francisco on September 30. The game would be broadcast back to L.A. on KRJ TV, sponsored by Hamm's Beer. Coach Schaus named Baylor team captain, the first such leadership position for a Negro National Basketball Association player. The new rules prohibiting coaches from bickering with referees prompted Schaus's move to name a surrogate. "Baylor was the absolute natural choice," Schaus told the *Times*, adding, "Not only is he our best player, but he is the type of superstar who commands the respect and admiration of our team off the court, as well as on it. Actually, I had no other logical choice. He has been the natural leader all along any way." The coach said the unofficial leadership role had "more or less been assumed by his fellow Lakers."

Baylor and the Lakers met the Syracuse Nats in a preseason game in Portland, Oregon. The many Pacific Northwest fans who recalled the Baylor of Seattle days—who scored 60 against the University of Portland in the Civic Auditorium—were not disappointed with the 1962 model. The Nats assigned a rookie from North Carolina, Lee Shaffer, to "guard" him. At one point Baylor hauled in a long pass in front of the Lakers' bench. Shaffer overplayed Baylor to force him left, but Baylor spun in a half circle and broke for an easy hoop, causing Shaffer to fall off balance on his rear. "Welcome to the league, rook!" quipped Lakers trainer Frank O'Neill in the *Los Angeles Times* account of the game.

* * *

The 1961–1962 season had hardly gotten under way when Baylor was called up by Uncle Sam on November 26. The Berlin Crisis forced many such men from their jobs and homes. Other pro athletes who did military service included Green Bay Packers halfback Paul Hornung, Yankees shortstop Tony Kubek, San Diego Chargers offensive lineman Ron Mix, and Redskins running back Bobby Mitchell. Just a few weeks before Baylor received the call, a young man from Seattle named Jimi Hendrix reported for military duty at Fort Campbell, Kentucky, home of the 101st Airborne. Baylor got to stay a little closer to home, serving as a reservist at Fort Lewis, Washington. Baylor's departure would leave the Lakers shorthanded and possibly create an opening for a new pro basketball rival in L.A.: the Los Angeles Jets, which Abe Saperstein had founded along with the new American Basketball League after he was passed over for the first NBA franchise in Los Angeles. Saperstein hired former Boston Celtics coach Bill Sharman to head up his upstart Los Angeles Jets, which he hoped might be more of a drawing card in their first season without Baylor in town.

The Lakers prorated Baylor's $50,000 salary so that he would earn his pay for the games he was able to play. He played in the team's first 42 games through New Year's Day. When Chamberlain and the Warriors visited L.A. on December 1 and 2, Baylor scored 33 in the first game and 20 in the second. Two days later, he scored 50 against Syracuse on December 4.

A December 8 away game against Philadelphia was particularly memorable, ending in triple overtime. Before the historic contest, Wilt Chamberlain greeted Baylor, who was entering Convention Hall with his travel bag, where The Big Dipper's long legs were draped over the arena's stage. According to Milton Gross in his 1961 *SPORT* profile of Baylor, Chamberlain asked, "Have you heard the news, big fella? I'm gonna be checking you one-on-one tonight."

"I get nervous enough before a game," Baylor shot back. "Don't shake me up, buddy."

Wilt egged further, "You're gonna be my personal pigeon tonight."

The Lakers–Warriors game was tied at the end of regulation, 109–109. Baylor had scored 47 points, Chamberlain 53, one of the few times that two NBA players had combined for 100 points in a game. Jerry West won the game for Los Angeles in triple overtime, 151–147. Baylor added 16 points in the extra sessions, giving him 63 total. Wilt scored 25 more, finishing with 78, breaking Baylor's league record. Baylor, however, had scored his 71 in regulation time, and he preferred not to quibble over numbers. "When I play," Baylor told Gross for the 1961 *SPORT* cover article on the NBA's scoring explosion, "I don't think about how many points I'm scoring. It doesn't mean anything to me. I like to win." And when asked specifically about losing his high-points record, Baylor asked, "Record? So what? We won the game, didn't we?"

On December 11, Baylor gave the St. Louis Hawks 52 points and, on December 13, dropped another 52 on the Hawks. While Baylor was helping the Lakers set attendance records and breaking NBA scoring marks, the Vietnam War officially began on December 11, when the first American helicopters arrived in Saigon, along with 400 U.S. advisors.

That season, as a couple, the Baylors were part of the Los Angeles social scene. They made the Phi-Delphians club's holiday party, a smartly dressed affair where guests reveled in the dance sensation called the Twist, a term also often used to described Baylor's basketball moves.

On Christmas Day, the Lakers trounced the Royals, 141–127, in Cincinnati. Baylor and Oscar Robertson both hit for 40, Baylor's points including 10 free throws. On December 26, the Lakers fell to Boston, 129–117. An estimated 3,000 fans were turned away from the Boston Garden's east lobby before the game, the second of a doubleheader that also featured Wilt Chamberlain and the Warriors facing the Syracuse Nats. Baylor played 40 minutes, more than any Laker, and scored 30 points. His 18 rebounds also led his club. Asked about losing Baylor for another stint of military service, Coach Schaus told the *Los Angeles Times*, "Basketball waits 75 years for a 6'5" player like Baylor, so he can't be replaced in a week, eh?" Schaus didn't want opposing coaches to relax, however. He told *Sports Illustrated* that Tom Hawkins and Rudy LaRusso would play more and that the team would "do the best we can." As far as the Celtics, the Lakers coach admitted that Baylor's absence "kills a nice rivalry" with Boston. "Without him, we'll not be the same team."

Celtic southpaw Bill Russell said the following to the *Los Angeles Times* concerning Baylor's imminent departure: "I'm happy. . . . Toughest man to handle ever on a court, I'd say. . . . [C]an't pick his teeth with his left hand. . . . Force him to the left and he's got that spin back and in with the right. Impossible to stop, and on a one-handed player."

Red Auerbach didn't share in the doom and gloom concerning the Lakers' fortunes. "Don't sell them short," harps the cagey Brooklynite in the *Boston Globe*. "They'll play good ball."

On December 27, 1961, Baylor, with 16 baskets, 16 free throws, and 20 rebounds, led L.A. to a 119–111 win over the Syracuse Nats at Philadelphia's Convention Hall. The next night, he poured in 44, in a 121–114 win over the Nats at Syracuse.

Commissioner Podoloff allowed Baylor to play in the 1962 NBA All-Star Game on January 16 at Kiel Auditorium in St. Louis. All the big names were on hand in St. Louis: Cousy, Chamberlain, and Russell for the East, and Baylor, Robertson, and hometown favorite Bob Pettit for the West, although the end of Pettit's stellar career was near. A highlight video survives, produced by the Brunswick-McCormack sporting goods company, in conjunction with the Chicago Zephyrs, showing many of Baylor's key moves and big plays. For the game's first basket, Baylor fills the right lane on a fast break and scores a gliding layup off a lead bounce pass from Oscar Robertson. In another early moment, Baylor sets up his defender on the left side of the lane, spins, and drives to his right, near the foul line, where he leaves his feet with his body at a 45-degree angle from the basket and launches a successful off-balance one-hander. On another possession, Baylor receives a baseball pass from Robertson on the right side and is confronted by East center Bill Russell. He dribbles and banks in a one-handed runner, despite a hard Russell foul. A third drive demonstrates Baylor's yen for improvisation, as he drives the right side, is challenged by East All-Star forward Tommy Heinsohn, and takes to the air, bringing the basketball down to protect it and then releasing it for the layup as he clears the defender.

On defense, Baylor thwarts a driving effort by Heinsohn by shadowing the Celtic and getting his left hand in the path of the shot. He challenges a Paul Arizin jump shot, forcing Arizin to change and miss the attempt. He does the same in making Bob Cousy miss a jumper. In his own end of the court, Baylor intercepts a corner pass intended for Cousy and lays the ball in. When West teammate Bob Pettit launches a long jumper from the side, Baylor boxes out the much taller Chamberlain as the shot lofts in.

In a beautiful offensive move, Baylor slashes from the left, is confronted by the towering East giant Chamberlain, and barely drives free of him to bank in a swooping one-hander. On the right baseline, he scores on a running one-hand loft eight feet out, despite having to steady himself in midair against East forward Johnny Green's back. He demonstrates his versatility in the lane by backing against Green and then leaving his feet to flip in a backward shot over Green without facing the basket. On the dribble, he begins in his backcourt on the ride side and blows by a chasing Green all the way to the basket, only to have the layup rim off.

Baylor initiated most of his moves from the left of the lane, from a rocking "triple-threat position" (one from which a player may pass, shoot, or drive). From there, he attempted to get his defender off balance or lean in one direction by giving a head fake, shoulder feint, or crossover step. His pet move was a runner off the dribble from that position. When a taller defender reached up to block the running shot, Baylor either pulled the basketball down to protect it, only to raise it again when free of the opponent to score, or used his body control to stay airborne longer than his foe, float by, and bank the ball in. He dribbled with his back turned, shielding the defender from the ball, bouncing it at a safe, low level. As a pro, his ability to float by multiple defenders along the baseline before releasing his shots was more impressive than his leaping.

In *SPORT* magazine, sportswriter Bill Libby says of Baylor, "His favorite shot is a going-away flip over his shoulder—like Minnesota Fats banking a poolball into a side pocket."

The Lakers' Fred Schaus coached the West All-Stars to a 150–130 rout of the Eastern squad, as Baylor scored 32 points in 37 minutes, grabbed 9 rebounds, and had 4 assists. He sank 12 of his 14 free throws, but MVP honors went to St. Louis's Pettit, who scored 25 in 37 minutes, adding 27 rebounds. Chamberlain scored 42, with 24 rebounds, for the losers. The more than 15,000 fans who attended the contest saw not only Baylor at his best, but the entire league's premier talent during an unforgettable, record-setting season.

While Baylor was away, Jerry West hit the big time on January 17, when he scored 63 points on 22-for-36 shooting against the Knicks in front of only 2,766 Sports Arena onlookers. The second-year man had opened the 1961–1962 campaign with four consecutive 30-point games, serving notice to the league that defenses had more to worry about than Elgin Baylor. Another boost for the Lakers came from third-year man Rudy LaRusso. LaRusso, who still holds Dartmouth College records for rebounds in a single game (32), single season (503), and career (1,239), scored 17 points a game for the 1961–1962 Lakers and grabbed an average of 10 rebounds.

Then Baylor only played sparingly—three games from Wednesday, January 24, to Sunday, January 28. By late January, he had missed nine games due to his service. Lakers rooters eyed the team schedule and hoped Baylor would be given passes to play in key games. Late that month, the Sports Arena hosted a second farewell tribute to Baylor. Just as with the first time, he was showered with two standing ovations. Since the Cincinnati Royals were the closest team to the Lakers in the Western standings, fans were glad Baylor was granted a pass to face Oscar Robertson and the Royals on January 24 and 25; he played a Chicago Packers team led by Walt Bellamy that same Sunday.

Baylor played three more games on Sunday, February 18; Sunday, February 25; and Monday, March 12. He had been limited to a 48-game season, at about $600 a game. The *Los Angeles Times*' Jim Murray did some math to figure out what Baylor's service was costing not only the Lakers, but also the government. He estimated that Baylor paid the government $10,000 in annual income tax and noted that 10¢ from each Lakers' ticket sale went to Uncle Sam. With the team losing a projected $100,000 in sales due to his absence, the IRS was also losing $10,000. Adding what the government would be losing from Baylor's reduced salary, decreased home ticket sales, and smaller crowds at road games, the writer guesses the government would be $25,000 short compared to a regular Baylor campaign.

After his last game with the team for a while, nearly 7,000 fans in the Sports Arena showered Baylor with two standing ovations. The Lakers dispatched team doctor Ernie Vandeweghe to Seattle to press for better military accommodations for their superstar, in hopes that Vandeweghe's former status as a U.S. Air Force major would help secure Baylor a bed rather than a G.I.-issue cot.

According to Terry Pluto in *Tall Tales: The Glory Years of the NBA*, Baylor once phoned an army captain at the base and, when asked who was calling, replied, "Captain Baylor," as he was captain of the Lakers. The dispatcher put him right through. Military duty or not, the world was

Elg's oyster. The U.S. Army paid Baylor $89 a month, and he would return to L.A. for weekend games as often as he could: "I would get a weekend pass that began on midnight Friday, and I had to be back on midnight Sunday," Baylor said. "I'd take the red-eye on Friday to wherever the team was."

Celtics coach Red Auerbach protested Baylor's weekend-warrior NBA participation, telling the *Los Angeles Times*, "That's not fair and should not be allowed. If Baylor plays four times against us, he should play four times against Cincinnati too! That's only right." Lakers fans jokingly argued the opposite: "Look at how many dependents this guy has—a wife and a child, 11 teammates, a coach, and a general manager," one protested in the *Times*.

Lou Mohs responded by telling the *Times*, "Auerbach is worried about meeting the Lakers with Baylor in the lineup, and he couldn't care less about how other teams fare against the Lakers." Mohs continued, "It will be a mighty cold day in Boston when Auerbach worries about how Baylor's playing will affect other teams in the Western Division."

In his absence, fans called the team the "Baylor-less Lakers." Without their teammate, the athletic Tom Hawkins got more playing time, and Jerry West asserted himself more as a scorer.

Baylor did reserve duty for most of the 1961–1962 season. While the military had given him a special month's leave for January, NBA commissioner Maurice Podoloff inexplicably forbade him from playing with the Lakers during that break, although Baylor managed to play three games in late January. Perhaps Bob Short's fellow owners, especially the Eastern contingent led by Walter Brown had ganged up against their Western foes, and Auerbach's squeaky-wheel tactic had earned some grease. But Lakers supporters made their own noise. City councilwoman Rosalind Wiener Wyman got involved, labeling Podoloff's decision "discriminatory" and unjust. She told the *Los Angeles Times* that the National Football League and American Football League had allowed its players to perform during leaves of absence. "It just doesn't make any rhyme or reason," said Wyman. "Podoloff in a sense is depriving one of the greatest athletes of our era from participating in a profession where he is highly skilled. If this isn't discrimination, I don't know what you would call it." But Podoloff's ruling stood, and for the balance of the season, Baylor only joined the team during leave granted by the military.

KHJ TV simulcast a half-hour radio and TV tribute to Baylor. His reserve duty also prompted a farewell tribute at the Los Angeles Sports Arena during the season, before his first deployment. During the Sports Arena ceremony, Baylor received two standing ovations from Lakers faithful.

* * *

In late February, Baylor came in from Fort Lewis for a game against Boston and led L.A. to a 125–99 rout. Two days later, he was gone, and Boston got revenge in the Sports Arena, 115–96. Rebounding from another March 10 loss to Boston, the Lakers set a NBA West record on March 12 by winning their 52nd game of the season, 119–106, over the Knicks. Baylor was back on the court and scored 37.

Los Angeles finished the season 54–26, winning the West by 11 games over a much-improved Cincinnati and ranking 17 spots ahead of the third-place Pistons. The racially divided, aging St. Louis Hawks club slumped to 29–51, down from a 51–28 finish the year before and back-to-back NBA Finals appearances in both 1960 and 1961.

The 1961–1962 campaign proved a banner season for the entire league, as teams averaged a record 118.8 points per game. The year had been good for rookie Wilt Chamberlain, too, who scored his historic 100 points against the Knicks in Hershey, Pennsylvania, on March 2. His feat earned him a guest appearance on the popular *Ed Sullivan Show* two days later. The league-wide scoring boom did not translate into additional television success, however; NBC canceled its contract with the NBA after the season.

Legendary sportswriter A. S. "Doc" Young, a leading figure in the black press for decades, writes of Baylor in the *Los Angeles Sentinel*, "Seldom in this town's history has the vast superiority of an athlete been so unanimously acclaimed as in Elg's case," which Young felt "is . . . also a great tribute to the fine gentleman that he is."

Baylor, the Lakers' weekend warrior, averaged 38.3 points and 18.6 rebounds a game that season. ESPN.com's Bill Simmons has marveled in retrospect at the accomplishment, especially in light of Baylor's sporadic schedule: "I don't see how this happened," states Simmons in an October 28, 2008, ESPN.com article about how unappreciated a historic player Baylor is. Simmons rates Baylor's accomplishments in 1961–1962 above

Oscar Robertson's triple-double average that same season and Wilt Chamberlain's 50-point scoring average that same year. Simmons continues,

> It's inconceivable. A U.S. Army Reservist at the time, Elgin lived in a barracks in the state of Washington, leaving only whenever they gave him a weekend pass . . . and even with that pass, he could only fly coach on flights with multiple connections to meet the Lakers wherever they happened to be playing. Once he arrived, he would throw on a uniform and battle the best NBA players alive on back-to-back nights—fortunately for the Lakers, most games were scheduled on the weekends back then—and make the same complicated trip back to Washington on Sunday night or Monday morning.

Despite his own challenging schedule, Baylor has fond memories of his time with the Lakers that season. "It was an enjoyable year," Baylor recalls in Roland Lazenby's 2010 book *Jerry West: The Life and Legend of a Basketball Icon*. "Our camaraderie was great. On and off the court, we did things together. We enjoyed one another. As a team we gave the effort every night."

The U.S. Army granted Baylor an 18-day leave to compete in the 1962 playoffs. His coach defended the decision in the *Los Angeles Times*: "He should have the games that are coming to him," Schaus said. "Elgin's saved his dates for the playoffs." To be closer to Baylor, the Lakers practiced in Seattle three days before the playoffs. While there, the players worked in a visit to the Seattle World's Fair.

The Lakers looked forward to the playoffs and thought that, this time, they were capable of the big prize. "I'd like to win a world championship," Baylor says in Phil Pepe's book *Greatest Stars of the NBA*. "The owners don't want to know how many points you scored but where you finished." Rod Hundley told the *Times* that three years ago his team had entered the NBA Finals "with stars in our eyes." He added, "This year we belong in the Finals." They saw Boston, the defending NBA champs, as their biggest competition but also believed they were beatable—especially with Baylor in their back pocket. Hundley says in the *Times*, "We feel we can lick the Celtics. With Baylor, we've beaten the Celtics four out of five times this year. Without him, we've been whipped five out of six. So that's what one man has meant to the club." They had actually beaten Boston three out of four with Baylor and lost all five of their games against the Celtics without him. Although always harassed by a fresh Celtics defender, Baylor had managed a season average of 31 points, 15 rebounds, and 5 assists versus Boston.

In the opening round of the Western Division Finals, the Lakers eliminated the Detroit Pistons, four games to two.

When the Lakers met the Celtics for the first game of the 1962 NBA Finals in Boston, only 7,617 Celtics fans attended. Boston won, 122–108, although Baylor scored 35 points on 14 baskets and seven free throws. The Lakers evened the series with a 129–122 win at Boston, as Baylor scored 36 points. In Los Angeles, game three brought stars Danny Thomas, Dinah Shore, Doris Day, and Pat Boone, among a record throng of 15,180, to the Los Angeles Sports Arena. L.A. took a 12-point lead going into the fourth period. In the final moments of the game, a contest in which Baylor scored 39, Celtic Sam Jones threw a bad pass intended for Bob Cousy. Jerry West intercepted, and as seconds ticked off, his teammates on the bench yelled for him to pull up and shoot. West kept going and scored on a breakaway steal as time expired in the 117–115 squeaker. Elated fans surrounded West and patted him on the back. In Aram Goudsouzian's biography of Bill Russell, *King of the Court*, West calls it the "greatest thrill [he] ever had in basketball," while Red Auerbach whines that there was no way West could dribble 30 feet and score in three seconds. "I had deflected the ball on the run," West says in NBA.com's Playoff Encyclopedia. "I knew I would have enough time, because I knew what the shot clock was."

The Lakers fell the next night, 115–103, when Krebs was supremely outplayed by Russell. Baylor had poured in 38 on 14 baskets and 10 free throws to lead both teams.

The Lakers' biggest show of the series occurred on the road during game five. At the Boston Garden, visiting teams were given every disadvantage. In the arena, located under the North Station rail terminal, in a noisy, gritty section of the city, visiting players dressed in a 15-by-20-foot area with only nails on the wall to hang their clothing. There was one toilet, a sink, and a couple of showers that dispensed chilly water. Temperatures inside the dressing space ran from ice cold to sweltering hot. Playing conditions were no better, another psychological and physical burden for opponents. The Garden's trademark parquet floor, while beautiful on television, had dead spots where a bounced ball behaved differently. Home fans pressed against the sidelines during playoff games like a rowdy crowd at a summer league game. Hub fans were also known to cast foreign objects, from eggs to cups, toward the court during play.

Despite the conditions, on April 14, Baylor displayed his mastery on Boston's home court. He scored on turnaround jumpers, one-hand push shots, backward floaters, and runners, as he exploded for 61 points and collected 22 rebounds. Baylor's ballhandling was so deceptive, it was impossible to tell when he would stop and shoot. His footwork was so precise, he stepped and jabbed his way free for shots. Baylor set up some of his buckets by turning his back to his defender on the dribble and crouching near the top of the key, only to suddenly rise and pop in a shot. He accomplished this feat despite the defensive efforts of 6'6" Tom "Satch" Sanders, one of the league's premier defenders, and the inside presence of Bill Russell, the greatest defender in NBA history. "Elgin was just a machine," Sanders says of the performance in Scott Ostler and Steve Springer's 1986 book *Winnin' Times: The Magical Journey of the Los Angeles Lakers*. Baylor also achieved the Finals scoring record (which still stands) against constant Celtic double-teams. Boston fans awarded him a huge ovation upon his exit, and the Celtics lined up to shake his hand. The Lakers won the crucial game, 126–121. Baylor said, "All I remember is that we won the game. I never thought about how many points I had." The important victory gave L.A. a 3–2 series lead. According to Goudsouzian's *King of the Court*, Bob Short declared, "If we win the championship this year, I think we will dominate the league for several years to come."

Baylor and West combined for 44 points in the first half of game six. At the break, L.A. led, 65–57, but Boston turned up the defensive pressure and won, 119–105. By the end, West and Baylor had both scored 34, but no one could stop Sam Jones, who had banked in 35 of his own. Neither team had held serve; Boston had dropped games two and five in the Garden, and L.A. had blown games four and six at the Los Angeles Sports Arena. Some of Boston's key players seemed to be losing ground. The aging Cousy was playing with an injured hand, Heinsohn had received stitches in his head, and Russell was still fatigued from their series with Philadelphia.

The deciding game was set for April 18, the first day of Passover, and Celtics owner Walter Brown proposed postponing the game to accommodate Jewish fans. But Baylor, who had been released from army duty for the playoffs, was scheduled to return to Fort Lewis on the morning of

April 19. Eight thousand fans jammed Boston's Causeway Street for tickets, the earliest arriving at 3 a.m. Some 7,000 hopefuls were turned away, prompting a 22-year veteran beat patrolman to say, "I have never seen anything like this."

When game seven got under way, Boston rushed to a 53–47 halftime lead, despite uncharacteristic 1-for-10 shooting by Sam Jones. Loscutoff, Sanders, and Heinsohn fouled out in their efforts to guard the swooping Baylor. Heinsohn's sixth foul resulted in Baylor sinking two free throws—his 37th and 38th points of the game. Auerbach inserted 13-year veteran Carl Braun, a 6'5" guard he thought the officials would respect. The champions led, 96–91, in the fourth, when Baylor followed a successful jump shot by West with his own clutch free throw. Baylor scored only three points in the final four minutes, giving him 41. Russell sank two foul shots, but West stuck another jumper to trim Boston's advantage to 98–96. Sam Jones blocked a jumper by Frank Selvy and made two free throws, making the score Boston 100, L.A. 96. Then Selvy grabbed a rebound and drove all the way down the court for a layup. He added another basket off his own miss to tie things at 100. For Selvy, the 100-point performance seemed propitious, since it was the astronomical scoring total he had achieved on February 13, 1954, in Furman's Textile Hall, against Newberry College.

Boston and L.A. were deadlocked at 100 points. For Los Angeles's final possession, Baylor was the first option; he had already scored 41. West was the second option, with his own 35 points. L.A. inbounded the ball at midcourt with four seconds to play. "Hot Rod" Hundley had the ball at the top of the key and looked for both of the high scorers. He was open but hadn't played much in the game, so he felt he might be too cold to take the shot. Baylor screened and cut, but Russell blanketed him down low. West came off a pick on the right side, but K. C. Jones was draping him. Although for an instant he considered shooting, Hundley pivoted and spotted a wide-open Selvy 15 feet from the basket on the left baseline. From Selvy, one of basketball's most celebrated shooters, the player who had earned the Lakers a tie, two points would suffice. Performing his swan song, Bob Cousy had cheated to quickly double-team West. Hundley pump-faked a pass to West, then passed to Selvy, and Cousy shifted to recover, running at the shooter. It was a 10-foot shot—a virtual layup for Selvy. The effort sailed, caught the back rim, and caromed off. Rus-

sell snared the rebound, in his 40th of this contest. The game entered
overtime.

Both Baylor and Selvy believed they were fouled at the end of regulation. "Selvy thought Bob Cousy fouled him," Baylor states in Roland
Lazenby's 1996 book *The NBA Finals: A Fifty-Year Celebration*. He
continues,

> I thought Cousy fouled him. He took the shot from a spot where he
> was very proficient. . . . I was in a position to get the offensive re-
> bound. But somebody behind me shoved me out of bounds right into
> the referee. There was no foul call there, either. I looked around and
> saw Russell and Sam Jones behind me.

In the 1991 book *The Golden Game: The Hot Shots, Great Moments and
Classic Stories from Basketball's First 100 Years*, Billy Packer and Roland Lazenby report that years later, when Baylor saw film of game
seven, it confirmed for him that Sam Jones shoved him out of bounds and
out of position for the rebound. In time, Jones joked with Baylor and
admitted to having pushed him.

In any case, Russell opened the overtime with a rousing stuff shot.
Boston was playing a small lineup, including Cousy and both Jones boys.
Frank Ramsey fouled out guarding Baylor. Auerbach inserted a young,
little-used forward named Gene Guarilia to check Baylor. Baylor missed
a couple of shots in the extra period and then a free throw. He then fouled
out. Boston drew ahead by as much as seven, and Cousy dribbled out the
clock while being frantically chased by Ray Felix and other Lakers—not
unlike the way the Washington Generals stooge players might try to
corner the Globetrotters in a comic exhibition game. There had been 15
ties and 13 lead changes. The combined shooting percentages were only
34 percent in the sloppy affair, but in the end, Boston kept their status as
NBA champions for another year.

Afterward, in the somber dressing room, Baylor mused to the *Los
Angeles Times* about his missed shots, while West lamented the "breaks."
Selvy, who drew the Lakers close with his baskets, said, "but I missed the
big one." According to *The NBA Finals*, Hundley fumed to Selvy, "You
only cost us about $30,000." "Baby" Ray Felix took an optimistic tack;
he is quoted in *Jerry West: The Life and Legend of a Basketball Icon* as
having said, "That's all right baby, we'll get 'em tomorrow." The adults
in the room knew "tomorrow" meant 1963.

Auerbach admits in his memoir, *Seeing Red*, "I thought it was all over when Selvy shot from the left corner." Yet, he would have thought the win unfair. Criticizing the timekeeper years later, Auerbach further claims, "We were cheated. The timer froze. . . . Selvy takes the ball and goes up for a shot and misses it. The rebound goes in the air, and the clock still hadn't gone off. Baylor got the rebound and put it up and missed it. It was more than Selvy's shot."

In the early 1960s, Hundley had a habit of ribbing Selvy about his college days by way of the 1962 Finals controversy. "Fabulous Frank Selvy, the pride of Furman, the player of the decade," he'd joke, as quoted in the 1961 *Sports Illustrated* feature by L.A.'s Jim Murray "A Trip for Tall Men," "once scored a hundred points in one game." "Hey, Fab," he would shout, according to Murray's feature, "didn't the horn blow before you got that last bucket in? You didn't really hit for a C note, did you?" Baylor recognized that Selvy didn't appreciate the jokes: "Frank is very sensitive about things," Baylor told the *Los Angeles Times'* Sam Farmer for a June 20, 2010, article, "and he's not the type of person that likes to be teased about anything." For his part, Selvy maintains that he did his fair share for the team that night. He told Farmer in the same June 2010 *Times* article entitled "He Missed a Shot at Changing History," "I was five for five from the field and was guarding Sam Jones, and he hadn't scored a point. We had a 17-point lead. Then I get put on the bench, and by the time I come back in we're down by 10. Maybe Hot Rod can explain that." In truth, Selvy only shot 2-for-10 and did not score until the final minute, and Jones finished with 27. Time can play tricks on the memory—L.A. never led the game by 17.

Baylor believes a different outcome in 1962 would have changed NBA history. "It could possibly have changed things," Baylor told Farmer for the 2010 article on Selvy, "We always thought that we could win. We never thought we were going to lose. We just felt that we were good enough to win."

Yet, 1962 had its share of winning players, Baylor among them. For the first time, four Negroes finished as NBA scoring leaders: Wilt Chamberlain, Elgin Baylor, Walt Bellamy, and Oscar Robertson. When the 1961–1962 expansion Chicago Packers played Walt Bellamy, Horace Walker, Sihugo Green, Andy Johnson, and Woody Sauldsberry together, it was an all-black lineup. Two years later, a much better team, the perennial champion Celtics, used an all-Negro quintet of Bill Russell, Satch

Sanders, Willie Naulls, Sam Jones, and K. C. Jones. Leonard Koppett writes in his 1968 book *24 Seconds to Shoot*, "Baylor, Chamberlain, and Robertson had shattered any lingering doubts that Negro players might be 'less appealing' at the gate, or that they could be persuaded to work for less money than they deserved."

Elgin Baylor was thought by many to be the cream of this impressive crop. An April 1962 cover article for *SPORT* magazine asks, "Who Is the Best of Basketball's Superstars?" Hawks owner Ben Kerner, also Bob Pettit's employer, answers in the *SPORT* piece, "My choice for the individual greatest is Elgin Baylor." Esteemed St. John's University coach Joe Lapchick agrees in the same piece, saying, "I'm only in love with one guy—Baylor. To me he answers all the questions."

NBA All-Star Gene Shue recalls players trembling in the locker room before games when they were assigned to guard Baylor, who scored 50 or more points on 14 occasions during his prime. Shue, whose Maryland A.C. team Baylor had destroyed when he played with the D.C. Stonewalls, says in *Tall Tales*,

> You couldn't defend Elgin. He had such a good outside shot. He could stare you down. He had a quick jab step. He would catch the ball at the top of the key or further out, and he'd get you going back and forth. He'd just explode by you. . . . He was very, very hard to defend. Not only was he a good outside shooter, but he had a good deceptive first step. He had incredible strength and could hang in the air with the ball. When you put all those things together you couldn't stop him.

Former NBA forward Earl Lloyd concurred: "Elgin, he was the toughest guy to guard, period. If you're looking for the real pioneer of the games these kids play today, he's the one. More of them should know his game." All-Star guard Richie Guerin said, according to *SLAM* magazine in November 2010, "Elgin's either got three hands or two balls. It's like guarding a flood." Jerry West used to bet people they couldn't knock a basketball out of Baylor's strong hands. He never lost that wager.

In the February 1965 edition of *Ebony* magazine, Celtic Tommy Heinsohn says, "Elgin Baylor can beat a team all by himself. He is the complete hoopster. If we can hold him below his average, even by two points, we figure we had a good night against him." Baylor's scoring feats were so astounding that some assumed he was taller than he was, even exaggerating his size. In a 1962 article in *American Legion Magazine*, Baylor is described as a "6-8 operator for the Los Angeles Lakers." That same piece also cites him as an exemplar of the high-scoring goon that seemed to be taking over pro ball. In fact, at 6'5", Baylor was an undersized professional forward who scored from all over the court. The inflation of his stature signified both the awe he inspired and the paranoia surrounding offensive production.

Baylor tended to be modest in demeanor, as well as size. Philadelphia Warriors player Al Attles says Baylor was not a particularly vocal opponent. "He didn't have to do any talking. Guys had to be careful what they said in the newspapers, because you would play those guys the next night. With Elgin, you had enough problems just with him lined up on the other side. He let his game talk for him."

But Baylor still commanded respect. One night a fellow African American NBA player, Shellie McMillon, was guarding him pretty roughly. Rod Hundley recalls in his book *Hot Rod Hundley: You Gotta Love It Baby*, "Shellie blew his stack and smacked Elj across the face. Elj just looked him in the eye and said, 'Shellie, have you lost your mind?' It was as if Elj was saying, 'Next time you do that buddy, you're a dead man.' Shellie didn't do it again."

Compared with other powerhouse players, Baylor kept a low profile, which sometimes worked to his disadvantage. In July 1962, the opinion periodical *Negro Digest* published an essay on charismatic, or what it called "colorful," Negro athletes. Baylor was lumped with football player Emlen Tunnell of the Green Bay Packers and baseball player Henry Aaron of the Milwaukee Braves in a group the article described as "not particularly colorful stars." The writer then backs off his stance, saying, "[I]n Baylor's case, perhaps the negative is being stretched." The article goes on to spotlight such nicknamed athletic heroes as "Satchel" Paige, "Big Daddy" Lipscomb, and Harlem Globetrotters principal clown "Goose" Tatum.

Perhaps more important, Baylor maintained a solid reputation as a nice guy and a gentleman. Former ESPN radio announcer and L.A. native Dave Stone recalls meeting Baylor after a game against the Detroit Pistons at the Los Angeles Sports Arena:

> Elgin scored 42 points and had 21 rebounds. I saw his wife Ruby waiting for him outside the Lakers' dressing room. Elgin walked out. I was transfixed. My father introduced himself to Elgin, and said, "This is my son David, I think he loves you more than he loves me." Elgin

laughed and put his arm around me. My father was so impressed with his grace and his warmth that, on the way home, he said to me, "He's a mensch!"

Stone has another memory from Baylor's 1961–1962 season:

A year later, when I was 12, the season Elgin was mostly stationed at Fort Lewis, I was with my father and uncle. I was going on and on about Elgin averaging 38 points and all that, and my uncle said to my dad, "Don't you think it would be better for him to emulate someone he has a chance of being like?" My father said, "I'd be thrilled if he grew up to be the gentleman Baylor is."

In a 1962 installment of the *Los Angeles Sentinel*, "Doc" Young writes of Baylor in L.A., "Seldom in this town's history has the vast superiority of an athlete been so unanimously acclaimed as in Elg's case," which the sports editor felt "is . . . also a great tribute to the fine gentleman that he is."

In his short time with the Lakers, Baylor had already established himself as one of the greats of the game. In its preview for the 1962–1963 NBA season, *Sports Illustrated* proclaims him "Elgin Baylor, the league's best all-round player."

When the Lakers 1962–1963 schedule was announced, fans learned the city would be hosting the 1963 NBA All-Star Game on January 16. In preparation for the big upcoming season, the Lakers began voluntary workouts on July 12, 1962, at Loyola of Los Angeles. Baylor was relieved of reserve duty in August, although the Cold War raged on. "While I have no regrets whatsoever about serving my country," he told the *Los Angeles Times*, "I am naturally anxious to get home and get into shape for the beginning of next season."

Baylor, who weighed 227 pounds, three shy of his listed playing weight, wasn't the only Laker getting into shape. Hot Rod Hundley had shed 15 pounds, and general manager Lou Mohs had offered to pay him $100 for every month he reported under 199 pounds but charge him $100 for every month he weighed more than that. "That's $200 difference baby," relates Hundley in the *Times*, attributing his weight loss to the health drink Metrecal. His wife, Flo, framed the agreement and hung it over their refrigerator, where it discouraged her husband's taste for beer.

Mohs promised Jim Krebs that if he logged 750 miles on an exercise bike, Mohs would pay for it. Teammates Frank Selvy and Rudy LaRusso asked for the same arrangement. Mohs and Schaus had shored up the bench by paying Syracuse $35,000 for the services of streak scorer and former small-college All-American Dick Barnett. No club had ever paid that much for one man. The *Los Angeles Times'* Jim Murray calls it the "biggest $35,000 bargain in NBA history."

They also decided to waive two unproductive big men, young Wayne Yates and an old "baby" named Ray Felix. In their stead, 6'11" St. John's All-American LeRoy Ellis and Wichita State star Gene Wiley were expected to shine. "Wiley has the potential to be of real value," Schaus touted in the *Times*, "and soon."

Mohs also liked his new young, big men. "Ellis has great speed," he beams in the *Times*. "Honestly, he's the fastest man we now have on the floor. Wiley's forte is his defense. . . . I think he can jump as high as Bill Russell of the Celts." Mohs, who had been aware of Wiley since his sophomore year at Wichita State, had scouted the young center when Wiley's industrial-league Amateur Athletic Union team, the Denver D-C Truckers, toured Central America. Mohs was delighted he was still available during the second round of the NBA Draft. Although he lacked the shooting touch, he was athletic, and his wide shoulders were an indication he could add some weight to his frame to assist him in battles under the backboards.

The addition of these Negro players to the Lakers roster showed how much the face of the game was changing. No longer were such men as George Mikan or Bob Cousy "Mr. Basketball." Of the league's 117 players, 47 were Negroes, including, arguably, its four top stars: Baylor, Chamberlain, Russell, and Robertson.

* * *

The 1962–1963 NBA season began on October 16. In the first game of a doubleheader in New York, L.A. routed Detroit, 122–106, as Baylor led all Laker scorers with 35.

Three days later the Lakers played the Knicks in Madison Square Garden. There were 13 lead changes and 12 ties during the first three quarters. L.A. led, 77–76, after three periods but was outscored, 40–28, in the fourth. With 5:13 to play, they were down, 100–89. Despite Baylor's

36 points—26 of which he scored before halftime—the Lakers lost, 116–105. New York's tough former U.S. Marine, Richie Guerin, had done a masterful job guarding Jerry West, limiting him to 15 points, while scoring 27 himself. New Laker Dick Barnett hit 21.

In a game against Chicago on October 24, 1962, Woody Sauldsberry, labeled the "human blackjack" by Jim Murray of the *Los Angeles Times*, shadowed Baylor, allowing him 17 points. The Lakers lost the game, 118–107, with Chicago's Walt Bellamy scoring 42 and Sauldsberry 24. "Woody does everything but frisk Baylor on the way down the floor," writes the *Times* columnist. "Russian freighters get better treatment."

After a rough start on the road, the Lakers played their home opener against the Pistons on Saturday, October 27, beating Detroit, 134–118.

Quiet rookie Gene Wiley showed early promise in a game against the new San Francisco Warriors, in which he grabbed 14 rebounds in one quarter and 27 in 28 minutes against Wilt Chamberlain and Wayne High-tower.

By early November, Baylor was averaging 31.2 points in the Lakers' 14 games, about 20 less than Chamberlain's seven-game rate. At the same point in the 1961–1962 campaign, Baylor had averaged 35.3; his scoring average by the end of the year had been 38. Baylor wondered if he was losing his competitive edge: In a *SPORT* magazine feature by Myron Cope, he comments, "I haven't had the same desire I had last season. Schaus and I have talked about it several times. There were games we could have won, we should have won!" Had the annual Finals losses to Boston taken a mental toll? Was the burden of scoring, rebounding, and playmaking too heavy? Or was his absence from the team for military duty to blame? "Maybe it's because I was away from basketball for too long. But I'm in better physical shape than I was at this stage last year," Baylor added. When asked if his generous salary had brought on complacency, he said, "It's not having money. I've always liked to play."

Schaus tried to tweak Baylor's game a little: "Within three years," Schaus told *Sports Illustrated*, "he's not going to be able to beat that man on the one-on-one drive. He's going to have to be cuter. We'd like to see him start taking the jump shot more." Schaus believed if Baylor shot more from the outside, defenders would no longer be able to solely play him to drive. But when Baylor stuck with what worked, Schaus shrugged. "I guess it's instinctive for a man to do what he does well." After a performance of 43 points at home against New York on December 4,

Baylor scored 33, 36, 34, and 42 in his next four games, 50 against Syracuse on December 12, and 51 at San Francisco on December 14. The next day he hit 52 against the Warriors in L.A.

The sport's future was on display each time Elgin Baylor donned his silky purple-and-white uniform. It was more than his aerial attack that made Baylor effective. In addition to his expert timing and deceptive fakes, Celtics rival Tom "Satch" Sanders, one of the league's top defensive forwards during Baylor's day, recalls in Ron Thomas's 2004 book *They Cleared the Lane: The NBA's Black Pioneers*, "He's arching his shot so he will clear your hand, and if the accuracy is still there you're in a world of trouble." Sanders tried timing his jumps to meet Baylor's shots at a certain interval but to little avail. No one could really anticipate Baylor's release time or angle, and he had some of his best scoring performances, including the one during which he set the 1962 61-point playoff record, against Boston. Baylor accomplished all this despite the inside menace of basketball's all-time premier shot blocker, Boston center Bill Russell. As astute as Russell was at observing opponents to learn to time their shots, Baylor frustrated the Celtics, as he did others.

Sportswriter Myron Cope provides an explanation for Baylor's unique abilities in *Ebony* magazine's profile of Baylor in February 1965: "He is tremendously strong in the thundering rushes to the boards, and so swift with his hands he is able to whip dangerously long passes diagonally across the floor before any of the five opponents in the ball's path can attempt to intercept." Such passing acumen placed Baylor in the rare stratum of Oscar Robertson. Longtime Philadelphia basketball announcer Sonny Hill told former UCLA basketball player Andre McCarter for the 2012 *International Business Times* article "LeBron 'King James' and Elgin Baylor, 'The Greatest Laker of Them All': A Comparative at Age 28," "He was not just a good passer; he was a superb passer."

One of Baylor's opponents, Al Attles, said,

> It was a pleasure playing against him, but also a curse. You hear so much about him, you think, "this man walks on water." But reading about him just doesn't do him justice. How much can a guy do? The basket is 10 feet. You dribble, you shoot, you rebound. He showed you how much he could do.

As the season progressed, Baylor recovered his usual superstar skills, while the scoring support provided by Barnett propelled L.A. to the top of the Western standings. Fans packed the Sports Arena for a game on the same day 81,000 filled the Rose Bowl to watch a University of Southern California–Notre Dame football game. One boon to the Lakers' attendance that Saturday was the preliminary game played by Marques Haynes's Harlem Magicians.

Los Angeles geared up to host the 1963 NBA All-Star Game on January 16, 1963, as the team relished the opportunity to showcase its city to the basketball world. The day of the game, Bob Short hosted a lavish luncheon at the Ambassador Hotel's Coconut Grove Lounge. The 1,000 guests, who paid $15 a plate to attend, were greeted by programs at each place setting that proclaimed L.A. the "Basketball Capital of the World." Boston's Red Auerbach followed Fred Schaus as a luncheon speaker. Pride trumped grace, as Auerbach declared, according to John Taylor in the 2006 book *The Rivalry: Bill Russell, Wilt Chamberlain, and the Golden Age of Basketball*, "I suppose you people expect me to make some more nice chitchat like Schaus. You're a bunch of bushers. That goes for the club, the fans, and all the writers." Auerbach held up the program and continued, "I come here today, and I see this—it's ridiculous! What do you people think this is? Win a couple championships first, then talk about being the basketball capital of the world. Right now, the basketball capital is Boston. And it's gonna stay in Boston for a long time!"

When 14,838 fans filled the Los Angeles Sports Arena for the All-Star Game that evening, celebrities Doris Day and Pat Boone were among the spectators, Day serving as the Jack Nicholson of that era of Lakers faithfuls. On the court, Baylor and West represented the host team. Baylor played 36 minutes, scoring 17 points on 4-for-15 shooting. He also had seven assists and 14 rebounds. The East won the game, 115–108, but Baylor's assist total topped those of East All-Stars Bob Cousy and Oscar Robertson, who had six apiece. The league still lacked a national TV deal, so an independent network broadcast the game. The commissioner hoped that arrangement would be extended to the 1963–1964 campaign, although what he really coveted—and the NBA needed—was a contract with one of the major networks.

That same month, the Boston Celtics proved their fame when they toured the White House before a game at the University of Maryland and were invited into the Oval Office by President John F. Kennedy, who had heard the current NBA champs were there. As the players were saying their good-byes, according to Bill Russell in his 1966 autobiography *Go*

Up for Glory, Satch Sanders reportedly shook Kennedy's hand and said, "Take it easy, baby."

The Lakers and Celtics continued their rivalry as they flew to Detroit for a February 12 game. At that point, the Lakers held a season record of 46–14, while Boston was 43–18. In those days, there was a NBA rule that gave the team with the best overall season record $2,000 and a better schedule for the playoffs. L.A. also had a goal to break the NBA record of 60 wins in a season, set by Boston the year before. In the previous meeting between Boston and L.A. on January 20, played in Boston, Russell had been knocked cold by a Laker elbow, after which Boston rallied to win, 133–121. That loss broke an 11-game Los Angeles winning streak and made the Lakers ready to get some revenge.

According to *Sports Illustrated*, the Lakers marched into Detroit's Cobo Arena on February 12, 1963, with their baby-blue gym bags, and Baylor watched as three Celtics—Sam Jones, Clyde Lovellette, and Dan Swartz—shot around. He took off his raglan topcoat with its red lining and, in a gesture of disdain, tossed a penny toward the Celtics. Satisfied with himself, he smiled and headed for the lockers. An hour before the game in Detroit, in the Boston locker room, Bob Cousy read a *Boston Herald Traveler* bearing the headline "L.A. Feels Celts Are Washed Up." According to *Sports Illustrated*, Bill Russell, Frank Ramsey, and Satch Sanders were looking over Cousy's shoulder as he read the sports page. Of the L.A.–Boston rivalry, Cousy said to *Sports Illustrated*, "It has gotten terribly difficult for me to get myself up for every game, to keep the image. But for a few specific games, I still can."

That night, Cobo Hall drew the largest attendance in Detroit basketball history—11,028—to see L.A. battle Boston. A high school coach from West Farmington, Ohio, brought his team 300 miles to see the game.

Said Red Auerbach to *Sports Illustrated*,

> The Lakers are a tremendous team, but they, and too many other people in Los Angeles, have a feeling that the Lakers are better than we are. There are a lot of people who are already saying that the Lakers can beat the Celtics for the championship. So far the Lakers aren't the champions of anything. The Celtics have great pride and great talent, and we don't lie down and die for anyone. The Laker organization has said that, "Los Angeles is the Basketball Capital of the World." Los Angeles has been in this league for two years, and it's the basketball capital of the world!

Auerbach followed his argument with a choice swear word.

For the Lakers, Schaus says in the *Sports Illustrated* article "Basket-ball at Its Toughest," "The Celtics have a great basketball team, and Red Auerbach has done a great job of coaching them for years. I respect Auerbach as a coach. But I don't like him. I just plain don't like him. And he knows it." Schaus and Auerbach never spoke to one another during the rivalry or acknowledged one another's presence, even at events where they sat shoulder to shoulder.

The second game of the doubleheader was to feature Detroit versus San Francisco. Of the Lakers matchup, San Francisco's Wilt Chamberlain told *Sports Illustrated*,

> This is one I wouldn't miss. I want to look over these ball clubs once. I think that the Lakers will probably beat the Celtics in the playoffs, but the more I consider things the more I'm not so sure. Both of them have great starting teams, both have good benches and, you know, they want *at* each other. I want to watch 'em, man.

Jerry West missed the game due to a hamstring injury. Early in the contest, Baylor elbowed Boston's Satch Sanders in the stomach. Sanders continued to bump Baylor, making it tough for the Laker star to score. Baylor managed only two first-quarter baskets.

When Boston jumped to an early lead, a fan in the seats shouted, "You are all bums without West!" On one play, Cousy fired the ball the length of the court to Russell, who guided it into the basket. L.A. ended up losing 120–93.

Cousy later said in *Sports Illustrated*,

> This game was my best of the season. We would have beaten them even if they had had West. We would have beaten anyone tonight because we were right all the way through. If only we didn't have to play the Lakers again tomorrow night, because this is the kind of a victory I could savor for a long, long time. We wanted this one, and we would have done anything to get it.

Auerbach barked to Jeremiah Tax of *Sports Illustrated*, "That ought to take care of those ——."

After the game, Schaus kept L.A.'s locker room door closed and gave a tough talk to his players in preparation for their next contest with the

Celtics, scheduled for the next night in Boston. He later told *Sports Illustrated*,

> I told them that there was a plane leaving for Boston the next morning. I told them that if anyone felt he couldn't play better tomorrow night than he did tonight he should fly back to Los Angeles instead. I said those who wanted to really play ball could meet me in the hotel lobby at 7:30 the next morning.

When asked about the Lakers, Heinsohn said to *Sports Illustrated*,

> Sure, we're mad at them. Why shouldn't we be? They're after what we've got. It's that Hollywood stuff, and everyone is on their bandwagon and off ours all of a sudden. Just about every story you read says that we've had it, that we're old and done. All those stories didn't just come out of the smog. The Lakers had something to do with them. We are not the oldest men alive, and we showed them tonight what we can do. When they play us they better be ready, because we love to beat them.

At 7:15 the next morning, according to *Sports Illustrated*, Schaus greeted his players in the lobby of the Sheraton-Cadillac hotel. "Well," he said, "it looks like they all want to go East for one reason or another."

The teams flew to Boston. Boston announcer Johnny Most told Cousy, "You beat them by 27 last night. Let's beat them by 40 tonight." The Garden was sold out, a rare occurrence in the 1960s, when even most playoff games didn't sell out.

As the game got under way, Cousy made three quick push shots and gave Boston the lead, 6–0. A bit later, Dick Barnett drove into Frank Ramsey en route to the hoop. Ramsey grabbed Barnett, and the two started swinging. The rival benches cleared, while even Auerbach and Schaus yelled at one another. When play resumed, Boston stretched its lead to 17 points.

To make matters worse, the Lakers had only eight players ("seven men and Hundley," joshes Rudy LaRusso in *Sports Illustrated*). Still, by halftime, L.A. drew within 10 points, 67–57. "Just keep after them," said Schaus to *Sports Illustrated*'s Jeremiah Tax in the locker room. "They can't shoot as well in the second half as they did in the first."

After intermission, Krebs did better on the backboards. ("There are nights when he can't jump high enough to get a half dollar under his feet," Baylor later said to Tax.) The Lakers cut the lead to five points, until the Celts eventually led by 12 with seven minutes left.

Then Heinsohn and Barnett collided under the Lakers' basket. For whatever reason, L.A. responded with a 13–2 run. With 1:13 left, they took the lead. Prior to the contest, Hundley had predicted to *Sports Illustrated*, "You just watch, I'll betcha $5 Heinsohn gets a technical foul called on him tonight just like he did last night. He's so crazy, he always does against us." With 30 seconds to play, Heinsohn drew a tech for swearing at a referee. On that final note, L.A. won, 134–128.

According to the article "Basketball at Its Toughest," Hundley said in the L.A. dressing room, "Well, we got by the easy one."

During the 1962–1963 regular season, the Lakers won five of their nine games against Boston. The team posted a 53–27 record, five games ahead of St. Louis. Without injured player Jerry West, the team soldiered on but grew fatigued. When the regular-season campaign ended, Baylor was second in the league in scoring, fifth in assists, fifth in rebounds (with 14.3 a game), and the third-best free-throw shooter. "Watching Elgin Baylor on a basketball court was like watching Gene Kelly in the rain," writes *Los Angeles Times* columnist Jim Murray.

In the Western Division playoffs, the Lakers ousted the Hawks, four games to three. Before one game in St. Louis, Bob Short bickered with L.A.'s Channel 9 to broadcast the game to the home fans. The station balked until local TV 11 began negotiating for the rights to the telecast. Short got his way, and the April 6 contest was televised by Channel 9 at 6:30 p.m. Pacific Time.

Against St. Louis, in a series that opened on March 31, 1963, the Lakers had Jerry West back after a seven-week absence because of a left hamstring pull. It was Cliff Hagan who gave L.A. the most problems. For the seventh game at L.A., Baylor guarded Hagan. Hagan scored only two points, as L.A. won, 115–100. The Lakers advanced to the Finals to meet the Eastern Division champions, the Boston Celtics.

"If my guys aren't up for Boston," said Schaus to the *Los Angeles Times*, "then, by heaven, they'll never be up for anyone."

Boston opened the NBA Finals on Sunday, April 14, winning, 117–114, at home. After a second home win for the Celtics, Baylor's 38 points, 23 rebounds, and 18 assists led his team to a 119–99 game-three drubbing of the champs in L.A. Boston won, 108–105, in game four, during which a charging call on Baylor against Russell proved pivotal with 1:45 to play. When asked the key to the loss, Schaus asked the *Times*, "How do you spell Russell?" On Sunday, the Lakers bounced back with three beautiful scores down the stretch to take game five, 126–119, at the Boston Garden (where an enraged fan charged a ref who had ejected Heinsohn). Baylor had hit for 43 and was averaging 35 in the series.

Fans created a mob scene at the Lakers' ticket office for the sixth contest, scheduled on April 21. In an administrative snafu, fans were told the box office would open at 9 a.m. on game day, but those who lined up found all sales windows locked and the game sold out. The Celtics, who usually stayed at the Sheraton West, were confined to the Olympian Motel because the Milwaukee Braves were in town to play the Dodgers. The motel's marquee read, "Welcome the Boston Celtics and Red Auerbach."

A closed-circuit theater broadcast drew an additional 6,000 attendees. At the Sports Arena, Doris Day, Pat Boone, and Danny Thomas turned out. Red Auerbach hated the Sports Arena, so modern and clean, and its home fans equally disliked him. The *Los Angeles Times* reported one Lakers fan stationed behind the Boston bench would yell into a bullhorn, "Hiya, Red, you're nothin' but a bum!" The L.A. sports press wasn't kind to Auerbach either. The *Times'* Sid Ziff wrote that a mummy could coach the Celtics to success. Jim Murray called the Boston coach a "bleeding shark."

The final game of the 1963 Finals was played on April 24. Baylor used a rocker step to initiate a move from the right lane after Gene Wiley controlled the opening tap. He then double-clutched in midair before passing to LaRusso on the weak side, who hit a jumper. Cousy responded with a basket to tie it. West scored off a touch pass from LaRusso to knot things up again at five. He followed with a beautiful runner while hanging at a 45-degree angle to give L.A. a 7–5 edge. Sanders was sticking to Baylor closely, but a LaRusso jumper widened the lead to 9–5. Russell then followed a Sam Jones miss with a dunk, after which Baylor missed a driving shot. A pair of Cousy free throws tied things nine even. Cousy hit off a give-and-go from Heinsohn, and it was 11–9, Boston. Cousy then came down the left side and went up for what appeared to be a jumper, until he flicked a blind pass to Heinsohn, who banked it in for a 13–9 lead. Baylor missed a turnaround hook that rimmed off. Heinsohn canned another jump shot that LaRusso appeared to have gotten a hand on, and the Lakers trailed, 15–9. When LaRusso scored his seventh point, the home team was down, 16–13.

Baylor went high to grab the rebound of a missed Russell hook shot, after which Wiley banked home an uncharacteristically long jumper to close it to 16–15. Baylor snared another rebound and threw a baseball pass to an open and running West, who put L.A. up, 17–16. They led, 21–18, after Baylor made a runner off his patented low-shouldered dribble drive. At that point, Dick Barnett came in as a sub. West went up for a short jumper but instead dropped a little pass to Selvy, whose basket made it 26–20, Lakers. Sanders fouled Baylor, who hit his one free throw. Jerry West put a double fake on his defender, shed him, and made a right-side jumper for a 29–25 advantage. Wiley's dunk off a Barnett miss gave L.A. a 31–26 lead. Baylor used a screen, crouched, and dribbled free for a jumper that made it 33–30. The Lakers led, 35–33, at the end of a quarter.

Barnett and LeRoy Ellis started the second period. Rookie John Havlicek went in for Boston, and his fast-breaking led Boston to eight unanswered points. With Sanders on the bench, Baylor was fouled by Frank Ramsey on a drive and hit both charity shots, but L.A. still trailed, 43–37, with 9:15 to play in the half. Baylor found Barnett on a three-on-one break for a bucket that made it 43–39, Boston. Boston led, 47–41, with 6:18 to go, as Russell was getting out on the wing to guard jump shooters and block their shots. When Lakers center Jim Krebs went out on the wing, Russell stayed inside to threaten drives into the lane. K. C. Jones spelled Cousy, who had scored 10. Boston expanded its lead to 57–46, with 2:40 before intermission. Baylor swept past Cousy on a drive to make the score 57–49. Then Cousy went to work, canning a long, one-handed push shot, followed by a running hook. The Sports Arena crowd was quiet as their team fell behind, 66–52, at the break. Cousy was 7-for-11 for 16 points, Heinsohn had 13, Sam Jones (who had been averaging 28.6 points for Boston in the series) only 1. For the Lakers, West had scored 20, LaRusso 13, Baylor 9.

In the second half, Sanders shadowed Baylor closely, even away from the ball. Baylor missed a running drive off the opening tap. Russell's defense was discouraging Lakers shooters. L.A. had narrowed it to 66–56 when Baylor fed LaRusso for a banked jumper from the left wing at 10:47. Baylor's own jumper made it 68–58, and he followed with another midrange jump shot, but the gap was still 10 points. When the defense played off him to guard for a drive, Baylor sank a jumper from the right corner that made the score 72–64.

Later, Baylor broke for a quick drive, but Russell blocked his shot, fouling him in the process. He netted both free throws, but Boston led, 78–71. Baylor had 17 points. Sanders continued to face guard him away from the play (the "weak side" of the Lakers offense). This was Baylor in his prime, the moves savvy and deceptive, the legs offering the necessary spring. He often set defender Sanders up with a crouched dribble from the right side—an unconventional angle for Baylor.

Rudy LaRusso buried another long jump shot to close things to 79–75 with 5:10 remaining in the third, rousing the Sports Arena faithful to life. Yet, the Celtics' defense and fast break were too much to overcome. Although he didn't do so with the basketball in his hands, Russell controlled clutch games. Boston led, 92–83, when Dick Barnett made a sharp cut, causing the backpedaling Bob Cousy to severely twist his ankle. Lakers doctor Ernie Vandeweghe came over to Cousy on the Boston bench and determined that he probably had a bad sprain. Celtics trainer Buddy LeRoux packed Cousy's foot in ice and covered it in tape like a cast. The old guard kept walking to test the ankle, and Auerbach sent him in for the rookie Havlicek with less than five minutes to play.

The Lakers trailed, 100–99, with 2:23 on the clock. L.A. fell apart, and the Celtics hit clutch shots to secure a 112–109 win and provide Cousy— who would retire after the season—a happy ending. In the closing seconds, the retiring guard launched the ball toward the rafters in celebration. There was no champagne in the winning locker room (no one thought of it) and no joy in that of the losers. Baylor and West had combined for 60 points.

According to Bill Reynolds's 2010 book *Cousy: His Life, Career, and the Birth of Big-Time Basketball*, when the Celtics' plane rose above the Los Angeles skyline on its way home, Bill Russell said, "And as the basketball capital of the world sinks slowly into the sunset, we can only say, 'Good-bye, Los Angeles. Good-bye, to the basketball capital of the world.'"

Despite the Finals loss, the season had been successful for the Lakers, a club that had earned more than $1.1 million in 1962–1963, based on sales of 285,462 tickets. *Sports Illustrated* reports, "Playing in the bright, airy Los Angeles Arena, the Lakers are the most enthusiastically supported team in the National Basketball Association, with movie stars like Doris Day, Dean Martin, and Bing Crosby leading the cheers."

But Bob Short still wanted to increase his profit margin, so he asked the Los Angeles Memorial Coliseum Commission to reduce his Sports Arena rent, which was as much as $175,500. Short threatened to play some home games in Long Beach's new arena if the rent was not reduced. The Sports Arena manager called his bluff and suggested the Lakers play their entire schedule in Long Beach. With USC and UCLA basketball, concerts, and other entertainment, arena officials figured they could fill the vacant dates. They also suspected that Short was merely invoking Long Beach as a bargaining chip.

Short was also the object of a lawsuit on the part of his co-owners. Eight plaintiffs were accusing him of using misrepresentations to acquire majority ownership. Short won his case in district court, and the others appealed to the California Supreme Court. In the decision, the eight sold their stock of 800 shares to the Lakers at $70 each, netting Short $56,000. He now owned 4,800 of 6,000 shares, or 80 percent of the franchise.

The business side of pro basketball was indeed difficult, not just for Bob Short, but also for many of the businessmen behind the scenes. The American Basketball League, which Harlem Globetrotters owner Abe Saperstein formed, in collaboration with National Alliance of Basketball Leagues owner Paul Cohen and AAU owner George Steinbrenner of Cleveland, did not last long. Saperstein's new league was intended to challenge the NBA, and he set up the Los Angeles Jets franchise to offer direct competition to the NBA's Lakers. But the Jets never made a go of it and folded during their first season, in January 1962. Less than a year later, the entire ABL would close, when Saperstein and Steinbrenner became embroiled in a legal battle over the Pipers' new signee, Jerry Lucas, and the Pipers' secret attempt to join the NBA. The ABL folded on New Year's Eve 1962, thwarting Saperstein's dream of revenge on the NBA.

The 1962–1963 season had been challenging for another franchise as well, the new San Francisco Warriors, the second NBA club to move to California. Eddie "The Mogul" Gottlieb had sold the Philadelphia Warriors to Marty Simmons and Tom Gray for $850,000, in hopes that the size of the Cow Palace (14,000 seats) and a natural rivalry with the Lakers would make the new team a hit with fans. Yet, despite the presence of Wilt Chamberlain and snazzy passer Guy Rodgers, Philly natives who had been popular with local fans there, Bay Area residents showed little interest. Where the Lakers outdrew all NBA franchises that year, the Warriors attracted less than 4,000 a game. The team went 31–49, missing the playoffs in a season when six of the league's nine franchises qualified for postseason play. In one stretch, the Warriors lost 11 straight.

But for Elgin Baylor and the NBA, the 1962–1963 season seemed to represent a new day. The time of players like "Tricky" Dick McGuire, Bob Davies, and Bob Cousy—the NBA's first showman—was waning, and new flash came from Guy Rodgers, Dick Barnett, and Baylor. Although Cousy had introduced the schoolyard game to millions, it was now the province of black players. Globetrotters owner Abe Saperstein no longer held a monopoly on fancy ball handlers and trampoline-type leapers. New York's "Jumpin'" Johnny Green and Cincinnati's Tom Hawkins could leap with the best of them. As much as Cousy's wizardry would be missed after his retirement that season, Oscar Robertson and Guy Rodgers ran precision fast breaks and fed teammates with blind passes in traffic, often off the dribble. St. Louis' lefty playmaker, Lenny Wilkens, a product of Brooklyn Boys High, was not far behind.

Among all this advancing talent, Baylor held his reputation as one of the best. The year 1963 marked the third consecutive year Baylor was honored as "Professional Cager of the Year" by the National Sports Awards Dinner selection committee. Baylor finished second to Bill Russell in MVP voting that season, 196 votes to 256. The same year, sportswriter Myron Cope wrote in *SPORT*, "Baylor . . . is widely regarded as the finest all-around performer in basketball history."

* * *

Throughout the years, Elgin Baylor has carved an extraordinary niche in basketball history. During his career, he finished in the top five of the MVP balloting seven times. He was named First Team All-NBA for 10 seasons; only Karl Malone and Kobe Bryant, with 11, have been so honored more often. Bob Pettit is the only NBA forward whose lifetime stats come close to Baylor's 27.4 points, 13.5 rebounds, and four assists per game. Before LeBron James, who, at this writing, has led his teams in scoring, rebounds, and assists four times, only three NBA players had led their teams in scoring average, rebounds, and assists during at least three seasons: Wilt Chamberlain, Grant Hill, and Elgin Baylor. Only Chamberlain has exceeded Baylor's 38.3-point scoring average of 1962, when Baylor was temporarily away with the U.S. Army Reserve. Not even Michael Jordan scored 70 points in a NBA game to equal Baylor, nor 61 in a playoff game, as Baylor did. Baylor played in seven NBA Finals, participated in 11 All-Star Games, and retired with the second-best scoring average in NBA history (to Chamberlain). Baylor was also a great player when it meant the most. Between 1960 and 1964, he scored at least 20 points in 49 consecutive playoff games. In the 1962 postseason, he scored 30 or more points in 11 straight games (Michael Jordan's longest string was eight games).

As statistically impressive as he was, Baylor's talent can never be completely captured with mere numbers. To quote Albert Einstein, "Not everything that can be counted counts, and not everything that counts can be counted." The things Baylor did on the court were uncommon in his time, and he was the NBA's first black scoring star. In the Lakers media guides of the early 1960s, no less than 33 basketball authorities proclaimed Baylor the finest player they had ever seen. Longtime Celtics player, coach, and announcer Tom Heinsohn considers Baylor one of the five greatest players of all time. Chick Hearn said in *Black Sports* magazine in 1977, "He might be the best player I ever saw." His teammates give him accolades as well. "He had that wonderful, magical instinct for making plays and doing things that you had to just stop and watch," said Jerry West to Roland Lazenby for the April 2010 ESPN.com article "The Rise of the Lakers." "He is without a doubt one of the truly great people who played this game. I hear people talking about forwards today. I don't see many that can compare to him."

"Cousy can't rebound, but obviously, Elj can," says Jim Krebs in *SPORT*. "Russell obviously is not a playmaker, but Elj is. Robertson's closest to him in all-around play, but . . . he can't rebound with Elj. And Elj can dribble around any forward in the league."

Fellow Laker forward Tom Hawkins said to the Web publication *Hoops Nation* in 2013, "Elgin could rebound with anybody, dribble, and score with anybody."

According to ESPN.com's Bill Simmons, author of *The Book of Basketball: The NBA According to the Sports Guy*, "There just isn't enough 'I can't believe how good he was' videotape of him." What Simmons has seen of early Baylor, he compares to the scene in the movie *Back to the*

Future, when Marty McFly astounds folks by playing an electric guitar before anyone has ever seen one.

In *Jerry West: The Life and Legend of a Basketball Icon*, West says,

> He was without a doubt, for many years, the most unique player I'd ever seen. . . . He was one of the first modern players. He was one of the first players that had that incredible ability and incredible knack to not only do the right thing, but the most spectacular thing. He had a unique magic.

Oscar Robertson says in his 2010 memoir, *The Big O: My Life, My Times, My Game*, "Elgin was the first real high-flier in the league. His aerial dynamics predated Connie Hawkins."

By the time Baylor became a less acrobatic player, basketball had become more established as a TV commodity. Baylor had played three seasons during his prime when the NBA had no national TV contract; once pro ball hit TVs throughout the country, the sporting media had shifted its reverence for the one-on-one game to such frequent flyers as the Hawks' "Pogo" Joe Caldwell, Baltimore's Gus Johnson, and the Virginia Squires' Julius Erving. By 1967–1968, players like Baltimore Bullets rookie Earl Monroe were bringing the full force of playground aerodynamics to mass audiences. Baylor's professional numbers exceeded Monroe's, Erving's, and Caldwell's best production. He played in seven NBA Finals and led his college team to a NCAA championship game. Baylor dropped 61 points in a NBA Finals game against the greatest dynasty in basketball history, facing the best defensive player of all time.

While Baylor was never was able to acquire a mass following, players throughout the decades have credited him with inspiring and teaching them. Julius Erving told *SLAM* editor Scoop Jackson of Baylor in January 2008, "He was special. He did things years before I was doing it. I think a lot of us patterned our styles, our games, after what he was able to do with the basketball. The funny thing is, he didn't have anyone to pattern his game after. Now how great does that make him?"

Longtime Philadelphia basketball announcer and summer league founder Sonny Hill says to Jackson in the January 2008 edition of *SLAM*, "C'mon! All of them come out of Elgin. If you talk to Hawk [Connie Hawkins], he'll tell you he got his stuff from Elgin."

Jerry West remarks in Thomas J. Whalen's book on the 1968–1969 Boston Celtics, *Dynasty's End: Bill Russell and the 1968–69 World*

Champion Boston Celtics, "Oftentimes you like to pattern yourself after a great player, but with Elgin it's hard to do. . . . Often you'd like to do some of the things Elg does, but if you don't have his tremendous strength and body control, the best you can do is just think about it."

In *A Sense of Where You Are*, John McPhee's highly acclaimed book with then-Princeton basketball star Bill Bradley, Bradley claims he emulated Baylor's "rocker step." Bradley says that when he practiced basketball alone as a boy, he would "try to remember a particular move that Laker forward Elgin Baylor had made, then imitate it." The copycat moves served Bradley well: His 58 points against Wichita State in the consolation game during the 1965 NCAA Final Four, scored on every shot from almost every possible angle, are still a Final Four record.

Rick Barry, All-Star forward of the 1960s and 1970s, states in the January 1976 installment of *Boys Life* magazine,

> Back when I was playing basketball for the University of Miami, I really admired All-Star forward Elgin Baylor of the Lakers. The things he did with his body and the ball while flying through the air were incredible. I'd watch him perform those acrobatic miracles in National Basketball Association games, then go out and try to duplicate them.

Barry told *Boys Life* he once saw a photograph of himself driving to the hoop as a rookie, with his right knee raised high. A few days later he saw an image of Baylor, "and it was astonishing how similar the two pictures were," he says. "I'm no Baylor," Barry comments in the article, "but I'd like to be. Most of the moves I've got I copied from Elgin. I've been studying Baylor's floor game for a long time." Barry, who led NBA scoring his second year in the league (1966–1967), said the first time he played against Baylor as a rookie, he had to pinch himself to realize he wasn't dreaming that he was sharing the court with the player he so admired.

Paul Westphal, the ambidextrous Boston Celtics and Phoenix Suns All-Star of the 1970s, says in the 2005 book *Boston Celtics: Where Have You Gone?* by Mike Carey and Michael D. McClellan, that while people compared him to Jerry West because they were both white, "to a large degree I modeled my game after Baylor." He continues, "He had that one-legged jumper, which became a part of my game. . . . I emulated him. I would go into the paint and create, sometimes throwing up those crazy shots like Baylor."

Kareem Abdul-Jabbar admired Baylor's game but says in his memoir, *Giant Steps*, that, as a young man, "It took me a while to realize I didn't have Elgin's physical talent." Calling Baylor a tough player to model one's game after, he made an early decision to pattern his skills after those of the elite pro centers.

George McGinnis, star of the 1970s Pacers and 76ers, says in the October 13, 1976, *Reading Eagle* (PA), he grew up dreaming of a time when he could move "nice 'n' easy" like Elgin Baylor. In August 1975, Cal-Berkeley basketball star Rickie Hawthorne told *Sports Illustrated*, "When I was younger, I admired Elgin Baylor; then it was Julius Erving."

Former All-Star guard Lenny Wilkens says in *Tall Tales*,

> Elgin Baylor would have been a great player in any era. People talk about the amazing things Julius Erving and Michael Jordan did athletically, but I saw Baylor do many of the same things—only this was in the early 1960s. He had the spin moves, the dunks, the head-above-the-rim attacks on the basket. He played way above the pack.

For all of Oscar Robertson's subtle fakes, lightning crossover dribbles, and beautiful floating lead passes, "The Big O" primarily played by the book, whereas Baylor wrote a new one. Robertson was considered the coach's dream, a player who beat you with textbook fundamentals. Baylor's style was more singular—more schoolyard—which spurred imitators. One Lakers media guide allowed that Oscar Robertson did some things better than Jerry West, and West did others better than Robertson, but that Baylor was in a category all his own: "[W]hen Oscar or Jerry do them basketball purists applaud appreciatively and politely at the precision of it all. When Elgin did (and does) things, you stood up and shouted and screamed and pounded the back of the guy sitting next to you, it was so fascinating and so impossible." Baylor brought elements of the outdoor game to the mainstream and helped bridge the gap between Globetrotter and textbook. Players of all ethnicities emulated him.

Baylor was a savvy shot blocker in his prime, challenging those who penetrated the lane. And rebounding is a facet of defense. Leonard Koppett writes in *24 Seconds to Shoot*, "He held, without a doubt . . . the record for sinking his own rebounds."

"That was by design," Baylor explained. "One of the coaches I had early in my career drilled 'follow your own shot' into my head. Then I learned you could create your own shot by missing one and getting the rebound. . . . Since I shot the ball, I had a better idea of where the rebound was going than the defense did." Former Knicks star and coach Carl Braun observes in *Sports Illustrated*, "He'll kill you off the offensive board because he has such a fine sense of timing for the rebound and the brute strength for the second effort."

Even as late as 1971, when Baylor was 36, the Knicks' Dave DeBusschere, a rugged NBA All-Defensive Team forward, shrugged and told *Ebony* magazine, "Every time I think I've got him figured out, he comes up with some tricky new move." The body control, the suspension in the air, the bank shots with English, Baylor could beat defenders so many ways.

As a passer, Baylor was so dangerous that the Celtics, no matter how easily Baylor was scoring on his defender, would never double-team him. Red Auerbach had been watching Baylor long enough to know he would just hit the open man. His 386 assists in 1963 placed him among the league's top-five feeders. Other clubs did double-team Baylor, however. "As a result," Coach Fred Schaus says in *Ebony* magazine's 1964 pro basketball preview, of the constant pounding that year, "Elgin was not at his peak during the championship series with Boston."

Baylor's accomplishments with the Lakers are still stellar by today's standards. The 38 points per game he scored while playing primarily on weekend leave in 1961–1962 is still the highest average by a player not named Chamberlain. In 1962–1963, Baylor became the first NBA player to finish in the league's top five in the four major statistical categories: scoring, rebounding, assists, and free-throw shooting. He prided himself on the accomplishment and its testament to his versatility: "Wouldn't it be great to make a clean sweep, to finish in the 'Top 5' in every department?" he asked *SPORT*'s Milt Gross.

In response to a feature about the play *Jesus Christ Superstar*, which credits Andy Warhol with coining the word *superstar*, then–*Sports Illustrated* writer Frank Deford wrote a letter to the editor of *New York Magazine* that appeared on November 22, 1970, stating, "I cannot offer proof of authorship, but I have often heard that the word *superstar* was first applied to basketball hero Elgin Baylor—at least, the word supposedly first gained regular currency with regard to Baylor." Deford traces coinage to the late 1950s.

The first superstar was not only the ballplayers' ballplayer, but a fan favorite. *SPORT* columnist Bill Libby wrote in 1965,

No matter what Jerry West does, which may be more than Baylor can do, the bigger ovations remain Baylor's, and he appears above criticism. It sometimes seems that if he kicked his mother on the court, the fans would boo her, the press would give her bad notices, and someone would circulate a petition to have Elg's toe bronzed.

Baylor consistently drew bigger crowds than his contemporaries. In November 1963, the first time Chamberlain returned home to play for the San Francisco Warriors against the new Philadelphia 76ers, only 5,800 fans showed up. Russell's 1961–1962 Celtics drew a mere 6,852 patrons a night, even though they were four-time NBA champions. Baylor held sway among his colleagues and rivals, played with the flair that fills seats, and was a big hit with fans. His status combined the elements that made Michael Jordan and Magic Johnson so popular a generation later.

By the end of the 1962–1963 season, Los Angeles fans—traditionally nonchalant in their sports interests—began to take serious notice of the Lakers. A year earlier, one home game during the 1962 NBA Finals against Boston had drawn 15,521 Lakers fans (and turned 6,000 prospective patrons away). In 1963, 285,462 Angelenos tipped the turnstiles, best in the league. By 1964, 322,331 patrons would make the Lakers the most popular team in basketball. In the mid-1960s, Elgin Baylor would continue to impose change upon basketball, and basketball left its most permanent mark on him.

Elgin Baylor, Seattle University star. *Courtesy Jason Behenna, Seattle University Athletic Department*

Baylor eludes Kansas State All-American Bob Boozer during the 1958 Final Four semifinal. *Courtesy Jason Behenna, Seattle University Athletic Department*

Elgin Baylor with the newly moved Los Angeles (former Minneapolis) Lakers.
Courtesy Jason Behenna, Seattle University Athletic Department

In November 2009, Elgin Baylor at Seattle U's ceremony honoring their top-29 basketball players of all time, with early 1950s SU legends Johnny and Eddie O'Brien. The O'Brien twins led SU to a win over the Harlem Globetrotters and later played for the Pittsburgh Pirates. *Courtesy Jason Behenna, Seattle University Athletic Department*

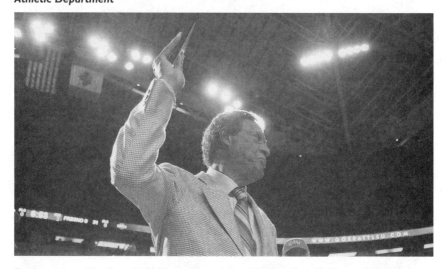

Baylor greeted by Seattle U fans in November 2009 at the ceremony honoring their top-29 basketball players. *Courtesy Jason Behenna, Seattle University Athletic Department*

8

A LEADER OF MEN

He grins like a baby but bites like a gator.—Dragline, *Cool Hand Luke*

In the early 1960s, the Lakers led all NBA teams in attendance as Elgin grew even more popular with local fans. In July 1963, both Bob Short and singing cowboy Gene Autry denied a rumor that L.A. Angels baseball owner Autry wanted to buy the Lakers for $3 million. Short admitted his franchise was costly, telling the press he was getting a raw deal on Sports Arena rent and that he had to meet one of the NBA's highest payrolls. He claimed Fred Schaus was the league's highest-paid coach and that Baylor was earning $50,000 and West another $25,000. Chick Hearn, according to Short, was making $25,000 for calling the games. But Short was keeping his team: The *Los Angeles Times* reported that Los Angeles Memorial Coliseum Commission head A. E. Englund had told Short, "I wouldn't give up the Lakers now for a hundred million. Something must be wrong with your management if this club isn't making money."

During his time off that summer, Baylor kept busy. In early July, he made a guest appearance at UCLA coach John Wooden's basketball camp at Palisades High School. At an event hosted by the Negro General Welfare Fund and black L.A. civic leader Woodley Lewis at his club, the Sportsman's Bowl, Baylor attended a ceremony naming scholarships in honor of the late football stars Ernie Davis and "Big Daddy" Lipscomb. On August 4, he played in a charity golf event at Los Serranos Country Club in Chino, California, with the likes of his former Amateur Athletic Union teammate and pro golfer Bill Wright and heavyweight legend Joe Louis.

At home, Ruby Baylor had resigned from teaching first grade so she and her husband could have more children. Little Alan had turned two on March 9. "I'd like him to be a fine son, to go to college, to be a good all-around athlete," his father said to *SPORT* magazine in 1963, "but not a football player. I didn't have a lot of things I wanted, and I'd like him to have them and be worthy of them. If he isn't a great basketball player, I wouldn't be disappointed, but I'd hope he could be. I'd like him to be a professional basketball player."

On August 28, 1963, Baylor joined 250,000 Americans in his hometown for the historic March on Washington. Although the police department feared the worst and nervous city officials closed the town's liquor stores, the great demonstration proceeded peacefully, as the Rev. Dr. Martin Luther King Jr. acquainted the world with his vision of black and white schoolchildren playing harmoniously.

The National Basketball Association was making its own strides in racial unity. At the time, 38 percent of the players were African American, and five of the league's nine teams had at least five black players on their rosters.

On media day in September 1963, Coach Fred Schaus insisted the Lakers club was improved. "In the first place, we'll have more depth at both forward and guard," he told the *Los Angeles Times*. In the same article, he calls LeRoy Ellis and Gene Wiley "much more advanced" than a season ago, when both "were green as any players [he's] had." Of guard Jim King he boasted to the *Times*, "He could be a great one. If you thought Hundley made us hustle, wait until this kid gets into action." Chick Hearn felt backcourt ace Jerry West was stronger and that Dick Barnett had some impressive new moves. Jump shooter Don Nelson of Iowa filled out the bench.

Of the back-to-back Finals losses to Boston and future chances of taking over the league title, Schaus reminded the *Times*, "We have lost our two best players for two months of each season. Two years ago the Army took Elgin Baylor, and last year Jerry West was hurt. I just hope we can get lucky this year." The Lakers' home opener would be played October 30, against the Oscar Robertson–led Cincinnati Royals.

In mid-October, Short signed a new deal with the Sports Arena, still paying 20 percent annual rent but lowering his ceiling for single games from $6,500 to $5,000. Rumors surfaced that Baylor would be dealt to the Baltimore Bullets for their 6'11" star center, Walt Bellamy. Short insisted to the *Times* that he wouldn't trade Baylor "for the whole Baltimore team, including the franchise." When asked about the likelihood of a deal, Bullets GM Paul Hoffman guessed that Baylor was not 29 years old as he was listed, but closer to "34 or 35 or maybe even 37." In fact, Baylor did tell the media conflicting stories regarding his years out of school, and he was always sensitive about his age. Jim Murray writes that the U.S. Army had more than one date of birth on record for Baylor. Center Jim Krebs would jokingly say to the *Times*, "The Elgin Baylor doll, you wind it up and it gets a year younger."

In late November, St. Louis led L.A. in a tight three-way Western Division race, with the gargantuan San Francisco Warriors in third. On Sunday, November 17, the Hawks shot 52 percent to beat the Lakers in a 117–112 thriller at the Sports Arena. Such stars as Lenny Wilkens, Bill Bridges, and Zelmo Beaty made the young Hawks formidable. Despite the imposing St. Louis front line, which still included Bob Pettit, Baylor scored 30, with 18 boards. His second and third efforts on the glass were impressive, and it was his third consecutive strong showing. Knowing that one of Baylor's knees had been bothering him, onlookers hoped the performance meant the knee was sound.

On Friday afternoon, November 22, President John F. Kennedy was assassinated. The *Los Angeles Sentinel* reported that the "tan population" hadn't shed so many tears since Mississippi NAACP field secretary Medgar Evers was gunned down the previous June. Along with the rest of the nation, L.A.'s black residents were riveted by the shocking developments unfolding on their television sets; one could drive down the streets of Central Avenue in the nightclub district and not see a car for blocks. Baylor mourned the loss as well, since he had supported JFK throughout Kennedy's presidential campaign and presidency. "Elg is the only born Republican I know who campaigned for Kennedy," said Rod Hundley to *Sports Illustrated*. New NBA commissioner Walter Kennedy canceled the league's evening games. As for Saturday's games, of the four scheduled, only two were played. Commissioner Kennedy (no relation to the president) decided to allow teams to play if they had already traveled to their host opponents' cities. The Knicks hosted Detroit, and St. Louis hosted Cincinnati.

By his sixth season in the NBA, Elgin Baylor not only led the Lakers in every major statistic, but he was also the figure most NBA players looked up to. He had earned this status despite the presence of contemporaries Wilt Chamberlain of Philadelphia and Bill Russell of Boston. "Actually, Elg is 'Chairman of the Board'—not only among the Lakers, but among all NBA players, regardless of color," writes sports columnist Bill Libby in the 1967 installment of *SPORT*. "If they were to elect a leader, [Baylor] would win in a walk." Longtime fan Dave Stone said, "He was majestic. He had a regal bearing." "His name should be Elegant Baylor," agrees Bob Cousy in *JET* magazine's April 4, 1963, edition.

In a 1966 *Sports Illustrated* cover feature on Baylor, writer Frank Deford marvels,

> On and off the court, he glides with a regal mien, carrying himself with such élan that it often has been said of him that he must surely descend from the giant black royalty of some Nubian empire. He dresses, always richly and impeccably, in the soft, tame shades, for he is one of those few who are able to accept simple quality as sufficiently ostentatious by itself. He is aware of his own great talent and thus is immune to flattery.

Bill Libby echoed this observation in *SPORT* a year later: "Elg's elegance off-court is even greater. A proud, sensitive man, he conducts himself with studied dignity in public."

Even Red Auerbach, coach of the Lakers' greatest rivals, respected Baylor. When asked in December 1961 how he would coach Chamberlain and Russell if they were teammates, he toyed with the idea of using a double-post offense or moving Russell to forward. "Of course, there'd be a third choice," he smiled to the *Boston Globe*. "It might be better to trade Chamberlain to the Lakers for Elgin Baylor! Then you'd have a better balanced Celtics team."

Compared with his fellow superstars, Baylor had the better personality. Chamberlain was friendly enough but not well regarded by coaches. Russell had a great sense of humor and commanded respect but wasn't the chummy sort. Baylor combined both the easygoing nature of Chamberlain and the leadership sensibilities of Russell. Chamberlain was well liked by some but also caused controversy at times. According to Aram Goudsouzian's book *King of the Court: Bill Russell and the Basketball Revolution*, Milton Gross once wrote, "Wilt has become the NBA's biggest problem." Goudsouzian writes that one Knick, when anonymously asked about MVP voting, said of Wilt, "Don't like the guy personally. I wouldn't vote for him for anything." *King of the Court* cites Knicks coach Fuzzy Levane as calling Chamberlain a "monster." In David Shaw's 1973 Chamberlain biography *Wilt: Just Like Any Other 7-Foot Black Millionaire Who Lives Next Doo*r, Bob Cousy mocked his annual threats to retire, remarking, "[W]e can all go back to playing real basketball again," and according to *King of the Court*, respected veteran Dolph Schayes chided Wilt for his immature remarks. When Wilt called the NBA a "bush league" in a *Sports Illustrated* cover story, teammate Johnny Kerr said, in an account in Wayne Lynch's 2002 book *Season of the 76'ers: The Story of Wilt Chamberlain and the 1967 NBA Champion Philadelphia 76ers*, "It's a good article, if you like science fiction." Some players resented Chamberlain's habit of glowering at players or the way he threw teammates Tom Gola and Guy Rodgers under the bus in a national magazine feature. Goudsouzian claims in *King of the Court* that others called Chamberlain the "n" word behind his back.

Baylor was easier to coach than Wilt, despite their shared superstar status. "I obey my coach," Baylor says in *SPORT*, "just like I obey my parents. That's what authority means." Baylor loved the game and mused, "I sometimes wonder if I'll miss this life when it's gone." In *SPORT* magazine in 1963, he expressed a desire to play another 10 years.

Under Coach Fred Schaus, and led by Baylor, the 1963 Lakers were a loose bunch, much as the late 1950s Minneapolis clubs had been, but with superior players. Sportswriter A. S. "Doc" Young described them as a "buddy-buddy team," comparing them to the great racially integrated Cleveland Browns squads of the 1940s and 1950s. Jerry West oozed both homespun charm and competitiveness, "Hot Rod" Hundley was a flake but also a loyal comrade-in-arms, Dartmouth grad Rudy LaRusso served as the resident intellectual, and Dick Barnett was always quick with a quip. They were a well-paid lot, too—Hundley with his $45,000 Malibu home and Krebs springing $350 for one of his wife's wigs.

Dick Barnett was known for his expensive taste in clothes. Teammate Hundley said Barnett seemed Broadway bound. According to a 1966 *Sports Illustrated* profile of Barnett, one morning in a Pittsburgh motel, Barnett rose before Hundley, who awoke to Barnett preening in the bathroom mirror. "He was dressed in spats," Hundley said, "and he had on a Chesterfield topcoat, matching tie and vest, a bright-red handkerchief in his pocket. He wore gloves and carried an umbrella and was carefully admiring himself." Finally, Hundley could stand it no longer. "Go on, go on," Hundley cried. "You got it, darlin'. Nothing going to stop you—all the way to Wall Street!"

Although Coach Schaus forbade poker games, his team members played them anyway, using the code phrase "prayer meeting" for their clandestine hotel room games. High-stakes poker would not have broken them, even in those days of meager meal money and shared taxis, but they kept the antes to a quarter limit. When Baylor's head twitch occurred during card games, guys accused him of peeking at their hands and teased, "Stop admiring your stripes" to the army corporal. Hundley says in his memoir, *Hot Rod Hundley: You Gotta Love It Baby*, "[W]hen he got a full house he'd twitch, and everybody folded."

The team also enjoyed cigarettes, even near game time. In his memoir, Hundley describes Lakers locker rooms in the 1960s as "one big cloud of smoke." The only nonsmokers were Jerry West and Rudy LaRusso. On one occasion, guard Slick Leonard was taking a drag while getting his ankle taped after spraining it. When he ran back onto the floor after a time-out, his cigarette was still in his mouth. His teammates had to yell for him to put it out. Baylor enjoyed a smoke, too, as Frank Deford, then a writer for *Sports Illustrated*, recalls from one halftime experience in the Lakers' locker room: "Elgin Baylor, the star forward, bummed a cigarette off me and then went for another set of double figures in the second half."

Those who spent time with Baylor enjoyed his company. "I've roomed with Elg a lot of times," LaRusso said to Deford for *Sports Illustrated* in 1966, "and he literally talks you to sleep. You know, he may even talk all night, because he is going as soon as you wake up. He talks in Technicolor. He's just one of the world's great conversationalists." Lakers GM Lou Mohs said if he were stranded on a desert island he would select Baylor for a companion. In the book *Basketball in America: From the Playgrounds to Jordan's Game and Beyond*, Wilt Chamberlain calls Baylor a "garrulous, fast-talking guy who likes to be the center of attention." Baylor was so fond of quizzing, challenging, and card playing with teammates, Laker Walt Hazzard said to Deford for his 1966 *SI* cover feature, "We call him the King of Gamesmanship."

But Baylor chose his conversational spots. Hundley told Deford, "Elj [*sic*] talks a mile a minute, and he's an authority on every subject, but the second a stranger comes into the room he shuts up and won't say a word."

"Pick a subject and he's got all the answers," echoed Jim Krebs to Deford for *Sports Illustrated*. "His wife Ruby is a nice girl who can outtalk him, and when the both of them get going, I don't think either one pays any attention to what the other is saying."

Baylor joked in a friendly way with his colleagues, giving some of his favorites pet nicknames. Baylor called Lakers center Darrall Imhoff "Headquarters" for the size of his head and referred to Dick Barnett as "Governor," after Mississippi governor Ross Barnett. Diminutive guard Gail Goodrich was "Stumpy." Coach Fred Schaus was "Beef," because when he yelled his nose looked like two pounds of steak. Another Laker was "Musty" due to the temporariness of his deodorant. Because Hundley already had a nickname, Baylor called him "Rodney."

Baylor became the Mr. Blackwell of the NBA for his chiding remarks about other players' wardrobe choices, which he often deemed hayseed. "There's too many country boys in their bully-woolly suits and Buster Browns in the NBA now," he told Deford in the 1966 *SI* feature. Jim Murray cites Baylor's taste for conservative neckties, Savile Row suits, and hand-stitched shoes. According to Deford, before a fall 1965 exhibition game against the Celtics, the Lakers discussed the color of their new team blazers. Seven players voted for light blue, Baylor for dark blue. "Mighty democratic of you Mr. Baylor," Bill Russell joked, according to Deford, "to let these gentlemen discuss the situation with you." The Lakers would be measured for dark blue blazers the next week. For all his ribbing, Baylor was considered good-natured by white and black teammates alike. "He's a big-hearted guy who'd give you the shirt off his back," said Jim Krebs to Deford.

Like any popular leader, it helped that Baylor could also take a joke. Once, after guard Dick Barnett finally beat his teammate in a poker game, he waited for Baylor to board the team bus. "When Baylor got on," recalled Darrall Imhoff to Deford, "Barnett made like a trumpet and blew taps for him."

Baylor's role as man among men was not limited to poker games and trivia contests. Teammate Jerry West says in Roland Lazenby's biography *Jerry West: The Life and Legend of a Basketball Icon*, "My best teacher was Baylor. I owe so much to him." Unlike many athletic costars, Baylor and West got along well. Although the *Los Angeles Times'* Jim Murray reported on April 19, 1965, that Baylor teased West about his Appalachian accent (saying he sounded like a "beagle with a sore throat") and called him "Tweety" because of his skinny legs and tweed jackets, West admired the team leader. When West became a star performer, this did not change. In his 1969 biography *Mr. Clutch*, West speaks about the Laker plays designed for the team's two bright lights. He says, "The Celtics never had two scorers like Elg and me. . . . Elg and I made our shots. Would it have been smarter basketball to let others who can't shoot as well shoot more?"

"I admire how they handled it," Fred Schaus states in *Tall Tales: The Glory Years of the NBA* of Baylor and West's relationship. "With two stars of that magnitude, you could have trouble on your team, but not those guys."

"We never had problems playing together," Baylor confirmed to Terry Pluto in *Tall Tales*. "History shows we were a very good combination, and I've always considered Jerry a great player." Rudy LaRusso felt there may have been a "bit of a rivalry," although he says he "never sensed any jealousy." Rod Hundley also granted, "I think there was some strain between the two guys. To me, that's natural, because they were such huge stars. But . . . I also sensed . . . the tremendous respect they had for each other." In the *Los Angeles Sentinel*, "Doc" Young writes that fellow Lakers, including West, spoke of Baylor "in tones of reverence. . . . West does not hesitate to call Elgin Baylor the greatest basketball player in the world."

The Lakers seemed somewhat progressive in terms of race, with the team's history of strong black players—Elgin Baylor, Dick Barnett, Ray Felix, Tom Hawkins, and the newly drafted Gene Wiley and LeRoy Ellis—and its camaraderie among team members. But the same spirit wasn't evident throughout the league. In the early 1960s, NBA commissioner Maurice Podoloff suggested a formal racial quota limiting the number of black players per team. Although such a measure was never drafted, Bill Russell opined in the *Saturday Evening Post* in 1964, "[W]hether they'll admit it or not . . . most teams in this league have a quota."

According to Baylor in *Tall Tales*, "Both black and white players said there was a quota, and I noticed it on some teams who really tried to stay white." Former 1960s San Francisco guard Al Attles said that when he entered the league, he heard the limit for black players was four to a team. "It was definitely an unwritten rule. There were eight teams, and my team had four African Americans. Some teams had three, nobody had five." Attles always felt that if he were competing for a guard position, he was really fighting for a spot against his fellow black guards. Center Charlie

Share, who played with the Hawks in the 1950s, said the prevailing notion was, "Give me two black players and I'll win a title. Three, and they'll take over and there will be trouble."

On December 16, 1963, when the Cincinnati Royals dealt Bob Boozer to the New York Knicks in a three-team trade for a journeyman named Larry Staverman, many suspected it was to preserve a racial limit. Of the one-sided deal, Royal Oscar Robertson told *SPORT* magazine in 1966, "A lot of good Negro ballplayers should be in the league, but only generally four or five spots are open on a team. We had five until Bob Boozer was traded." Bill Russell felt the Royals' racial quota would prevent them from seriously contending for a league title later that season: "[A]s despicable as the quota system was, it won a title for the Celtics," he says in the June 8, 1970, *Sports Illustrated* article "Success Is a Journey." "The Royals could have beaten us, but in my opinion they virtually gave Bob Boozer away to get down to their black quota." For the balance of the 1964 season, Boozer would average 17.5 points and 8.5 rebounds for New York.

Team owners continued to have concerns that the game might be becoming too black to appeal to paying fans, although NBA attendance passed the 2.75 million mark in 1964–1965 and ABC's package of 17 NBA games drew a respectable 20 percent audience share. In the 1965 All-Star Game, seven of the 10 starters were Negroes. One anonymous white former All-Star found the racial makeup distasteful and told *SPORT* magazine in 1966, "I was disgusted. There were just too many of them. I couldn't get interested in watching them play." On November 16, 1965, during a St. Louis–Philadelphia game, all 10 players were Negroes. "Nobody wants to say anything," one anonymous coach says in the same *SPORT* article, "but of course the owners are worried. How are you going to draw with 11 colored players on your team?" None of the white sources in the *SPORT* feature on whether the pro game was too Negro were quoted by name, for reasons of anonymity.

The wave was irreversible. In the college ranks, Negro stars like Cazzie Russell, Jimmy Walker, and Dave Bing were destined for large NBA contracts and potential stardom. In the 1966 National Collegiate Athletic Association championship game, Texas Western started five Negro players against an all-white Kentucky team.

Baylor recognized the increasing number of Negroes in the NBA and said it was due to lack of other opportunities for them in the world at large. Black players, he told Deford for "A Tiger Who Can Beat Any-thing," "all work hard to get in this league, because it is one chance we have. And besides, we have to be that much better to beat out a white player. And then everyone asks where the white players are. I've seen many of them come into this league, and they've had great talent." Baylor told Jim Murray for the *Los Angeles Times* in 1963, "A Negro, to make it, has to be just a little bit better." The trend of Negro players outnumbering white would continue, he said, unless racial discrimination changed on a larger scale. White players sometimes decided against pro sports because, he explained to Murray, "They married some money or got a good out-side job, things that don't happen to us. . . . You give us a chance in other things, and you'll get your white players back right away." Lee Shaffer was a good example of what Baylor meant; the former North Carolina Tar Heel averaged more than 18 points for Syracuse in 1963, and, when traded as part of a deal for Wilt Chamberlain the night of the 1965 NBA All-Star Game, opted for a job with a transportation firm rather than reporting to his new team.

Says Hot Rod Hundley in *Tall Tales*, back then the saying went, "It's a white dollar," a reference to the majority fan base. According to a *SPORT* magazine article entitled "Pro Basketball's Hidden Fear: Too Many Ne-groes in the NBA," one anonymous announcer told writer John Devaney, "I'm only being realistic when I'm saying that if a white center were to come along and challenge Chamberlain or Russell, the ratings for those games would jump at least 50 percent."

Wilt Chamberlain once told Howard Cosell in a radio interview that the prevalence of black players and stars was a hindrance to NBA popu-larity: "I think there has been sort of like a stagnant box office attraction due to the fact that we are somewhat overpopulated with . . . first-class and star Negro players." NBA publicist Haskell Cohen says in "Pro Bas-ketball's Hidden Fear" that the numbers did not back Chamberlain's claim. "During the past five years," he relates, "our attendance, on the average, has increased by 10 percent each year." Cohen, who worked as the league's publicist from 1951 to 1969, felt that winning teams drew well and losers did not. Commissioner Walter Kennedy agreed with him and cited the San Francisco Warriors as an example; the team had drawn poorly after it first moved West but gained popularity as Western Divi-sion champs in 1963–1964. The Lakers were perennial winners, and in Jerry West and Elgin Baylor they had appealing stars who were white and black. "I must say that with the Lakers, race was never an issue," Baylor states in *Tall Tales*. "All Bob Short cared about was winning." He credited part of the team's success to its colorblind attitude and owner.

Yet, Jerry West garnered more national and local endorsement opportunities than Baylor, including deals with Jantzen sportswear, Wilson Sporting Goods, and Karl's Shoes of Los Angeles, as well as a magazine ad for ChapStick and ads for Wheaties cereal. Most of Baylor's ad work was limited to African American publications. Decades later, Jerry West, in his 2011 autobiography *West by West: My Charmed, Tormented Life*, said, "I had witnessed the indignities visited upon my black teammates and admired the way Elgin Baylor, Oscar Robertson, and other black athletes had spoken out. . . . I was no crusader."

Baylor did crusade on some important occasions. Guided by a strong sense of right and wrong, he stood up to injustice in key moments and used his influence for the good of his sport. One notable instance happened at the 1964 NBA All-Star Game, scheduled to be played in Boston on January 14, 1964. In addition to the main contest, an old-timers game was planned, as well as a pregame ceremony to honor the old touring team the Original Celtics for the first time in years. It was to be a grand night: The East would feature Bill Russell, Oscar Robertson, and Jerry Lucas, while the West included Elgin Baylor, Jerry West, and Wilt Chamberlain. But a behind-the-scenes campaign by the NBA's leading players threatened to halt the event.

At the time, the NBA minimum player salary was $7,500 (about $53,000 when adjusted for 2014 dollars). Frustrated by low wages, excessive traveling, and the lack of a pension plan, the National Basketball Players Association, headed by the Celtics' Tom Heinsohn and counting Baylor, Robertson, and Russell among its members, thought it was time to put the NBA owners' feet to the fire. In addition to the salary limit and pension plan, the athletes had a long list of grievances. For one, team trainers did not travel on road trips, which left players to fend for their own injuries. Team members were not paid for preseason games, and they stayed in second-class hotels. There wasn't even a real All-Star break; teams played less than 24 hours after the showcase game.

Heinsohn scheduled a meeting for 3 p.m. on January 14, the day of the game, to discuss a boycott of the All-Star match that night; however, on January 13, 12 inches of snow blanketed the Eastern Seaboard from Boston to New York. Some 26 players—most of whom had planned to arrive that day to attend a pregame party hosted by Celtics owner Walter Brown at the Sheraton Plaza—were stranded en route to the city. Oscar Robertson, Jerry Lucas, and Wayne Embry of Cincinnati and Detroit forward Bailey Howell were stuck at Chicago O'Hare Airport, where they were told flights were being delayed by eight hours. Flights to New England had been canceled, and the All-Stars in Chicago eventually finagled their way onto a flight to Washington, D.C. Early on January 14, the weary giants left their hotel to catch a 6:30 a.m. express train to Boston. Most players, including Baylor and Bob Pettit, spent much of game day traveling to Boston because of the inclement weather. Fatigued players straggled into Boston after enduring long train rides and sleeping on airport floors.

Heinsohn went ahead with the players' association meeting, joined by counsel for the association, Larry Fleisher, a former Bronx schoolyard player who graduated Harvard Law School at age 22 and was vice president of a corporation by the time he was 34. As each player arrived, Heinsohn handed him a petition declaring that none of the All-Stars would play unless the owners agreed to a new pension plan. The player reps for the teams—including Baylor, Heinsohn, Robertson, the Warriors' Guy Rodgers, Johnny Kerr, and Tom Gola—huddled with Fleisher for a quick update and skull session. Highly respected and admired, Baylor possessed a charismatic leadership that was integral to the evolving solidarity of the players' union.

The players prepared to inform Commissioner Walter Kennedy that they weren't playing without a pension agreement in place. The petition proposed that the players and owners each contribute $500 a year to such a plan to create a 30-year life insurance policy and annuity. This group of NBA players had a strong bargaining chip: The scheduled ABC broadcast of the All-Star Game was to be the first national TV exposure for the league in nearly a year. A few of the stars, including Wilt Chamberlain, wanted to play the game and negotiate later. Later in the evening, 11 men voted for the decision to play, nine against. At 8:15, ABC told the league if the players didn't come out in five minutes, the network would proceed with other programming. Celtics owner Walter Brown, who stood to lose the $30,000 he had spent promoting the game, wanted the league's board of governors to bar the 20 striking players from the NBA.

Not long before tip time, Commissioner Kennedy tried to gather the owners for a vote, but they were determined not to bow to the players' use of the telecast as a bargaining chip. Kennedy came into the locker room where the East and West squads were sitting. According to Thomas J. Whalen's *Dynasty's End: Bill Russell and the 1968–69 World Champion Boston Celtics*, he nervously told the players that they and the owners had a problem. He said he had met with the owners and that Fred Zollner of the Pistons had apparently spoken to his fellow owners and gotten an agreement. There was, however, no signed statement, Kennedy said. Apologizing profusely, he agreed on the need for a pension plan. The players asked him to leave.

According to Oscar Robertson's memoir *The Big O: My Life, My Times, My Game*, Robertson, Pettit, and Heinsohn told their peers, "If we go out and play now, we'll never get what we want." The veteran players thought about how genuine Kennedy had sounded but also remembered how his predecessor, Podoloff, had also seemed sincere. Others considered that the commissioner was operating from a position of weakness and would say anything to get them out on the floor. Maybe this was the time to take a stand. No one spoke for a while. Then, one by one, the players voiced their feelings regarding the new league head and their own bargaining.

Every few minutes, the NBA's PR man, Haskell Cohen, ducked into the tense room and tried to persuade the stars. He told them if they didn't come out now, the network would never air NBA games again. When Cohen left, as Robertson recalls in *The Big O*, owner Red Auerbach came in and threatened to fire his players for their protest. While the players discussed their options, according to Heinsohn's memory in *Tall Tales*, there was an Irish cop that the players asked to stand guard at the locker room door. Lakers owner Bob Short came down the corridor and demanded the guard let him speak to his players. The guard repeated his orders. John Taylor writes in his book *The Rivalry: Bill Russell, Wilt Chamberlain, and the Golden Age of Basketball*, Baylor spat back, "Tell Bob Short to f--- himself!" Author Harvey Araton states in his 2011 book, *When the Garden Was Eden: Clyde, the Captain, Dollar Bill, and the Glory Days of the New York Knicks*, that basketball millionaires from Michael Jordan through LeBron James owe their largesse to that moment.

According to *The Rivalry*, Short barged into the training room next door and loudly harangued the players: "If any of my players are in on this, they're through!" Baylor and the others could hear him, which was his intent.

As the old-timers hit the court at 8:30, a half hour before the showcase game, the players voted a second time, and two more voted to play. One player, fearful of his owner's reprisal, sat on his trembling hands.

Kennedy worried any potential TV contract would go up in smoke if the players left them hanging with dead air. He insisted they would ruin the game, echoing Philly owner Eddie Gottlieb's statement when NBA owners had voted for racial integration almost 15 years earlier. Heinsohn sent Bob Pettit to the commissioner's hotel suite with the ultimatum: No pension plan, no game. Pettit's teammate Lenny Wilkens accompanied him.

In his 2010 memoir *Unguarded: My Forty Years Surviving in the NBA*, Wilkens says Kennedy asked him, "Lenny, you mean to tell me that you're really going to strike this game?" "Yeah," Wilkens deadpanned. Kennedy shook his head in disgust.

Finally, Kennedy relayed through Pettit to Heinsohn that if the game was played, he'd facilitate a pension deal with the owners. There were only 15 minutes until tip-off. The men took another vote about whether to play. Five minutes later, Pettit exited and went to tell the league president the game would be played. TV viewers were none the wiser, as the network delayed the tip-off time by 15 minutes. The All-Star teams took the floor at 8:55 p.m.

This was the first real victory for a players' union in major sports history. It happened eight years before baseball's Curt Flood lost his Supreme Court case regarding the reserve clause, which bound a player to his team unless he was traded, forbade athletes from contesting trades, and severely hampered any means of players negotiating contracts, since they could not declare themselves free agents. The proposed walkout, although little discussed in sports circles today, helped pave the way for strong players' unions in major-league sports, free agency, and multimillion-dollar salaries. As he had in Charleston in 1959, Baylor risked his career for a larger cause.

Several days later, on January 17, Bob Short denied he had sent word into the All-Star locker room threatening to fire West and Baylor. He told the *Los Angeles Times*, "I have always given my players whatever they ask. If they want a pension, I'll give them one." Short added that neither the league nor a players' association had the right to demand he do so, however. "I ordered Baylor and West onto the floor, but I did not say they would be fired." In the same article, he blames Tommy Heinsohn for influencing his players to do "foolish" things. Short says the players should realize that NBA owners, unlike their counterparts in pro football and baseball, didn't receive $500,000 in TV revenue. There wasn't as big a pie to divide in basketball. He claims that the net profit from the 1963 NBA All-Star Game in L.A., which drew more than 14,000 fans, was only $2,000.

When the Lakers returned to Los Angeles from Boston, Ruby Baylor greeted her husband, and they went to thank Schaus. *Sports Illustrated* reports that as Schaus watched the Baylors walk away, he felt he had never been so touched or so proud of a man.

Baylor was always a huge favorite with fans. In a March 1964 letter to the editor of *Ebony* magazine, a New Yorker critiques the publication's annual NBA season preview, writing, "Newspapers selecting Bill Russell and Wilt Chamberlain over Oscar Robertson are crazy. The only one who is better than him is Elgin Baylor." In fairness to *Ebony*, the season preview states, "In some circles Baylor is considered the greatest man-for-man, size-for-size athlete ever to lace on a pair of basketball shoes."

Yet, Baylor never really pursued the attention or favor of the media. At awards banquets, he kept it short and sweet. He seldom called attention to himself, telling *SPORT's* Milton Gross, "I sometimes duck interviews. When sportswriters telephone me I'm sometimes not there. They want to ask me about myself, and I just don't like to talk about myself." Of the media, he relates,

> If you've just lost a game or even won one that was hard-played, you're at a loss for words. So when they ask me a few questions I say no comment. They've been a little irritated several times. But once the game's over, I like to forget it. Maybe if people get to know me well enough they might think different of me.

He was no more comfortable with or enthralled by the limelight than when he was a high school kid, embarrassed by the attention he drew when he made Washington's All-Met team. Of stardom, he says to Gross in *SPORT*, "[A]fter a while it comes to a point where you get tired of it and you just want to get away from it. It's just the same questions all the time." People would ask Baylor the difference between college and pro ball, who the best player was in the league, and how a player goes about checking Chamberlain—although Wilt was a 7'1" center and Baylor a 6'5" forward. Others wanted to know how many points he was going to score that night. As with Chamberlain, who tired of being asked how tall he was, for Baylor the questions got old fast. Bill Russell didn't give autographs—not even to teammates and trainers whose relatives asked for them.

Baylor did what he needed to do to market himself and be a successful businessman, however. By 1963, he was making $60,000 a year. By the mid-1960s, he owned a sporty Jaguar automobile. He told the media he owned "only" 15 suits and "only" eight pairs of custom-made English shoes. Baylor also owned part of a shopping center in Falls Church, Virginia, as well as the duplex apartment near Wilshire Boulevard where he, Ruby, and little Alan lived. Ruby Baylor appeared in an *Ebony* magazine ad for Virtue Bros. Furniture of Los Angeles. The ad encouraged women to "Follow the example of the charming Mrs. Elgin Baylor" by purchasing a modernistic gold inlaid Micalite dining table. Its tagline read, "The Smart Set Selects."

Baylor had other local real estate, too. After working two years in the escrow department of Great Western Savings & Loan, he knew something about property values and construction expenses. Baylor said to *SPORT* magazine in 1963, "I'm always looking to the future. Ruby is expecting a baby next spring, and probably there'll be other children coming along. I don't con myself that I can go on playing real good basketball for more than four more years or so. Mister, I'm making sure I don't wind up driving a truck."

Baylor took a stand during the 1966 NBA All-Star Game. While Coach Fred Schaus was in Cincinnati at the All-Star Game, which was played at Ben Kerner's outdated and undersized Kiel Auditorium, Baylor was in a hotel room in Boston, coaching the Lakers. It was the first time he had not been chosen to play in the game. In Cincinnati, Schaus and GM Lou Mohs discussed Baylor's exclusion. Schaus called Baylor to tell him it had been decided he should sit on the bench as an honorary All-Star. Baylor told Schaus he would consider it and call him back.

As he weighed the offer, Baylor thought about Dick Barnett. His teammate hadn't been voted an All-Star, even though he was the third-leading scorer in the NBA. Bullets coach Paul Seymour called Barnett's jump shot the "best in the league." A white player had been selected instead, some felt, because there were not enough white faces on the team. Just as Baylor had decided not to play that game in Jim Crow Charleston, West Virginia, he also decided to sit out the All-Star Game that had already excluded him. Baylor called Schaus back and said he wouldn't be coming to St. Louis. The All-Star Game was played, without Elgin Baylor, on January 11, 1966.

Baylor generally kept his focus on basketball, and it was his game that earned him his fame. "Everybody wanted to be like Elgin," said basketball Hall of Famer and Detroit mayor Dave Bing, who, like Baylor, was a product of Spingarn High School. "I wore his number all the way through high school and college."

Kids throughout the United States idolized Baylor. Historian Jeffrey T. Sammons writes in his 1990 book *Beyond the Ring: The Role of Boxing in American Society*, "I imitated Elgin Baylor, nervous twitch and all."

Pro Bowl and Hall of Fame Kansas City Chiefs wide receiver Otis Taylor was also enthralled with Baylor. "I tried to do the things Elgin Baylor did," he states in the November 1, 1971, issue of *Sports Illustrated*. "I saw this man while I was in high school, and I just fell in love with him." For the athletes of Rick Barry, Billy Cunningham, Eddie Miles, and Otis Taylor's generation, Baylor was the gold standard. His appeal and influence crossed racial lines.

For Baylor and the Lakers, the move to Los Angeles had ushered in a new era of professional basketball. NBA attendance in 1963–1964 grew by more than 20 percent from the previous season, and the Lakers drew more fans than any other team in the league. In 1964–1965, Commissioner Kennedy signed a new TV deal worth $650,000, and ABC Sunday-afternoon telecasts were extended from three years to five. In 1965, ABC agreed to televise league games for $600,000 a year, with a clause to pay $1 million a year if the contract lasted five seasons.

As basketball gained a following throughout the country, so did Baylor. When he first established himself in Southern California in the early 1960s, local white youth were obsessed with hanging 10 at Doheny, Malibu, and San Onofre. Basketball was of little consequence. By the late 1960s, enough boys had followed in Baylor's footsteps that many wanted to hang 10 feet from the floor like their hero, fortifying high school basketball teams from Redondo Beach to La Mesa. This shift in interest provided the supporting cast for the great UCLA teams of the 1960s, which starred Gail Goodrich from L.A. Polytechnic, Keith Erickson of El Segundo High, and John Vallely of Corona del Mar High in Newport

Beach. John Wooden had been coaching at UCLA more than a decade before gaining national prominence, and in the three seasons before the Lakers moved to L.A., UCLA's conference records had been 10–6, 7–5, and 7–5. The 1959–1960 team finished only 14–12 overall. After Baylor and his Lakers helped establish the game among Southern California boys, UCLA went 30–0 in 1964 and 15–0 in the Pac-8, winning their first NCAA title in 1964. The 1965 Bruins won 28 games and lost only two, were 14–0 in the Pac-8 Conference, and won their second consecutive NCAA championship. The success of that team played a large part in UCLA's ability to recruit New York phenom Lew Alcindor (now better known as Kareem Abdul-Jabbar). The first title with Alcindor would happen three seasons later.

Crosstown rival University of Southern California also benefited from the bonanza in local talent, although to a lesser extent. The Trojans hired former Seattle University coach Bob Boyd in 1967. During the next 13 seasons, as interest in the sport grew and local talent became more abundant, Boyd's teams went 216–131 overall and played in four postseason tournaments, including a National Invitation Tournament and NCAA appearance (back when the NCAA field was limited to 32 teams, generally only one per strong conference). In 1971, Southern Cal went 24–2 and was ranked fifth in the nation, after being ranked first at midseason. They also won 24 games in 1974. Star guard Paul Westphal, who would go on to play for the Celtics, was a product of Redondo Beach's Aviation High School; center Ron Riley came from L.A.'s Jordan High; and sixth man Monroe Nash graduated from Morse High School in San Diego. Los Angeles became a basketball capital in the Baylor years.

Baylor was also popular with East Coast youngsters. In the 1960s, Scott Russell, now a sportswriter, told the author he was playing pickup ball one day in the South Bronx with a group of young men that included NBA star Kevin Loughery's younger brother John. All of a sudden, John Loughery began crying during the game. "What's wrong?" the guys asked him. "The ball!" he cried. "Huh, nobody touched you!" they protested. "No, the ball. My brother gave me this basketball, signed by Elgin Baylor, and I forgot. Now we've ruined the autograph!"

In his 2013 autobiography *Dr. J*, Julius Erving, who was raised on Long Island, says that watching Baylor really showed him how beautifully the game could be played.

9

"THE MORE DETERMINED I BECAME TO PROVE THE DOCTORS WRONG"

I have got two reasons for success, and I'm standing on both of them.—Betty Grable

The Lakers' 1963–1964 preseason began in Honolulu against the 76ers. Dick Barnett sank a 40-footer as the buzzer sounded to give them a 106–104 win. Baylor led the team with 24 points, but Barnett had scored the last six, including two free throws, to tie it at 102, and his trademark jumper, to tie things again at 104. He finished with 19.

Baylor's knees were already an issue. In fact, he had been taking painkiller shots for them since 1960. Fans and teammates feared the worst. In one telling play in November, San Francisco's Nate Thurmond threw a cross-court pass, and Baylor picked it off. A physically sound Baylor would have dribbled in a dash toward his basket before the Warriors could catch him and laid in a bunny. Instead, 10,834 Sports Arena onlookers watched as the 6'11" Thurmond hustled to reach Baylor from behind and tied him up. Two nights later, L.A. played the Hawks in St. Louis. Baylor suited up with a high bandage wrapping his left leg and heavy canvas-elastic supports on both knees. He managed only eight points on 2-for-12 shooting. It was the least he'd ever scored in a pro game. His lifetime average was 32 a night.

On Wednesday, November 27, the day before Thanksgiving, the Celtics toyed with the Lakers, 114–78. Baylor's weakened status was getting to Jerry West, and he shared his concern with the *Los Angeles Times*.

Rubbing his sore thigh in the locker room, West lamented, "I'm just sick about it. Tonight Elgin couldn't do anything, and the Celtics handled us like babies. There was a loose ball out there. Sam Jones and Elgin both had an even chance to get it. Elgin prides himself on his speed and can beat Jones in any head-to-head race," referring to the man most players and sportswriters considered one of the league's swiftest players. "You saw what happened," West continued. "Jones left him behind. . . . Elgin had to make one little turn . . . but he simply couldn't make it."

Baylor was having none of it. "I have no time to talk to gravediggers!" said the prideful Lakers leader to the *Times*. The team traveled to Baltimore the next week and played the Bullets on December 4. Again, Baylor suited up, but 6'6", 235-pound Bullets forward Gus Johnson held him to 3-for-21 from the floor. This was not the Elgin Baylor who gave defenders nightmares the evening before games. Not only did L.A. lose, 118–98, to the young Bullets, but a few times Johnson stood by as Baylor took his shots. Baylor, aware of rumors about the calcium deposits in his knees and his imminent demise, did damage control with his wife. He told *SPORT* magazine that he called her from Seattle. "Something else happened in the game tonight," he told her. "Somebody stepped on my foot, and it swelled so bad, I can't get my shoe on." He added he had a bad cold.

"I can hardly understand you," she replied, and suggested he come home and rest. Baylor begged off, citing a slim one-game division lead over the Hawks. "If we can pull out in front, I'll think about resting." Pride trumped performance.

Sam Jones told the *Boston Globe* in 1964, "It's a crying shame what they're doing to Elgin."

"Hot Rod" Hundley told the *Los Angeles Times*, "I'm not a doctor, but it seems to me he shouldn't have been suiting up these past weeks. If they don't know what's wrong with him—all the more reason he should be sidelined."

Disagreeing, Frank Selvy said to the *Times*, "Red Auerbach and his guys would just love to get Baylor out of action," calling the apparent Celtics' concern "psychological warfare."

Fred Schaus responded to the critics, especially those in the green shamrock shorts. He asked the *Times*, "Listen, do you think Bob Short would let me jeopardize a quarter-of-a-million-dollar ballplayer? Don't you think we have solid medical opinion that exercise is more liable to help his legs than to hurt them?" Schaus said the Celtics and other clubs "have too many self-appointed orthopedic specialists on their squads. None of them know a piece of calcium from a watermelon."

By then, Baylor was so stiff, the defense didn't even bother to foul him—another first. At that point, Short called Baylor and put his foot down: "You're going to the Mayo Clinic!" he said for a *Times* report on Baylor's debilitating knee.

"I'd rather not," Baylor said. "There's plenty doctors here in Los Angeles giving me treatment." Some people close to Baylor thought he didn't want to go to the famed Rochester, Minnesota, clinic because he didn't want to go under the knife. Baylor spoke to the *Times* about his hesitancy to go to Mayo, saying, "I was already . . . getting all the X-rays, deep heat, and cortisone-shot treatments that were necessary." He finally relented to Short's wishes, however, saying, "Mr. Short is the boss, so I went."

According to Myron Cope in the *Ebony* article "Elgin Baylor Comes Back," on December 10, 1963, Baylor and Short flew to Rochester in the owner's private Beechcraft. Noted orthopedist H. H. Young took blood tests and X-rays that same day. After reviewing the test results, Young believed Baylor was either suffering from a "calciumated condition above the knees" or a bone growth. More heat treatments and future X-rays would determine which. "It could be serious," Young said. When Baylor got home, Ruby drove him to L.A.'s Freeman Hospital to have a separate virus treated. His foot was also extremely swollen, and they reduced that. But the staff in L.A. was reluctant to offer an opinion on Baylor's knees; who were they to attempt to one-up Mayo Clinic?

In early December, Baylor missed his first game since the 1962 playoffs. Some folks felt the Lakers should have declared him inactive the rest of December. Boston's Tom Heinsohn was one, harping to the *Boston Globe*, "The Lakers are ruining Baylor. He can't do anything, and he shouldn't be out there."

The first opponent after the Mayo Clinic visit was St. Louis on December 15. Baylor played 13 minutes before he scored. His timing was off, as well as his accuracy, but he snared 14 rebounds. He scored only 19 points, and the Lakers lost by seven. John Taylor recounts in his book *The Rivalry: Bill Russell, Wilt Chamberlain, and the Golden Age of Basketball*, that one Lakers fan yelled from courtside, "Take a vacation, bum; do us all a favor!" Baylor heard the wag, and it showed on his face. But he kept on playing. He felt obligated to do so. By the 1963–1964 season, Baylor was well aware that during his year of reserve duty, the team had drawn 2,000 less fans each night he was absent from the lineup. In addition, after 1960, Short had signed Baylor to one of the longest contracts in pro sports—six years of salary on a sliding scale. On December 21, Baylor put some doubters to rest, scoring 31 points, with 13 rebounds and 9 assists, against Philadelphia.

But he continually had to answer the critics. "First of all, the Mayo doctors, and every other doctor I've seen—seven in all, have told me that running on my legs isn't likely to hurt them," he told the *Los Angeles Times* in the Sports Arena locker room before a Sixers game right before New Year's Eve. Baylor said, if anything, running could break up the calcium.

"Second, I owe this club a lot," Baylor added. "Bob Short signed me out of college for a lot of money. He and his partner in the trucking business, Frank Ryan, have advised me on a lot of investments that have paid off. They've seen I've learned about stocks and bonds until now I can pretty much look after myself." He said he would play for them with one hand cut off, if he had to. In 1959–1960, he had played through a gash that required eight stitches on the third finger of his shooting hand—defying docs who suggested that he rest—because he was the team's primary gate attraction. Bob Short, the starstruck owner who exhibited such faith in Baylor that he banked the Lakers' westward move on it, engendered such loyalty among pro athletes.

That night, Baylor took the court against Philly without leg braces. "I'm gonna do myself some sashaying!" he warns in the *Times*. The Sixers' 6'7" Chet "The Jet" Walker drew the defensive assignment. The second-year former Bradley All-American jostled successfully against Baylor. West hit Baylor with a pass, who looked for a free man but found no one. He backed against Walker, dipping from side to side as he dribbled and positioning himself closer to the hoop. Larry Costello came over to help Walker, but Baylor appeared to split himself in two as he slipped between the two defenders, drove, and hung in the air. When he finally did shoot, all Walker could do was foul him, but the ball went in. Baylor sank both free throws, and L.A. led the game for the first time. He continued to play well, floating in long hook shots, lofting them in from the lane, and arching in jumpers. When the game was over, he'd scored a conventional 26, collected 10 boards, and handed out 7 assists. Was he back? "I'm 28," Baylor says in the *Times*, "which means I've got some time left." But some sportswriters wondered if he wasn't 29, after hearing that the age on his 1954 Spingarn High School graduation transcript read "19." If so, he would turn 30 on his upcoming birthday, September 16, 1964. And in team sports, 30 was the beginning of the end—especially if the "wheels" were gone. Schaus, ever the optimist, contemplated moving Baylor to a guard position.

On January 17, the Lakers faced the Celtics in front of 10,061 in the Boston Garden. Fred Schaus often complained that in the Garden's visitors' locker room the windows were stuck open so the players would freeze. Others said visiting teams got shortchanged on towels. When the game got started, Baylor was hot early, and L.A. led, 23–15, with 1:30 to play in the first. John Havlicek started hitting, and Boston scored nine unanswered points. The Lakers never regained the lead. They shot poorly and scored only 35 points during the next two periods. They missed Dick Barnett's jump-shooting; suffering from a sore hamstring he had injured in Cincinnati, he had been advised to sit out until at least the following week.

When Boston went up, 80–65, early in the final period, Schaus sat West and Baylor for the balance of the game. West had scored 15, Baylor 22. "I had to save them for an all-out effort against Philadelphia Saturday night," the coach explains in the *Times* article on the game. "We have to have that one for a split on the trip." The Celtics crushed the Lakers, 99–79. Of the team's effort in Boston, Schaus says in the *Times*, "I know we're tired, but we're not that tired." Havlicek ended up with 27, although none of the other Celtics played particularly well. Baylor had lost weight and was down to 212 from his usual 220 pounds.

On Friday, February 7, Baylor scored a season's best 40, but the Pistons beat the Lakers, 111–103, in front of 8,116 disappointed Sports Arena rooters. Detroit forwards Bailey Howell and Ray Scott combined for 56 points, and substitute guard Don Ohl hit three key baskets down the stretch to turn back a Lakers rally. L.A.'s only lead was at 83–82, and Baylor got almost no scoring support. "Pops" Selvy contributed 17 but tired in crunch time. It was also the club's eighth straight game without Jerry West.

The Lakers defeated Boston, 113–109, on February 11, but both Baylor and West were limping combatants as the teams flew to L.A. for a rematch on the 16th. This time the Lakers lost. Auerbach, as always, dismissed the regular-season contest. Schaus told the *Los Angeles Times*, "I know damn well he doesn't mean that. We'll take it any way we can get it." He credited the team's recent success to better defense and rebounding.

On Sunday, March 1, 1964, they downed St. Louis, 114–91. On March 7, Baylor twisted and pumped for 35 points against the Warriors. Days later, he told the *Times*, "A lot of people have my career finished, but I intend to keep on playing this year and next. I've got a lot of basketball left in me." The Lakers won nine games and lost eight of their final 17 that season.

* * *

In a season of physical ups and downs for Baylor, the 1963–1964 Lakers landed in third place, their 42–38 record four games behind second-place St. Louis and a half dozen behind Wilt's Warriors. Baylor had averaged 25.4 points per game, almost nine points a game less than 1963, and 13 less per game than 1962, when he had averaged 38. His 12 rebounds per game in 1963–1964 were a career low, but he averaged 4.4. assists, a good figure for a forward, and made 80.2 percent of his free throws.

In the opening round of the playoffs, the Lakers faced St. Louis. As the Lakers faced the Hawks in the division playoffs, Schaus deemed Baylor "as good as he ever was." He went on to tell the *Los Angeles Times*, "That's why I think we have a great chance in the playoffs." They would open with Saturday and Sunday games at St. Louis and return to the Sports Arena on March 25. Baylor's season had been up and down because of knee strain. The *Los Angeles Sentinel*'s A. S. "Doc" Young writes that Baylor heard the "boos of the crowd. People who hailed him as 'the greatest ever' mere months earlier began to put him down." Of the stories that continued to surface claiming that Baylor was much older than his listed age of 29, Young says, "You would have thought, from some yarns, that Elg was ready for the ol' rockin' chair. But gentleman that he is, Elgin never cried the blues." John Hall of the *Times* praises Baylor, saying he "came back in pain to give us another great season" and was "still the most electric basketball player most of us have ever viewed."

L.A. lost the opener at St. Louis, 115–104, despite 30 points from Baylor. In the second game, also on the road, Baylor only scored 20, and

West 18, and the Lakers fell, 106–90. L.A. recovered in their first series game at home, edging St. Louis, 107–105, in a game where Baylor scored 23. The Hawks went on to eliminate the Lakers, three games to two. In two of the postseason games, the Lakers were held to less than 100 points.

* * *

In April, the Lakers lost a key player when center Jim Krebs was offered a job with United California Bank, a once-in-a-lifetime opportunity that led him to retire from the National Basketball Association after seven seasons. In his best season, 1961–1962, the former Southern Methodist University All-American had averaged 10 points and grabbed 616 rebounds.

On May 4, the 1964 NBA Draft was held in New York City. Fred Schaus and Lou Mohs had flown to Denver to pick up Bob Short, and from there they flew to New York. Schaus made no secret of his wishes for a certain UCLA guard: "I want Walt Hazzard. I know he's a winner," Schaus told the *Los Angeles Times*. L.A. could select Hazzard with its territorial pick and still own a first-round choice. Size was the main concern—even more so with Krebs gone. Oregon State's Mel Counts was a prospect, but, at seven feet, he was more shooter than shot blocker. Schaus hinted that the club might trade up for a high pick.

The Lakers selected flashy UCLA guard and Philly schoolyard product Walt Hazzard with their first pick in the NBA Draft. Baylor welcomed Hazzard to the fold. "It's a really nice thing," Baylor told the *Times*. "Walt called me the other day and said he wants to play in Los Angeles. . . . I'm quite sure he will be able to help us." Hazzard had also been offered lifetime employment to play with the Phillips 66ers on the Amateur Athletic Union industrial circuit, and he was selected for the U.S. Olympic basketball team slated to play in the 1964 Tokyo Games. Looking ahead, the Lakers' weakness was up front. New York got the best big men in the first two rounds of the draft, as Baylor observed: Texas Western center Jim "Bad News" Barnes and Grambling All-American Willis Reed.

Some in the local sports press felt the club had made a big mistake by cutting former Pepperdine star Bob Warlick, a kid who the *Times* reported had "so many great moves" and who, along with Cotton Nash, had stood out during rookie camp. The *Los Angeles Sentinel*'s Brad Pye writes of Warlick, "[H]e was a much better ballplayer than second-year man Jimmy King. He was giving Jerry West fits in practice." The Lakers had selected Warlick as a future pick in 1963 but had not invited him to camp. Sportswriter George Watson of Grenada, California, calls the 6'4" prospect the "finest Negro basketball player to come out of Pepperdine," saying he and Walt Hazzard were the best two basketball players on the West Coast in the 10 years or so since Bill Russell left college. But Mohs and Schaus had released Warlick, who went on to play seven seasons with the Pistons, Warriors, expansion Phoenix Suns, and American Basketball Association Los Angeles Stars.

In the summer of 1964, the Lakers convinced Baylor to consult Dr. Robert Kerlan, Sandy Koufax's physician, about the ongoing issues with his knees. When Baylor entered Kerlan's office on an initial visit, he saw the orthopedist bent over in apparent pain. "He seemed to have a problem and couldn't even help himself," said Baylor to the *Times'* Gary Libman in a September 14, 1992, profile of Kerlan titled "No Time-Outs." "I told the receptionist I was there for a cold and had come to the wrong doctor. And I left." Kerlan had developed arthritis in the early 1940s, and his condition worsened. By the late 1960s, he sometimes used crutches, but his mind was not weakened. When other doctors could not relieve or diagnose Baylor's knee pain, the player came back to Kerlan. "Once we sat down and talked, I was very impressed," he told Libman. Kerlan determined that the calcium deposits were not in the knees, but rather in the quadriceps muscles—a condition more common among football players. "By using a peripheral vasculator on Baylor, we hope to work him out of this condition without surgery," Kerlan told the *Times* in 1964. The procedure, which involved air pressure massage, was already working for Baylor's friend and homeboy, Dodgers shortstop Maury Wills. "Going in, cutting, would do more harm than scraping out the calcium would do good," Kerlan told Baylor, according to the 1992 *Times* story.

"Baylor missed one day that whole summer," said Lakers trainer Frank O'Neill to *Ebony* magazine in February 1965. "And just like Elg all he wanted that day was to take his little boy to the zoo." Therapeutic heat treatments and weight lifting strengthened the quadriceps muscles around Baylor's knees, and, for the most part, they held up. Mel Counts, who was a rookie in 1964, says in an online article for Hoops Nation dated May 11, 2013, "Elgin had a tremendous drive and self-motivation."

On August 6, 1964, Los Angeles kicked off its city summer basketball league with a free clinic by Elgin Baylor at perennial power Jefferson High School. GM Lou Mohs was happy with Baylor's physical progress, telling the *Times* that the management team was "not only elated for the Lakers, but more so for Elgin himself." He added, "We expect to see again and enjoy the greatest basketball player, pound-for-pound, inch-for-inch, that has ever laced on a sneaker." Schaus also assured the *Times* that Baylor "had four deep X-ray treatments to his knees since the playoffs, and it appears definite now he won't have to have surgery." Baylor persisted with his weight-training and stretching regimen, and Dr. Kerlan told everyone who asked that the main man would soon be better than ever.

Baylor also stayed politically active during that long, hot summer. He appeared alongside such sports celebrities as University of Southern California fullback "Big" Ben Wilson and former Rams bruiser "Deacon" Dan Towler at voting drives organized by the Students Committee for the Improvement of Watts, a neighborhood in South L.A. At a rally on August 22, Baylor, Wilson, and Dodgers hero Tommy Davis—along with jazz luminary Benny Carter and actor Tony Franciosa—urged prospective voters at the Imperial Housing Project at 114th Street and Gorman Avenue. The citywide aim was to register 50,000 new voters for the 1964 elections. Baylor also glad-handed at a ribbon-cutting for Unimart, a membership food and department store in Northridge, where he was joined by Negro assemblyman Mervyn Dymally, who would become one of the first black elected U.S. lieutenant governors a decade later.

The Lakers inaugurated their fifth season in L.A. by opening preseason camp in September at Loyola University of Los Angeles. Newcomers included 6'5" Cotton Nash from the University of Kentucky and veteran center Darrall Imhoff, a former Cal-Berkeley standout acquired from Detroit. Gene Wiley, LeRoy Ellis, Jim King, and Dick Barnett were still on hand. The team would be subject to Schaus's two-a-days and play an intrasquad scrimmage at Costa Mesa High School on September 18. Schaus split his Lakers into two teams, the white squad, featuring Baylor, Barnett, Imhoff, Ellis, Jerry Grote, and Don Nelson, and the blue, with Nash, Wiley, West, King, Rudy LaRusso, and John Savage. As 1,354 fans watched, LaRusso emerged as the star of the scrimmage, with his 30 points leading the blues to a 94–84 win. Nash scored 24 for his blue team.

Baylor and West were used sparingly, so Schaus could gauge the progress of the younger players.

On the 21st, the team scrimmaged again at Loyola. Early reports indicated that Baylor looked fit and strong, having responded to off-season treatment. Many basketball writers believed that, if Baylor was indeed 100 percent, this was the year L.A. could finally dethrone Boston. They had youth, bench strength, the best one–two scoring combo in the game, and the size to combat Bill Russell. They would open the preseason against the Warriors in Santa Maria.

After an off-season spent making public appearances, giving basketball clinics, helping push voter registration, rehabilitating his knee, and working as a PR man for Pepsi-Cola, Baylor felt confident and ready to face NBA opponents—and his staunchest critics. He saw Baltimore as the most improved club in the West, since the Bullets had acquired star forward Bailey Howell and scoring guard Don Ohl in trades. In the East, he felt Cincinnati, led by Oscar Robertson and Jerry Lucas, would push Boston for the division title.

Sports Illustrated's 1964–1965 NBA season preview was titled "The Pack Closes in on Boston," although Celtic Tommy Heinsohn displays an unworried expression on the cover, bearing the bold white letters, "We'll Win Again." The magazine forecasts that the Lakers would again rely on the one–two punch of Baylor and West, and that the new men, Walt Hazzard and Cotton Nash, would be limited by Hazzard's understudy role to West and Nash's inability to score as much as Dick Barnett. LaRusso was granted credit as a rebounder, but in his opinion, other frontcourt players demonstrated little promise. The *SI* scribe finds LeRoy Ellis inconsistent and questions whether Darrall Imhoff would be much help to Gene Wiley. The L.A. prognostication ended on a cautionary note: "Baylor's knees are a big question; he applied heat to them every halftime during exhibition games." In the East, Boston's challenge was John Havlicek's ability to "replace" four strong bench players. Young Mel Counts's backup role to Russell was unimportant; the writer says of the starting center, "With him, this will always be the team to beat." The Celtics also had added incentive: On Labor Day weekend, their beloved owner and founder, Walter Brown, died on Cape Cod. They dedicated their upcoming season to him.

In a game promoted by Greater Seattle, Inc., Baylor returned to Seattle on October 6, 1964. His 24 points led the Lakers' 127–102 exhibition victory over Wilt Chamberlain's San Francisco Warriors in front of 6,850 fans at the Seattle Coliseum.

In early November, the Lakers swamped the Warriors, 130–103. Rudy LaRusso's frontcourt play was making a big difference. What the Lakers lacked in a fearsome big man, they boasted in the rebounding tenacity of LaRusso and, when healthy, Baylor. Still, not only were they limited by their centers' lack of defensive and rebounding prowess, but neither Ellis, Wiley, nor the newly acquired Imhoff were efficient scorers. That deficiency allowed the Chamberlains, Bellamys, and Russells to cheat on defense and wait in the lane for penetrating Lakers like West and Baylor. Baylor was playing quite well early in the month, quelling doubters in the stands and the media. Lakers publicist Mitch Chortkoff told *Ebony* in February 1965: "He's scoring about the same as last year, but there's a difference. He's rebounding more, turning, twisting, making the moves. But it isn't just the scoring or the rebounds. It's the whole system that revolves around him."

On Friday, November 13, the Lakers beat the Celtics in the Boston Garden. Muhammad Ali's Louisville ownership brain trust attended the Lakers game until finding out during a restroom break that Ali had suffered a hernia in his Sherry Biltmore hotel room. His fight to defend the title against Sonny Liston, scheduled for the following Monday in the Garden, was called off.

Then Baylor's knee problems returned, and he watched a 108–98 loss to Boston in civilian clothes in early December. Doctors from Hawaii to L.A. had examined the most valuable legs in basketball, and the problem was, they disagreed in their diagnoses. The calcium deposits did reduce Baylor's efficiency. Opponents noticed the hesitancy in his game—some of the assertiveness was gone. Jim Murray writes in his *Los Angeles Times* column, "The lion has a thorn in his paw. It's heartbreaking to see the jackals come out of the woodwork in the forest. Guys who used to take a head cold on the nights they needed to stop Baylor now volunteer." Baylor was playing at about two-thirds of his normal effectiveness. He found it more difficult to spin, explode off the dribble, and spring for tap-ins. In Phil Pepe's 1970 book *Greatest Stars of the NBA*, Jerry West is quoted as saying, "To see him crippled and scoring less points than some of the subs on the other team just makes you want to cry."

The Lakers started the season winning 15 of their first 21 games. On December 10, they held a slim game-and-a-half lead over St. Louis in the standings. L.A. edged Detroit, 116–115. Before Christmas, they dropped the Sixers, a game in which Baylor scored a season-high 40 points. *Los Angeles Sentinel* columnists objected to the big-city sportswriters who maintained that West was a more important player than Baylor, and the one the team had missed more in his absence. Baylor's advocates in the Negro media insisted that when Baylor was down, or not at full strength, it was not only his scoring the Lakers lacked, but his abilities to rebound and find open teammates with passes. "I certainly hate to keep harping on this, because it looks like we're trying to 'pan' West, when actually we are not. . . . Jerry has the rep of being a real 'right' guy. . . . It just peeves us when some of the local scribes and others stress that West is THE most important player on the Lakers," writes L. I. Brockenbury in the *Sentinel*.

Baylor told the *Los Angeles Times'* Jim Murray that the most important contributions by a basketball player to his team—for instance, a steal or keeping the ball alive on the backboard—often are not reflected in the box score.

The Lakers faced the Hawks in St. Louis in front of 8,609 fans on the first Saturday of the new year. The lead changed six times in the first half, as Baylor hit for 21 points. He contributed 40 total, despite missing two key free throws in the final minute (as did West), and L.A. won, 115–112. Baylor made up for the lapse by sinking his last four foul shots, as the Hawks resorted to fouling in desperation. LeRoy Ellis scored key fourth-period baskets to help seal the win. Zelmo Beaty's 27 points and Bob Pettit's 28 led the losers. On Sunday, L.A. beat St. Louis again, 99–92, with West hitting 34. They led the division by three and a half games. Before assembled basketball writers at the Olympian Motor Hotel, Fred Schaus said in the AP wire report on January 4, 1965, "I was really pleased with the St. Louis series, but I was more pleased when I returned home to read a local report that I had saved my job." Bob Short had extended Schaus's contract earlier in the month in Minneapolis. Schaus was also encouraged by the recent play of LeRoy Ellis.

After playing four games in as many nights, the Celtics came to the Sports Arena on Thursday. A minute into the game, Baylor cut through the lane to the right corner, received a bounce pass, deftly faked his man twice, eluded him, and swooped in for a reverse layin. Like a high jumper loping toward the pit, Bill Russell took a long stride, lifted up, and swatted the shot away. The champs coasted to a 10–0 advantage, and before anyone knew what hit them, the score was 16–2. "Wake up, you bums!"

screamed a Lakers fan from the third row, according to the *Los Angeles Times*.

Although not accorded the superstar status of Robertson, Baylor, and Chamberlain, Sam Jones proved unstoppable. "We put four different men on Sam Thursday night," said a frustrated Coach Schaus to the *Times*, "and we couldn't stop him. We didn't even slow him down." After seven and a half minutes of play, the Lakers trailed, 29–6. The home team did wake up, aroused by some nifty passing by Baylor and West. L.A. led, 38–30, at the end of the first period. Rookie sub Walt Hazzard was doing well. Boston pulled within one at halftime.

L.A. fought back and led by 10 with seven minutes to play. On defense, the Russell factor was too much to overcome. John Hall of the *Times* observes, "Baylor and West, in particular, completely change their shooting style when Bill is on the floor. Players are afraid to breathe." Boston won the game, 107–103, its 12th straight victory despite a murderous schedule. Baylor had scored 23 on 9-for-18 shooting, and West hit 33.

Of Hazzard's play, Schaus beamed to the *Times*, "I'm completely satisfied with Walt . . . and if he keeps up his performances of the Celtics games, he's going to be a starter for the rest of the year." The rookie fit right in with sartorial leaders Baylor and Barnett, sporting a fur-collared topcoat and favoring a beret and alligator shoes. His socks, tie, and breast handkerchief were color coordinated. The *Times'* Jim Murray quips, "[Y]ou half expect the accent to be one-part Maurice Chevalier and two-parts Peter Lawford." But Hazzard was still relegated to the duties of a first-year pro: In one hand he carried a bag that contained a hydrocolator, the machine that heated the moist pads for Baylor's knees; in another, he carried the team's basketballs.

In their last game before the All-Star break, the Lakers visited the Pittsburgh Civic Center to play Detroit. Baylor and the guys had never played in Pittsburgh, which Jim Murray of the *Times* calls the "only city in the world with a downtown of pure tinfoil." Jerry West gave Detroit a 127–126 edge on a free throw with 36 seconds to go. He had scored eight points in the final three minutes. After the Pistons' Ray "Chink" Scott sank a 10-footer with 18 seconds to play to put his team in front, Dick Barnett missed a one-hander from the side, and Baylor's attempt to convert on the rebound fell short. Young Pistons coach Dave DeBusschere snared the rebound and held the ball until the buzzer. Detroit won,

128–127. Baylor had scored 26 on 12 baskets, West 43, and Barnett 20. Reggie Harding's 29, Scott's 28, and Terry Dischinger's 26 balanced the victors.

When the NBA All-Star teams were selected for the January 13, 1965, game in St. Louis, 11 of the 16 players were Negroes. Five pro teams had black captains: the Celtics' Russell, the Royals' Wayne Embry, Philly's Hal Greer, Chamberlain with San Francisco, and Baylor. By contrast, there were no black captains in the National Football League, and in baseball, only Willie Mays had been given the responsibility.

The big news surrounding the All-Star Game concerned Chamberlain. Deep into the night following the game, owners bid and listened to offers of his services from the Warriors. Bob Short was among the interested.

On January 2, 1965, United Press International had reported the Lakers were negotiating for Chamberlain's services, although Lou Mohs said to UPI, "We haven't talked to anyone about Chamberlain for 30 hours." He also confirmed that neither Baylor nor West was on the table for any such transaction. Lakers fans salivated at the idea of facing Boston with three of the league's best players and a center who could occupy all of Bill Russell's attention. The *Los Angeles Times* reported that the Lakers offered as much as $500,000 for "The Big Dipper." Mohs told the *Times*, "In the first place, I don't know if the Warriors are interested in selling him. Certainly there's a price for everything. . . . In fact, you might say we're withdrawing from the market at this time."

Warriors owner Franklin Mieuli said the figure was an exaggeration but admitted discussions were taking place. Mieuli knew Chamberlain was unhappy. Chamberlain had spent the summer in Philadelphia, where he was diagnosed with pancreatitis. At Temple University Hospital, he lost 35 pounds and most of his muscle tone. John Taylor writes in his book *The Rivalry* that Chamberlain felt Mieuli had ignored him while he was ill. When the Warriors had won the Western Division, Wilt suggested the owner give the players diamond stickpins rather than the usual rings. When Mieuli greeted his underweight star center at the San Francisco airport with a diamond stickpin, Chamberlain scowled at the gift and asked, "What is this piece of s---?" Before the 1965–1966 season began, Mieuli offered Chamberlain to the Lakers. The 76ers and Hawks were also in discussion for his services. Mieuli believed if he traded Wilt, he could reduce operating costs enough to keep the team afloat while he built a fan base. To leverage his negotiating stance, Chamberlain entertained offers to train as a professional boxer or play football for the American Football League's Kansas City Chiefs.

Hawks owner Ben Kerner told the media he was bidding for Chamberlain (although St. Louis' Kiel Arena, which seated 9,000, was too small to attract enough fans to recoup Chamberlain's cost). The Lakers front office consulted Baylor, West, and player rep Rudy LaRusso, who thought the likely asking price, streak-shooting guard Dick Barnett, was too steep. Barnett had averaged 18 points a game in both 1963 and 1964, and was a 45 percent shooter during the latter year. Schaus told *Ebony* for its January 1964 pro basketball preview, "Dick Barnett is the best sixth man in basketball. He contributes plenty of scoring, and he is a tenacious defensive man who can irritate opponents with his tenacious close guarding."

In the end, the Warriors dealt Chamberlain to his hometown 76ers, for journeyman players Paul Neumann, Connie Dierking, Lee Shaffer, and $150,000. The Lakers held on to Dick Barnett.

* * *

On January 14, in their first game after the All-Star break, Baylor scored 38 (12 on free throws), and West scored six straight down the stretch to break a 96–96 tie, as the Lakers avenged the Pistons in Detroit, 104–100. Barnett hit 17. On the 17th, the Lakers met the Hawks on national TV. Jerry West was out with an injury. Baylor went 2-for-15 in the first half. His third-quarter scoring spurt put L.A. ahead, 67–66, halfway through the period. St. Louis responded with 12 unanswered points, eight of them by the quicksilver lefty playmaker Len Wilkens. They led, 78–67, and then 84–71 going into the fourth, before ultimately overpowering the Lakers, 118–105, led by Bob Pettit's 34 points. Baylor had finished with 26 on 10 buckets; Barnett had 20. The teams were tied at 24–20 in the standings.

On January 23, Phil Ederkin of the *Christian Science Monitor* wrote that young NBA forwards Jerry Lucas and Gus Johnson were only a "half-a-step behind Elgin and Pettit," who were "still great, but not quite as formidable as they used to be." Ederkin adds, "Baylor, in particular, has trouble maintaining a high rate of efficiency in back-to-back games."

On national TV, Boston shellacked the Lakers, 117–93, in a game played after the Sixers had snapped a 16-game winning streak by the Celts. Baylor had scored 30, but Boston led all the way, including 57–46 at intermission and 87–66 after three periods. In the third quarter, K. C. Jones assisted on five baskets and scored three others, as Boston outscored their rivals, 31–19. Sam Jones scored 27; Russell took 31 rebounds; and L.A. was outrebounded, 97–61. The victory was Boston's 24th in their last 26 games.

Schaus felt NBA referees swallowed their whistles when the Celtics body- and hand-checked his players. "It's pretty well felt throughout the league that there are two sets of rules," he remarked to John Hall of the *Los Angeles Times*. "One set is for the Celtics, the other for the rest of the teams." Sportswriter Hall cites John Havlicek for bumping and shoving, Satch Sanders for hooking his arm around Jerry West's elbow, and K. C. Jones for slapping the arms and hands of Lakers ball handlers.

The Lakers and Knicks met in a January doubleheader in front of nearly 16,000 fans at Madison Square Garden. In a nationally syndicated January 28, 1965, column by Milton Gross, reprinted that day in the *St. Petersburg* (Florida) *Independent*, Jerry West was popping antacid tablets before the game. "I guess," he said, "that all by myself I can keep the company in business that makes those tablets." L.A. beat New York, 111–99, behind 47 from West and 36 from Baylor. The Lakers had trailed, 37–27, after Knicks rookie Artie Heyman got hot. They recovered to lead, 52–47, at the break, lifted by Baylor and West. In the third, they widened the margin to 17, as Baylor scored 13 in the period. He had made 15 of his 29 shots and six of seven free throws.

On January 27, L.A. faced Cincinnati and Robertson in front of 10,294 onlookers in the Sports Arena. Sparked by a crisp fast break featuring Wiley, LaRusso, and Jim King, the Lakers led by 10 at the half. In the third quarter, Royals coach Jack McMahon posted Robertson up against King. Robertson, who nearly skipped the game because of the flu, rallied the Royals to a seven-point edge by either scoring or hitting Jerry Lucas for open jumpers. Then Schaus stuck West on him with two minutes left in the third. West outscored Robertson, 18–6, the remainder of the way. L.A. trailed by as many as five in the fourth until a three-point play by LeRoy Ellis tied the affair four minutes into the final quarter. West canned three straight jump shots. Adrian Smith and Jerry Lucas brought Cincinnati within one, with 2:46 on the clock. The Lakers won, 119–112, as Baylor and West scored 24 of the team's final 32 points. Baylor finished with 35, including eight rebounds and five assists, and West netted 42 in the outstanding show for home fans. Robertson had tallied 34 but needed 31 shots to make 12. Schaus felt it was their best win in quite some time.

"I said it in October and I'll say it again," says Schaus in the *Times*, "46 victories will win the West. And if nothing happens to Baylor or Jerry West, I have to like our chances." He adds, "There are still some things about Hazzard's defense I don't like, but I can go with him in clutch situations now and not worry too much." In terms of winning the division, Schaus states, "We have four games left with St. Louis—three here—and we'll have to get no worse than a split."

On February 2, in a game against the Detroit Pistons in Cleveland, Baylor fell on his left knee. The basketball floor there covered a layer of cement, and the shock damaged his knee. A few days later, he banged the same knee in a collision with an opposing player. "I'll be glad when the season's over," Baylor admitted to the *Los Angeles Times*.

On February 21, 1965, the Lakers avenged a recent loss to Boston, with a 129–114 drubbing in front of 14,814 in the Sports Arena. Celtics coach Red Auerbach, annoyed by the noisy regular-season throng, asks in the *Boston Globe*, "What's all the excitement about? They are fine fans here, but why don't they take a good look at the standings?" Playing with a dilated eye, West scored 47, and he and Baylor both hit clutch shots to secure the team's sixth straight win since a February 12, 1965, drubbing of the Warriors at home. Baylor was "brilliant clearing the boards, starting fast breaks, and making fine passes," according to Mal Florence in the *Los Angeles Times*. L.A. had led, 11–1, before Tom Heinsohn sank some difficult shots to close the gap. Then Baylor made his first bucket, and West sank a jumper. The Lakers led, 18–11, and by nine at the end of the first quarter. Their halftime lead was 15. Boston got to within six in the third, when Baylor broke their momentum with a three-point play. West sat out the start of the fourth, so Baylor scored seven in one stretch, as they widened their advantage from nine to 12 points. West returned, and his and Baylor's hoops made it 115–98, with 5:21 to play. It may not have been a big deal to Auerbach, but symbolically the strong performances by West and Baylor (29 points and 15 rebounds) meant a lot to a Lakers club that had endured injuries, shooting slumps, and media doubts.

"We may dilate West's eye again on Tuesday," jokes Schaus in the *Times*, as the two teams would meet again on Wednesday.

In mid-February, with just 14 games to play, San Francisco—in next-to-last place that same time the previous season—was in first place, ahead of the St. Louis Hawks and the defending Western Division champs, the Lakers. It helped teams like the Warriors that Elgin Baylor and Jerry West had been injured.

On March 11, the Lakers hosted the Bullets in Long Beach, the site of Bob Short's arena trump card. There were but five regular-season games remaining, and L.A. had already clinched the third playoff slot in the Western Division. They had recently beaten the young Baltimore club, coached by former Laker Slick Leonard, 122–112, at Sports Arena. With a front line that already featured Walt Bellamy and young former Purdue All-American and 1963 NBA Rookie of the Year Terry Dischinger, Leonard felt he was a draft pick away from coaching a contender. The Lakers beat Baltimore in overtime, 121–116, including Baylor's 25 points. The Bullets' forwards, Gus Johnson and "Jumpin" Johnny Green, only scored 17 between them.

In February 1965, *Ebony* magazine had celebrated Baylor's return with a profile entitled "Elgin Baylor Comes Back." He finished the season averaging 27 points and almost 13 rebounds in 74 games—improving on averages of 25.4 points and 12 boards from 1964. Happy, he asked his teammates, "Wasn't I a beast, baby?" In his career, Baylor had scored 49 points or more in 42 NBA games.

Los Angeles closed the regular season at 49–31, winning the West by four games. Ticket sales were up 13 percent, and the team drew 7,000 fans a game. Rumor had it that Bob Short had turned down an offer of $2 million for the club at that point, although other rumors about a change in ownership would prove true in the coming months.

In the opening game on April 3 against Baltimore during the 1965 playoffs, Baylor went up for a twisting shot and lost his balance. When he landed on the floor, Lakers players and sideline spectators heard a loud, frightening crack of bone. To the Bullets on the opposing bench, it sounded like a "pop." Baylor got up and tried to take a step, but pain shot through his leg when he attempted to put weight on his left foot. In the stands, 16,000 Lakers fans rose in hushed astonishment, many covering their mouths. Trainer Frank O'Neill helped Baylor, but surprisingly, in a move that was encouraging to most, he walked to the lockers on his own. Onlookers read his lips, as he swore to himself.

"Something pulled," he later told Frank Deford for *Sports Illustrated*'s cover feature, "A Tiger Who Can Beat Anything," October 24, 1966. "I didn't know what it was. I forgot about the ball as soon as I felt it. But I could run. I went up and down the court a few times [on the sidelines], but it hurt so much and I didn't know what it was, so I decided I better get out." It was a wonder Baylor could test the knee at all in the game after the injury. His kneecap had shattered in half. The top third of the left patella had broken completely away from the rest of the kneecap.

Baylor was transported to a hospital. As he writhed in pain, the receptionist asked his name and occupation, and handed him a lengthy questionnaire. Dr. Robert Kerlan showed up just in time and carted his patient into X-ray. After the X-rays, Kerlan gave Baylor a sedative and let him rest.

Dr. Kerlan operated on Baylor the next day. He cut the left knee open, extracted the shattered portion of the patella, and smoothed the rest of the kneecap. Kerlan then drilled miniscule holes in it and attached the torn tendons. He also removed small granules of calcium. An hour and a half later, Baylor was fitted into a hip-to-ankle cast and wheeled to a room.

While he told Baylor he hoped he would be fit to play basketball again someday, the doctor thought he would be really lucky to be able to play just a couple more years, even in a supporting role. Even after rehabilitation, Kerlan expected Baylor to walk with a limp. "My first thought was that if he would simply be able to move around normally again, we'd have accomplished a great deal," he says in Pepe's *Greatest Stars of the NBA*.

The day after the surgery, Kerlan gave Baylor a jagged piece of calcium the size of a quarter that had been floating about in his leg. The calcium had been the cause of the intermittent pain. Lakers GM Lou Mohs spoke to five other physicians who had operated on broken kneecaps. "They say the odds are one-in-a-hundred, that Elg ever will be his old self again," he says in the *Los Angeles Times*. Trainer O'Neill felt Baylor faced as daunting a mental road as physical.

In the Western Division playoffs, the Lakers escaped a hungry Baltimore team by a decisive four games to two. After the deciding game, which L.A. took, 117–115, at Baltimore, Schaus declared to the *Times* of his Baylor-less group, "This club won it with heart."

Bob Short said to the *Times*, "Even when we lost Baylor, I felt we could do it." In reality, the "we" was mostly "W-E-S-T," as West scored 46.3 points a game in the series, which is still a NBA record. He scored 42 in the deciding game, while Barnett shot 13-for-22.

The 1965 NBA Finals were anticlimactic. The Russell–Chamberlain rivalry's latest chapter had been settled by John Havlicek's deflection of an inbound pass from Hal Greer during the deciding game of the Eastern Division finals—a moment that became an audio legend because of Celtics announcer Johnny Most's frantic radio call: "Havlicek stole the ball. It's all over! Johnny Havlicek stole the ball!" With Baylor sidelined for the Finals, the Lakers offered limited opportunity for a classic confrontation against Boston. Bill Russell missed the challenge of his respected rival—the man he felt was the best player in the game. Baylor made the trip with his teammates, his left leg covered in a cast as he got around on crutches.

Boston stormed to a 142–110 game-one victory, setting a record for points scored by a team in a final. Boston had left 64–49 at intermission, when Russell already had 19 rebounds. Dick Barnett led Lakers scorers with 13 at the break. Television viewers were treated to ABC colorman Bob Cousy interviewing Chamberlain about Havlicek's timely steal and Wilt's latest threat of retirement. Jim Murray of the *Los Angeles Times* writes that the game was "as one sided as a firing squad." Jerry West, who had averaged 46 points in the series against the Bullets, tallied 45 in game two, but a balanced Boston attack prevailed, 129–123. Five Celtics scored 20 points or more, while the Lakers lacked a second fiddle for West's courageous effort. The series then moved to Los Angeles, where Doris Day, Dean Martin, and tennis star Jack Kramer attracted attention in the stands. Gene Wiley played the best ball of his career, and West's 43 triggered a 126–105 victory for L.A. Lakers fans mocked Red Auerbach by throwing cigars in his direction.

The results in Boston and L.A. were so different, some fans accused the NBA of staging dramatic outcomes, as in pro wrestling. But Lou Mohs defended his club in the *Times*, declaring, "You'd better not say that to Rudy LaRusso or any of the guys on our team. Whoever does will get a bust right in the mouth." He did acknowledge the psychological home-court advantage provided by NBA crowds. For his part, Short created a local controversy by pulling popular Chick Hearn off the radio and TV broadcast to work a closed-circuit theater telecast of the game into such markets as Minneapolis and Boston. The team's TV sponsor, Union Oil, fumed at Short's move.

The fourth game, played in L.A., demonstrated both the Lakers' inability to consistently score without Baylor and the NBA's continuing struggle for major-league status. L.A. lost, 112–99, and in the closing minutes of the game, ABC cut away to a previously scheduled program.

On April 25, Boston ran away with game five, 129–96, again holding their Baylor-less opponents to less than 100 points. Jerry West had averaged a league-record 40.6 points throughout the playoffs, but Boston had a more balanced team. "There was a time when Minneapolis dominated the game just as Boston does now," claims Lou Mohs in the *Los Angeles Times*. "The entire league has improved, but the Celtics seem further out of reach than ever. No team in the past could rate with a team that has Russell." Fred Schaus agreed, telling the *Times*, "It's the quickest and best five-man defensive club I've ever seen."

* * *

In the upcoming NBA Draft, Lakers brass had their eye on Walt Hazzard's former UCLA backcourt mate Gail Goodrich, a Hollywood native. "We've been looking at Goodrich of course, and feel he can play in the NBA," relates Short in the *Times*. "But you hesitate to decide too quickly on a man who only goes 6'1"." L.A. could exercise their territorial draft pick to take Goodrich and still draft "big" later.

The Lakers selected local hero Goodrich, and although the ball club had no shortage of talented guards, Short had to defend the choice to the *Times*. "We kept trying to find the big center, and there just aren't any more Bill Russell's. We wasted a lot of time." From now on, he was sticking to the Hazzards and Goodriches.

Tragedy struck the Lakers family on May 6, 1965. While trying to remove a tree from his neighbor's yard, a limb struck retired center Jim Krebs in the head as the tree fell, killing the popular center. "Of all the lousy breaks for all of us," Jim Murray writes in the *Times*. Krebs, who had joined the team a year before Baylor, was a humorous, popular teammate and a fixture in the Lakers family, even after his retirement.

After the season ended for the Lakers, Baylor was bedridden for one week and on crutches for much longer. "[M]y first thought was that my career might be ended," he admitted the *Los Angeles Times*. "After all these years, that was a hard thing to face."

Baylor spent the next six months in his hip-to-ankle cast and still had to get around on crutches. When Dr. Kerlan removed the cast, the knee was stiff and painful. Kerlan first limited Baylor to walking; he progressed to jogging and riding a bike. Next, he was told to run stadium stairs. From there, Kerlan had Baylor do leg lifts with weights attached to his ankles. Yet, the stiffness and soreness remained.

Baylor wanted to return to the game, but that seemed impossible based on the way his knee felt. The more he worked out, the more pain he suffered. His game was predicated on explosion, body control, and sudden changes of direction. How could he play in this condition? He talked with Ruby about other career options. Outside of basketball—but based on the status he achieved in it—he was working as a Los Angeles public relations representative for Pepsi-Cola. Ruby later told *Ebony* magazine, "He seldom let on how much he was suffering or how much he was concerned." She continued, "That's his way. We'd talk about what he might do outside of basketball, but he insisted that was just in case. I tried to encourage him, but I saw he was discouraged. Still, he kept on trying. That's his way too."

Because of concern for his injury, Elgin lost sleep, and Ruby knew how troubled his mind was. After one game, the *Los Angeles Times* reported he muttered in the locker room, "I wonder how much they're paying bricklayers these days." Still, he adhered to Kerlan's program of physical therapy. In a July 22 news brief headlined "Elgin Baylor Romps Like a Rookie," the *Los Angeles Sentinel* reported that Baylor was riding a bike and running to rehabilitate his knee.

When the team opened preseason camp in September, Baylor was far from ready to play. Schaus let him scrimmage for short spurts but noticed how stiff-legged his movements were. "It was pathetic watching him punish himself," relates Schaus in the *Times*. "I don't suppose any of us will ever really know how bad it was for him, but I was close enough to him to know it was very, very bad."

Not only was Baylor sore, but he also favored the bad leg. Later in camp, he convinced Schaus to let him play in a game. Kerlan agreed, and Baylor received an extra dosage of Novocain before the exhibition contest. While his shooting accuracy had not suffered, his hobbling made him a liability on defense. His confidence was also shot. He tried to play more, with the doc wrapping the knee in ice after games.

September 1965 brought a new era in Lakers history. Early that month, Chick Hearn's status as the voice of the Lakers was uncertain, as Bob Short and TV sponsor Union Oil continued to bicker over the playoff broadcast from which Short had pulled Hearn during the NBA Finals.

L.A. Dodgers owner Walter O'Malley advised Short that he could parlay the sale of the Lakers into a Major League Baseball ownership. But, on the 15th, UPI reported that Short denied having sold the team for $3 million. "The ballplayers aren't my wife and kids so I suppose it's possible I might sell the club," he told UPI in his customary double-talk. The next day, Short's denial was proven false, as the *Los Angeles Times* reported a $5 million ownership change.

Jack Kent Cooke bought the Lakers from Bob Short for $5.175 million, by far the largest purchase price for any NBA team. The other NBA owners had the right to approve or disapprove the sale, but the Lakers franchise was worth far more than other teams in the league, including the champion Celtics. The Lakers averaged 9,000 fans per game, despite being the only NBA club with a top ticket price of $7.50 (at a time when a gallon of gasoline cost motorists 33¢ and a pack of cigarettes about the same). "I worked long and hard to swing this deal," says Cooke in the *Los Angeles Times*. His first bid of $4.5 million had been turned down. "It's a high price, but I think the Lakers are worth it."

The 52-year-old Cooke, born in Hamilton, Ontario, in 1912, had always been an enterprising type. As a teenager, he sold encyclopedias door to door, later became a runner on the floor of the Toronto Stock Exchange, and was running radio station CJCS in Stratford, Ontario, by age 22. He bought his first station in 1945 and was well on his way to a radio and magazine empire. Cooke had owned the Toronto franchise in the 1959 Continental Baseball League that never got off the ground, and in 1961, he purchased a 25-percent share of the Washington Redskins. After moving to the swank Bel Air district of Los Angeles in 1962, he founded the American Cablevision Company within the next two years.

While he still owned a quarter share of the NFL Redskins, Cooke was quoted in the *Times* as calling pro basketball the "most exciting game there is." And in Elgin Baylor, he believed he employed the game's most exciting player. "Why would anybody bother to go to the Royal Ballet when they can see him?" the new owner asked the *Times* in his patrician accent that September. "He's poetry in motion. . . . I mean he's Shakespeare in motion." Cooke called Baylor a miracle.

He also expressed votes of confidence in both Lou Mohs and Fred Schaus. Of Short, Cooke states in the *Times*, "He doesn't believe in logic. That's why I had to pay $5,175,000 for the Lakers when experts valued them at a little under $4,000,000."

Prior to the 1965–1966 NBA season, Red Auerbach declared in *Sports Illustrated*'s pro basketball preview issue, "I'm announcing it now so no one can ever say I quit while I was ahead. I'm telling everyone right now—Los Angeles, Philadelphia, everyone—that this will be my last season. You've got one more shot at Auerbach!" That summer, Auerbach, Walter Brown's widow Marjorie, and Lou Pieri sold their shares in the team to the Ruppert Knickerbocker Brewery, and Auerbach planned to stay with his Celtics for one more year. Soon afterward, a holding company paid $3 million for the team, $2 million less than Jack Kent Cooke's purchase of the runner-up Lakers.

Baylor played in the Lakers' October 1965 season opener. He began to favor the left knee, which made the right one—still full of calcium—worse. In a November game, he made a sudden, off-balance move that strained the ligaments in his right knee. Schaus placed him on injured reserve, and by late November, Dr. Kerlan had to put a new hip-to-ankle cast on Baylor's right leg. He missed a month of the season, returned to the team out of shape, and had lost even more athletic confidence. Fred Schaus played Baylor against San Francisco, whose rookie forward, Rick Barry, swished by his idol for easy buckets. Seven minutes into the game, Schaus yanked him.

Baylor realized he either had to retire or patiently approach rehab. He reasoned that he'd had only five months of therapy before training camp of 1965. Little by little, he tested his legs during the season. He never tried to go all out, fearing permanent damage. Dr. Kerlan called Baylor into his office. "It was about a month before the season ended," the doctor said to *Sports Illustrated*'s Frank Deford for the profile "A Tiger Who Can Beat Anything." "I sat him down and told him it was now—he had to find out right now. I told him that he either had to go out and test it and find out, or otherwise he might as well come over and rest with me." Convinced, Baylor was up to the challenge. In a late 1966 game, he played full speed and jumped with confidence, buoyed by Kerlan's encouragement to go for it. When he landed, twisted, and turned on each testing play, the knee held up. Although he knew he was physically not the same man who had scored 71 points in a game, he had turned a psychological corner. Coaches, teammates, opponents, and fans noticed the change.

While in 1965–1966 Baylor was not the dynamic scoring force he had been, there were flashes of previous brilliance: a 28-point game, as well as a 46-point, 17-rebound effort against New York.

Dr. Kerlan proved important to Baylor's mindset. "I'd never broken anything before," Baylor told Deford,

> so at first I just didn't know what to think, whether to be scared or what. Dr. Kerlan kept assuring me, but as soon as I'd get some confidence something would go wrong again. Finally, I just accepted the fact that I would never play again. I just worried about being a normal person—could I fish or play golf, just move around ever again? I thought that way. And then, just about then, it all got better.

Sensing a key to Baylor's recovery, Kerlan helped restore Baylor's confidence to return to the game.

Not only were Baylor's legs stronger, but he also began to rely more on deception, change of pace, and strength to beat defenders. He may have lost the former quickness, but not the smarts. "Listen," he told the *Los Angeles Times*, "I am playing better basketball than I ever have been playing. You have to watch action at both ends of the court. You have to look for statistics that no sportswriter ever looks for."

Baylor scored 29 and grabbed 21 rebounds in a February victory over Robertson's Cincinnati team, a ball club with burly forward Happy Hairston, silky leaper Tom Hawkins, and heavyweight big men Wayne Embry and Jerry Lucas. The *Times'* Jim Murray reports, "The old pro with the aching legs wound up the big man."

On February 13, 1966, the Lakers beat Boston on "Red Auerbach Day." Characteristically, the cigar-chomping Celtics coach earned a technical foul. According to Lew Freedman's book *Dynasty: The Rise of the Boston Celtics*, during the ceremonies, retired Bob Cousy joked that he "sweated out the whole first half" worrying what they would all do if Auerbach were ejected from the game.

On February 23, against Cincinnati, Baylor hit 35, including 14 in the final period, for a 140–133 win. Brad Pye of the *Los Angeles Sentinel* notes Baylor "was the Elg of old. He made shots only Baylor can make." The sportswriter urged the Lakers to sign Baylor for five more years.

Baylor averaged only 16.6 points per game for the 1965–1966 season. He played 1,975 minutes in 65 games. He was stronger toward the end of the campaign, scoring 25 a game, with 14 rebounds in the last 20 games. L.A. finished 45–35, seven games ahead of an improving Baltimore club.

"It was the furthest thought from my mind that he would ever be outstanding again," Kerlan told the *Times* of Baylor, looking back. "I wasn't optimistic, frankly. . . . It was an amazing recovery, certainly, but only if you consider it simply overcoming an injury. The man is often the most important thing, and in view of the sort of man Elgin is, then, maybe, we should have even expected it."

By that time, Elgin and Ruby had moved into a beautiful new Beverly Hills home, and Baylor would tool into the city proper in his Jaguar. Alan was six, and daughter Alison was two. They owned two large German Shepherds, Brutus and Caesar. Through a telescope from his second-story front window, Baylor could see Catalina Island 23 miles away. Both his personal and professional future seemed bright.

By playoffs time, Baylor was even stronger. *Sports Illustrated*'s report of the postseason notes that Red Auerbach listened to the Western Division games by radio and couldn't believe his ears. "Baylor twisting . . . Baylor jumping . . . Baylor drives," the announcer repeated. It seemed just yesterday that Auerbach saw Baylor wearing a cast from his hip to his ankles.

The Lakers advanced to the NBA Finals against their annual rival, the Celtics. Boston's average player was 30 years old. Jim Murray writes in his *Times* column, "The Celtics are the aristocrats of basketball—arrogant perfectionists who play with almost insulting contempt . . . the score is psychologically 20–0 before the tip-off."

In the first game of the 1966 NBA Finals, Baylor demonstrated the progress of his recovery by scoring 36 points against Boston. The Lakers overcame an 18-point first-quarter deficit, and Jerry West contributed 41 in the team's 133–129 overtime victory. After the loss, Auerbach complained to the media about the officiating, including a controversial goaltending call. He then shocked the reporters with a bombshell: He announced that Bill Russell would succeed him as coach, making Russell the first Negro coach of a major sports team. During the season, Auerbach had offered his job to Cousy, who liked coaching at Boston College, as well as Frank Ramsey and Tommy Heinsohn, who preferred business careers. Russell accepted the appointment only after careful consideration. The *Los Angeles Times*' Jim Murray writes that Russell would now become a "functioning member of the Establishment" who would have to throw away his Thelonious Monk records. Although Murray's comment was a joke, Auerbach's expert timing of the announcement was altogether serious.

The Celtics responded to the historic hiring with a 129–109 rout in the second game and then beat L.A. in the Sports Arena, 120–106, in the third match. Boston continued to ride the wave of the Russell appointment with a 122–117 win in game four, putting the Lakers at a 3–1 deficit. Their backs against the wall, the wounded Angelenos traveled to Boston. Game five was played on April 24. ABC color analyst Bob Cousy praised the officiating, saying, "This entire series has been handled extremely well." The Lakers led by 17 at one point, only to relinquish an eight-point advantage to Boston. Rudy LaRusso one-hand pushed in the closing free throws as L.A. escaped, 121–117.

On Tuesday, April 26, the series returned to L.A. for the sixth game. and the Lakers faced elimination. 15,069 packed the Sports Arena. The home team led 32–29 after one quarter, and were up 68–58 at intermission. Boston woke up in the third quarter, outscoring the Lakers 32-21 to take a 90–89 lead. Riding a strong fourth quarter, and a total of 25 points, 14 rebounds, and six assists from Baylor, L.A. won 123–115.

In game seven, Fred Schaus went to a three-guard lineup to take advantage of the quickness of such players as West and Goodrich. Forward Rudy LaRusso sat out. Boston surged to a 19-point third-quarter lead before a home crowd. Baylor had missed eight of nine shots in the first half, while West shot 2-for-9. "K. C. Jones used to tackle West rather than let him get off a jump shot," Schaus recalled to NBA.com. The Celtics led by 10 with a minute to play, when Massachusetts governor John Volpe lit Auerbach's signature victory cigar. Boston was ahead by six with 16 seconds left. Boston supporters crowded the boundaries of the court, yelling for Lakers blood. While the game continued, some fans hung on the basket supports; others actually stormed the court before the game ended. Orange juice containers littered the parquet floor, and a Celtics player lost his footing on some of the citrus, allowing Jerry West to slip free for a layup. West then stole the ball from Russell and scored again. Fans were reminded of Frank Selvy's two late game-changing buckets in the 1962 deciding game. But Selvy was not nicknamed "Mr. Clutch," like West. Boston committed an offensive foul, and L.A. scored on their next possession. The lead was cut to two, but K. C. Jones dribbled out the clock, much as Cousy had done four years earlier. Boston pulled out another Finals victory, with a score of 95–93, and another NBA championship.

Baylor improved on his late-season averages in the playoffs, averaging 27 points, with 14 rebounds, in 14 games. He had overcome his status as a sidelined player, although his injury still made national news. Proving that Elgin Baylor transcended the boundaries of basketball in 1960s America, his shattered knee was included in the pages of *Popular Science* magazine in May 1966 in a feature sportswriter Milton Gross called "Baseball's Fragile Superstars." While the piece focuses on the injuries and surgeries of Mickey Mantle, Whitey Ford, and Sandy Koufax (also a Kerlan patient), it offers another example of a wounded warrior: "Elgin Baylor, one of the scoring leaders of the National Basketball Association, lost his effectiveness for the Los Angeles Lakers when stricken with knee trouble. A portion of his kneecap had to be cut away before he could play again." In the off-season, Dr. Kerlan and colleague Frank Jobe reattached the tendons of Baylor's thigh muscles to what remained of his patella, through tiny, carefully drilled holes.

Baylor and the Lakers opened the season on October 15 against the Bullets in Baltimore, and Baylor hit 36 points on 10-for-15 shooting in a 126–115 victory. On October 18, the Lakers visited the Knicks for New York's home opener at the old Madison Square Garden. Young Knicks center Willis Reed had been exchanging elbows all night with Rudy LaRusso. Sitting in a cheap upper-deck seat, St. John's University guard Johnny Warren had never seen such bruising play underneath the backboards. Reed told referees Richie Powers and Mendy Rudolph that LaRusso was playing dirty. The veteran refs admonished Reed to shut up and play ball. Baylor was at the free-throw line nearest the Lakers' bench, shooting foul shots in the third quarter. Reed shot LaRusso an elbow to the head as they jostled for position alongside the key. As they ran upcourt after the foul shots, Reed tripped LaRusso, who swung a right cross at a ducking Reed. Darrall Imhoff grabbed Reed from behind, and Reed lost his cool, in part because the refs did nothing to intervene. He punched Imhoff, then chased LaRusso to the bench. Rookie John Block emerged from the Lakers bench swinging, but the southpaw Reed decked him with a left hook, and when Imhoff attempted to hold him, he turned and again slugged Imhoff, who collapsed. In what has become a famous sequence, the 6'9", 235-pound Reed tagged five successive Lakers from the bench, domino style. He belted LaRusso twice more and Imhoff once. Bleeding from above the left eye, the big center from Cal dived under the bench, where Block was cowering with a broken nose.

When Reed asked his teammates why they had not intervened, Dick Barnett—now a Knick—told Reed it was because he was winning the brawl by himself.

The Lakers lost that game to New York, 122–119, but Baylor looked strong, scoring 31 to lead the team.

The expansion Bulls beat the Lakers, 134–124, in Chicago, led by 34 points from little Guy Rodgers, whom Baylor upstaged with 45 points on 17 baskets and 11-for-12 free-throw shooting. Baylor hadn't scored like this in three years. On October 21, Chicago beat them again, 108–101, as the new franchise improved its record to 4–1, and L.A. dropped to 1–3, but Baylor contributed 29 to lead his club.

On October 24, 1966, the NBA preview issue of *Sports Illustrated*, featuring the article "A Tiger Who Could Beat Anything" by Frank Deford, hit newsstands, with Elgin Baylor posing on its cover. Deford describes the regard in which Baylor was held throughout the league, his fierce pride, his jovial manner, and his sense of racial justice. The article also covers his recovery from knee injury and surgery. In addition, Baylor's picture graces the cover of the *Sporting News' 1966–1967 NBA Media Guide*. In an action photo, Baylor twists for a reverse layup in his prototypical style. At the time, he was the leading playoffs scorer in league history.

L.A. fell again, this time to the Knicks, 133–122, on October 26, although Elgin's 31 points again led them in scoring. On October 28, 1966, in a game with New York with two minutes left in the first half, Baylor dove for a loose ball, and the Knicks' Dick Van Arsdale landed on his left knee. Baylor rolled away, grimacing in pain, as the arena grew quiet. Another knee injury. More rehab and physical therapy. What would become of his career?

Baylor aggravated his knee injury again in a November game against the Warriors at the Sports Arena. Jerry West also had nagging injuries, and he and Baylor didn't play in a game together until the 10th, against Detroit. The Lakers were mired in last place when Baylor came back on Saturday the 19th, in a return match with San Francisco. He had been averaging almost 32 points a game before the injury.

* * *

In January 1967, the National Basketball Players Association delivered a set of grievances to their attorney, Larry Fleisher. The player representatives met at Leone's restaurant in New York City, making their collective case for some of the same issues they had contested during the 1964 All-Star Game boycott: a better pension, an All-Star break, elimination of back-to-back Saturday night–Sunday afternoon games, and roomier airplane seating sections. At that time, the players still flew coach when traveling to away games. Former *Sports Illustrated* writer Frank Deford recalled to *Sports Illustrated* on April 28, 2012, "In 1966, when I was doing a cover story on the Celtics' John Havlicek, we were on a coast-to-coast flight, and I was in first class, according to Time, Inc. policy. He came up to see me, and then I went back to interview him in steerage, where the NBA champions were sitting."

Although they worked together on their case, white players and black players did not always possess the same attitude toward management. As a rule, Negro players were skeptical of the owners' lofty promises, dodges, and delays. They remembered Commissioner Walter Kennedy's stall tactics that led to the 1964 All-Star Game boycott, and some even recalled his portly predecessor, Maurice Podoloff. Negroes were less likely to have father–son relationships with white owners, general managers, and coaches. Baylor had expressed his recognition of racial prejudice in the NBA to *SPORT* magazine 1963: "If a white and a Negro have equal ability—and play up to it—they keep the white."

White players tended to believe things would improve as long as the NBPA maintained a unified front. But they, rather than their black counterparts, also tended to be on the receiving end of beneficial relationships with NBA leaders. White team members often played poker with the coaches (and even, in the case of the Hawks, with their owner, Ben Kerner), and there was a coaching carousel of former players like Buddy Jeannette, Paul Seymour, and Alex Hannum, who were always prime candidates for new vacancies. Auerbach offered the Celtics coaching job to a series of former white players—Bob Cousy, Bill Sharman, Jim Loscutoff, Tommy Heinsohn, and Bob Brannum—before hiring Bill Russell during the 1966 Finals in Los Angeles.

During the NBPA's 1967 negotiations, the players threatened to boycott the playoffs, but a collective bargaining agreement was eventually reached. The players would be paid a pension after retirement; they had asked for $600 a month for 10-year veterans, almost half of the Major League Baseball retirement pay. The NBA owners argued that basketball players didn't need the same size pension as baseballers, because they had their college educations to fall back on. The stipend also did not apply to the pre–1955 players upon whose contributions the NBA was founded.

The 1967 NBA All-Star Game returned to the West Coast, in San Francisco's Cow Palace. Baylor started for the West team. In one sequence, he wrestled a rebound away from the East's John Havlicek, faked Havlicek out with a nifty up-and-under move, and shoveled a pass to Wilt Chamberlain, who scored on a bank shot.

In an early February game against the Knicks—played in front of less than 2,700 fans due to a blizzard in New York City—Cazzie Russell, Dick Barnett, and Walt Bellamy triggered a third-period rally that gave New York a 91–84 lead going into the final stanza. A Bellamy bucket and a pair of free throws stretched the advantage to 105–94 midway through the fourth. Baylor and West then outscored the Knicks, 10–2, on a run that made it 107–104 Knicks with 4:20 on the clock. Imhoff made a basket and a foul shot to put L.A. up, 114–113. Cazzie Russell responded with a hoop, but West's last basket gave his team the lead for good with 1:40 to play. Two free throws and a jumper by Baylor, along with a couple of free throws from Goodrich, sealed the deal. L.A. won, 122–117, supported by 34 from Baylor (14 in the fourth quarter) and 27 from West (12 in the fourth). Barnett led the losers with 27.

The 1966–1967 Lakers were a travesty. The team finished 36–45, in third place—three behind second-place St. Louis and eight back of the division champion, the San Francisco Warriors. The real winners were in the East: Philadelphia finished with a league record of 68–13, led by Chamberlain, who sportswriters throughout the United States were calling the "new Wilt Chamberlain." An aging Boston club was 60–21. Baylor was a bright spot for the Lakers, and *SPORT* magazine ran a feature about his recovery called "The Elgin Baylor Miracle." Despite starting the season with an injury, he averaged 28.4 points in 70 games, snared 898 rebounds, and dished 215 assists. His best scoring nights were 46 against tough, young St. Louis and 45 against Chicago.

Rick Barry, in his second season with San Francisco, led the NBA in scoring in 1966–1967, with 35.6 points per game. A *Life* magazine profile compares Barry with Baylor: "A rebounder, a ball hawk, a fine passer, Barry, most of all, is a superb shotmaker, with moves recalling Elgin Baylor at his best." Warriors coach Bill Sharman said, "He and Elgin Baylor are the best passing forwards in the game."

The first round of the Western Division playoffs matched Baylor against Barry, and the best veteran forward would be tested against the young hotshot. Injuries plagued the Lakers, as big man Jim "Bad News" Barnes had to miss the series. Jerry West broke his hand in the first minutes of game one. This put additional pressure on the rejuvenated 32-year-old Baylor, but it also gave him an opportunity to shine. Bill Libby writes in *SPORT*'s miracle comeback profile, "For these beautiful moments it was 1961 and all the other good years all over again for Baylor. He dribbled, shot, rebounded, passed off, and turned and twisted like the Baylor of old." In the locker room, Baylor declared to the *Los Angeles Times*, "It's good to be back."

Yet, the young Warriors swept the Lakers, three games to none.

Baylor's comeback after such a series of injuries proved his mettle as a powerhouse player—but those injuries couldn't help but weaken his overall legacy. Had Baylor remained as healthy as Oscar Robertson or Bill Russell throughout his career, he would have compiled incredible career statistics. On two sound knees, he could have averaged 30 points a game rather than his 27.4 lifetime mark (which is still the third best of all time, trailing only Jordan and Chamberlain among past players). The 1965–1966 season, during which he averaged only 16.6, pulled his numbers down considerably. The setbacks also impacted his image. Unlike such oft-injured white athletes as Mickey Mantle, Joe Namath, and Jerry West, Baylor was not lionized by sportswriters as a courageous, tragic hero. He never received sufficient credit for more than salvaging a career as a scoring threat on two badly damaged legs. Meanwhile, teammate Jerry West was portrayed as a gutsy warrior because of the nine broken noses he obtained in collisions for baskets and loose balls. West became the personification of the walking basketball wounded, even though Baylor was four years older and played hurt. On January 21, 1965, Baylor had told Jim Murray of the *Times*, "I will give Jerry my nose any day for his knees. I need two good knees. My nose can take care of itself."

While another of Dr. Kerlan's patients, Sandy Koufax, retired from baseball in 1966, at age 30, due to arthritis in his pitching elbow, Baylor soldiered on into the early 1970s. "After the operation, all that long time I lay in bed," recalls Baylor in Libby's *SPORT* article on his recovery of his torn kneecap, "I just figured I'd do what I had to do to get better, and I'd wind up playing again as good as ever."

Few fans knew Baylor also had a natural back condition that made playing basketball painful. Lakers trainer Frank O'Neill referred to it as a pseudo-vertebra, which was "not as strong as a true vertebra." When aggravated by anything, from bad hotel beds on the road to bumpy train rides and basketball collisions, the condition caused spasms to shoot down Baylor's back and hamstring. "That back could go at any time," an unnamed team authority told the *Los Angeles Times*.

"[H]e'll tolerate a great deal before he lets you know he's hurting," O'Neill says admiringly of Baylor in Libby's *SPORT* feature. Baylor, never one to miss a debate or a barb, would even rise up on his elbows while the trainer worked on his back on the training table. On top of that, Baylor told *SPORT* that he also experienced a bronchial condition during his playing days, saying it "seems to get worse, not better with age." One Lakers official said if Baylor was not a famous athlete, he would have been physically disqualified to serve National Guard duty.

Baylor's stoicism in the face of physical and mental challenges didn't always work in his favor. While he remained the proud Roman warrior in the Forum, his teammate, Jerry West, played his tragedy like a Greek. As a result, perhaps because his emotions were more apparent than Baylor's, sportswriters always described West as "competitive." "When he commits a glaring mistake," writes Myron Cope in the *Saturday Evening Post* for a 1960 profile called "The Unpredictable All-American," "he almost invariably acts out a little ritual: He punches the palm of his left hand and casts a sheepish glance at Schaus. . . . One can see the words 'My fault' form on his lips." Thus, it was the brooding West who was portrayed as the battler, more pained by the annual bridesmaid role to Boston than any other Laker. Yet, Baylor was every bit the competitor Jerry West and Bill Russell were. This was demonstrated when Baylor said to Milton Gross in the 1961 *SPORT* feature on the NBA's scoring explosion, "If I score a hundred, and we lose, what good is it? This is a team sport—not boxing."

On June 27, 1967, Elgin and Ruby Baylor were guests of President and Ladybird Johnson at a White House state dinner honoring King Bhumibol Adulyadej and Queen Sirikit of Thailand. Three days before the White House event, Baylor was one of 10 "athlete immortals" of the 20th century honored at the first annual City of Hope Sportsmen's Club banquet at the Beverly Hills Hilton.

Despite the public recognition he was enjoying off the court, Baylor was not happy with the terms of his NBA contract. He had a year left on a two-year deal that paid a reported $37,500 annually. The *Los Angeles Times* said he never felt he was paid "anything close to what the other top names in the game were and are making," despite the Lakers being the NBA's best box-office draw. Baylor was also upset because when the league approved a Seattle franchise for the 1967–1968 campaign, the Lakers led him to understand that he would be free to go there as a player-coach but then changed their minds. Hot Rod Hundley says in his memoir, *Hot Rod Hundley: You Gotta Love It Baby*, "When Seattle got an expansion team in 1967, Gene Klein, who owned the San Diego Chargers football team, talked to me about coaching the SuperSonics. He offered me a one-year contract for $17,000, but I wanted a guaranteed three-year deal if I was going to coach an expansion team." Hundley instead took a $15,000 gig as Chick Hearn's partner on Lakers broadcasts.

Baylor also entertained the idea of jumping to a new rival league, the American Basketball Association, which would begin play in the 1967–1968 season. The ABA's commissioner was Minneapolis Lakers legend George Mikan, and the league was placing charter franchises in both Anaheim and Oakland—cities that had recently welcomed Major League Baseball. The upstart circuit courted such NBA stars as Oscar Robertson, Wilt Chamberlain, Dave Bing, and the 1967 scoring king who had idolized Elgin Baylor, Rick Barry. There was a charter franchise in Baylor's former showcase—Minneapolis—and Hawks rookie Lou Hudson, who played his college ball there, flirted with the idea of jumping leagues. The ABA was looking into placing a team in Los Angeles Sports Arena, once the Lakers moved into the Forum in 1967, as long as Baylor could play for the new franchise. Baylor would not be able to play for such a team at first, because the Lakers owned his contract, but he could work in the front office during its first season. His attorney, Fred Rosenfeld, told the *Times*, "It's still a little premature to go into full detail, but there has been a lot of conversation along these lines."

Pro basketball was big business in 1967, with a deep national talent pool and widespread fan interest in the game. The San Francisco franchise was financially healthy, there was a new team in Chicago, and the Lakers' success spurred expansion West Coast clubs in San Diego and

Seattle. As the business of basketball grew, so did players' opportunities to capitalize on it. Former Cal basketball star Larry Friend and Lakers forward Rudy LaRusso had formed a firm called the Professional Management Association to advise pro basketball players on contracts and investments. Friend was vice president of L.A. brokerage house McDonnell and Co., for whom the actively playing LaRusso was a licensed broker. By the summer of 1967, they had signed Lakers Gail Goodrich, Archie Clark, and Elgin Baylor as clients. If Baylor jumped leagues, there was a good chance younger players Goodrich and Clark—talented guards laboring in the shadow of Jerry West—would follow.

In early June, *Los Angeles Times* sportswriter John Hall dined in Minneapolis with ABA commissioner George Mikan, who hinted that big things were ahead for the new league in Southern California. Hall told Mikan that what the ABA really needed was "a Chamberlain, Russell, West, or Baylor." "What makes you think we haven't got one?" smiled Mikan. Hall writes, "It would be a stunning irony if Mikan, the man who originally put the Lakers on the map in Minneapolis, and Baylor, the man who made the Lakers in L.A., got together to bury them in Inglewood."

Other reports stated that an offer was on the table for Chamberlain and Baylor to receive $600,000 and part ownership in a proposed L.A. franchise. The two superstars were holding out for $1 million.

NBA scoring champion Rick Barry jumped to the ABA's Oakland Oaks in late June but would be ineligible to play for them while the San Francisco Warriors owned his rights. In L.A., rumors of an impending Baylor jump grew stronger.

With the help of Rosenfeld and others, Baylor diversified his business ventures. A July 13, 1967, *Times* real estate classified ad lists a "2 Bedroom Garden-Like" apartment in the city's Wilshire district, with carpets and drapes, for $105 a month, "1 Child OK." The contact person was Elgin Baylor, "937-1285."

10

WILT: THE UNLUCKY NUMBER 13

He sinks shots one-handed, two-handed, underhanded, flatfooted, and out of the pivot, jump, and set. . . . That his touch still lives in his hands elates him. He feels liberated from long gloom. But his body is weighty, and his breath grows short. It annoys him, that he gets winded. When the five kids not on his side begin to groan and act lazy . . . Rabbit quits readily. "O.K.," he says. "The old man's going. Three cheers."—John Updike, *Rabbit, Run*

On Sunday, August 13, 1967, former Lakers general manager Lou Mohs died. Mohs, 70, had only recently left his position with the Lakers to serve as vice president of California Sports, Inc. It was Mohs's business savvy and Baylor's exciting play that had transformed a fledgling Minneapolis team into the National Basketball Association's most popular home team. Now, Elgin Baylor wanted to join the elite group of professional athletes earning $100,000 a year. He and attorney Fred Rosenfeld were hashing out the details with Lakers management for a pact that paid Baylor $90,000 in the coming year and $60,000 as salary, with a $30,000 signing bonus. The parties finally agreed to terms a few days after the exhibition season began in Honolulu, where Ruby had accompanied Elgin for the team's three-game series with San Francisco. Baylor was to earn a one-year extension that did not affect the current terms. It covered him from 1968 through 1970. Thus, he joined Bill Russell and Wilt Chamberlain in the fraternity of pro basketball players earning $100,000 a year. Rick Barry and Nate Thurmond of San Francisco, Oscar Robertson, and bonus babies Cazzie Russell, Bill Bradley, and Jimmy Walker were also members. (Bradley had signed for $500,000 over four years—$25,000 more than Cazzie Russell.) A few of those six-figure earners benefited from the bidding war initiated by the new American Basketball Association, which began play that year. Baylor's higher salary was further evidence of his physical recovery, as some sportswriters felt he was now 95-percent sound. His upper-body strength and physical control helped compensate for the knee damage. "The man was so strong," says former NBA guard Rod Thorn in Terry Pluto's *Tall Tales: The Glory Years of the NBA*. "You would try to lean on him and he'd fend you off with his left arm, using it like a hammer."

On Wednesday, September 20, four days after his 33rd birthday, Baylor reported to preseason camp. He was an eight-time All-Pro who had led the Lakers in rebounding for seven seasons and scoring for four years. The Lakers would host their first Southern California preseason game of 1967 against the Cincinnati Royals in Long Beach on October 1, as part of a doubleheader that also featured the Warriors against the Baltimore Bullets. It would be the Lakers' sole preseason game in Southern California that fall.

The late 1960s became known as the years of the "long, hot summers" in urban America, as such cities as Chicago, Detroit, and Newark had exploded in racial unrest in the aftermath of the 1965 Watts Riots. The more "militant" black athletes were considering a boycott of the following year's Summer Olympic Games in Mexico City to prove a point about the racism that persisted in the United States. Meanwhile, Baylor helped make a difference in L.A. by continuing to appear at events that benefited city youth. In the August 17, 1967, issue of *JET* magazine, the world's premier long jumper, Ralph Boston, said, "A lot of Negro athletes in Los Angeles, people like Elgin Baylor of the Lakers, John Roseboro, catcher of the Dodgers, and Junior Gilliam, Dodger coach—have done wonders since last summer's tragedy in Watts."

The Lakers underwent a series of changes in the 1967–1968 season, including a new GM, a new coach, and a new venue for their home games. In the summer of 1967, Fred Schaus left his position as Lakers coach to become general manager of the club. In thinking about a new coach, owner Jack Kent Cooke had no interest in participating in the NBA's "musical chairs" practice of hiring a coach who was available merely because another team had canned him. Seeing a *Sports Illustrated* cover story on Princeton basketball, he asked who the Tigers' coach was.

That man was former U.S. Marine Willem Hendrik "Butch" van Breda Kolff. Hailing from Montclair, New Jersey, van Breda Kolff was a 45-year-old former Princeton and New York University player who, during a brief pro career, was a member of the late 1940s New York Knicks. He was only a 30-percent shooter with New York, but his tenacity earned him a role as team captain. Before the Bill Bradley era at Princeton, van Breda Kolff coached at Lafayette College and Hofstra University.

The team was also preparing to move their games to a new arena. Since purchasing the Lakers two years earlier, Jack Kent Cooke had become embroiled in a bitter dispute with city officials regarding rental of the municipal Los Angeles Memorial Sports Arena. In 1966, the National Hockey League had announced that it intended to sell six new franchises, and Cooke had prepared a bid. The Los Angeles Memorial Coliseum Commission, which operated the Sports Arena, supported a competing bid and advised Cooke that if he won the franchise he would not be allowed to use that facility. Cooke threatened to build a new arena in the Los Angeles suburb of Inglewood. City officials would not budge, so Cooke bought a huge tract of land near the Hollywood Park Racetrack. The surrounding area featured iron-barred liquor stores and one-pump gas stations, yet Cooke claimed the Forum would be the "most beautiful arena in the world." He had it designed by the same architect who drafted Broadway Plaza and Houston's Manned Spacecraft Center, and spent $16.5 million on the construction.

The Fabulous Forum opened on December 30, 1967, and the Lakers would play their first game there the next night, on New Year's Eve. Spectators, media, and basketball players loved the new facility. Ushers dressed in Roman togas escorted patrons to their goldenrod plastic seats. Male ushers sported orange togas, and women wore miniskirts and suede lace sandals tied at the calf. There were handmade tiles featuring the building's design throughout the arena. An innovative scoreboard messaging feature was called the Magic Message Board. The corridors and playing areas were spotless and bright, and the building breathed cool air-conditioning. Private press rooms could host pregame and postgame interviews. There were bars and restaurants, and it was the first NBA arena to boast a luxurious club lounge for special postgame affairs. Cooke ordered his staff to "never call it an arena," adding, "It's the Fabulous Forum, or sports theater." It was a case of venue as extension of owner, unlike any other pro basketball arena of that time. Although locals dubbed the Forum the "House That Jack Built" after owner Cooke, it was Elgin Baylor's success in attracting Hollywood types to cheer on the Lakers that truly set the stage for the grand arena.

For Baylor, it was a palace suited to his Hollywood status and tailor-made for his sensitive knees. The baskets were sufficiently loose, and thus more forgiving on a shot, affording friendly roll-in baskets. For shooters, the lighting provided some distance between the court and the crowd. The Forum's playing surface gave nicely beneath a player's weight, due to a separation of four inches of air between the court and the ice hockey surface below—a tremendous improvement on standard NBA floors, for example, the outdated Minneapolis Armory where Baylor began his career. In most other arenas, Baylor risked injury because the cooling pipes for the NHL ice were directly underneath the portable court, and in some arenas, condensation from the ice leaked up onto the hardwood. In addition, no press members were allowed at courtside, so there was no danger of a player colliding with reporters' tables.

Players could park their cars near the employee entrance, and the Forum's lots accommodated 4,000 cars. The spacious locker room featured mirrors, wash basins, benches, and showers designed with men 6'5" and taller in mind. A man of Jack Kent Cooke's height, 5'6", could not see himself in the mirrors.

The 1967–1968 Lakers were an enigma. Baylor was back strong, but the old Achilles' heel of a subpar frontcourt seemed to limit the team's chances. In September 1966, the Lakers had traded LeRoy Ellis to Baltimore for former Texas Western All-American Jim "Bad News" Barnes. Barnes, whom the Knicks had selected as the third pick in the 1964 NBA Draft (ahead of the likes of Joe Caldwell, Luke Jackson, Jeff Mullins, and Willis Reed), was a flop. Veteran Tom Hawkins was no longer a dependable rebounder. Rudy LaRusso was gone to the rival San Francisco Warriors, where he would average a career-best 21.8 points per game. On the bright side, young guards Archie Clark and Gail Goodrich added scoring punch—but the Lakers had always been strong in the backcourt. Their young guards were generally groomed as temporary tandem men for Jerry West, then traded when their development attracted attention from opposing general managers. Such had been the case with Dick Barnett and Walt Hazzard.

Part of the problem with the Lakers' big men was recent coach Fred Schaus's taste—or the lack thereof. L.A. drafted bigs who could shoot:

Jim Krebs, Darrall Imhoff, LeRoy Ellis, and Mel Counts. None of the men were spirited rebounders, a deficit Bill Russell and his Celtics comrades exploited when the money was on the line. At 6'10", Gene Wiley was a sensitive, quiet sort who was a better artist than athlete. Although Wiley, a commercial art major from Wichita State, would be employed as a successful artist by the Atlantic Richfield oil company from 1968 to 1984 and sell works to Brent Musburger, Jerry West, Mrs. Jesse Owens, and Elgin Baylor, the Lakers struck dry ground with him when they selected Wiley 15th overall in the 1962 NBA Draft, after taking LeRoy Ellis with the eighth selection.

In 1967, Schaus exerted even more authority over personnel moves, after being named general manager of the club. As for the coach, *Sports Illustrated* opines that van Breda Kolff "rails at them all, one by one, and then quickly forgets."

In midseason, they picked up Erwin Mueller from the Bulls and Fred Crawford from the Knicks. Warriors coach Bill Sharman told *Sports Illustrated*, "Those two gave the Lakers an opportunity to keep up their quick. Before, if you saw West and Baylor leave the game, you knew the pace would be slower. Now, if anything, it's faster."

According to the April 15, 1968, edition of *Sports Illustrated*, van Breda Kolff dubbed Erwin Mueller "Mules," telling him, "I can't possibly call you Erwin, and I can't call you Dum-Dum, because if I did every guy on this team would turn around."

In February, the Lakers dealt the Celtics their worst home loss ever, drubbing them, 141–104. Jerry West was happy. "This whole team gets along better together than any I've ever played on," he told *Sports Illustrated* in the April 15, 1968, feature, continuing,

> That's part of the reason I was so discouraged when I was hurt again a few weeks ago. We're a more aggressive team. I play against better defense in practice than in a lot of games. And this is absolutely the best-shooting team I have ever seen. I mean shooting. Not drop it in or beat it to death on the backboard.

The Lakers won 30 of their last 38 games after January 17 (around the All-Star break, when they acquired Mueller and Crawford). At the end of that stretch, after mid-March, the team played outside California only once, visiting Philly on the 18th. Van Breda Kolff instituted his Princeton offense, which required all five players to touch the ball—not just Baylor and West. Although the coach felt Baylor, West, and company dribbled the basketball too much for his taste, he found the stars and other players cooperative.

While the Hawks led the Western Division that season, helped by center Zelmo Beaty and playmaker Len Wilkens, van Breda Kolff's first club finished 52–30, a marked improvement from the Lakers' 36–45 record in 1967. In the new Forum building, they were 21–5 toward the end of the season.

In the first round of the playoffs, the Lakers eliminated Chicago in five games. Baylor and West scored 293 of the team's 533 points—55 percent.

The Thursday, April 4, *Los Angeles Sentinel* was published on the eve of the division playoff finals, and says of Baylor, "[T]he PERFECT example of the MONEY player, the guy always comes through when the chips are down and the real money is smack on the line."

At six o'clock that evening, Memphis time, Rev. Dr. Martin Luther King Jr. was shot dead on a hotel balcony in Memphis, while addressing his colleagues and Southern Christian Leadership Conference staff who were gathered in the hotel parking lot. King was in the city to lend support to striking black sanitation workers. Baylor told *JET* magazine in April 1968, "It was really a shock to me. I'm awfully sorry it happened." He thought of King's young family: "I'm especially saddened because of his wife and kids. I think he did more than anyone else in the civil rights movement and for our people."

Commissioner Walter Kennedy left the decision whether to play Friday's playoff games up to the league owners. According to *King of the Court*, Aram Goudsouzian's 2011 biography of Bill Russell, one NBA official said, "It would be different if this were the president." The Celtics, who had seven black players, including their coach, Russell, voted to play. When the team met to discuss their options, Mississippi State product Bailey Howell asked, "What was his title? Why should we call off the game?" Their division finals opponents, the Sixers, who had six black players, voted, 7–2, for postponement, with Wilt Chamberlain and young guard Wally Jones on the side of postponing. In Lew Freedman's book *Dynasty: The Rise of the Boston Celtics*, an emotional Wilt said, "I would personally like to see the whole day taken off as some kind of memorial to Dr. King. But I'm only one individual. . . . I don't want to instigate anything. I'll follow the majority."

Three hours before tip-off, Russell reached Chamberlain by phone, and the big men agreed the game should be postponed, but Philly fans were already en route to the Spectrum. Although the Friday game was played, many of the players went about their duties as if in a fog. Sunday's games were postponed because President Lyndon B. Johnson declared a national day of mourning.

In their playoff series with San Francisco, Lakers forwards Tommy Hawkins and Elgin Baylor were matched against the Warriors' beefier Rudy LaRusso and Fred Hetzel, the latter 6'8", 230 pounds, and selected first overall in the 1965 NBA Draft, before Bill Bradley and Rick Barry. The Lakers outrebounded San Francisco and won the opener at home, 133–105. LaRusso had trouble scoring against his longtime teammate Baylor, and the Lakers fans rode him all night.

Meanwhile, as Philadelphia jumped to a 3–1 series lead over Boston, *Sports Illustrated* reported that the Lakers wanted a rematch with their nemeses, the Celtics: "In Los Angeles the Lakers watched the final game on TV, rooting for Boston. To a man, they believe they can handle the Celtics, matching their speed, giving Russell the boards but outshooting the rest." Boston's veterans fought back from the deficit and became the first team in NBA history to win a seven-game series after losing three of four.

At the time, Brock Brockenbury of the *Los Angeles Sentinel* reported his belief that Baylor was the "greatest all-around player in NBA annals," but said, as nice as it would be for L.A. to capture a league title, "we find ourselves pulling for the Boston Celtics. . . . Reason is simple: Bill Russell is the coach of the Celtics." Brockenbury writes that all the years Red Auerbach earned the sole credit for the team's banners, it was actually Russell who held the key to victory.

In the 2010 book *Jerry West: The Life and Legend of a Basketball Icon*, by Roland Lazenby, Jerry West relates, "If we can rebound, we can win. We're little, but we match up well with Boston. We're quick and we shoot well, and that can be enough in any seven-game series."

In the first game of the 1968 NBA Finals, on April 21, the Lakers blew a 15-point lead to lose, 107–101. According to *Sports Illustrated*, "Despite that loss, the Lakers have an excellent chance of becoming the first Western team to win the title in exactly a decade. Certainly it does not seem likely that West and Baylor will repeat their shockingly poor shooting performances. West hit on only seven of 24, Baylor on 11 of 31."

In game two, L.A. rode a strong third-quarter effort by Baylor and West to a 123–113 win. For the tiebreaker, 17,000 fans packed the Forum, and Boston raced to an 18-point advantage. Then Baylor caught on fire, but it wasn't enough, as L.A. fell short, 127–119.

In the fourth match, a sloppy affair new TV analyst Red Auerbach called a "lousy game," Baylor and West combined for 68 points as the Lakers won, 118–105, tying the series at two games apiece. When van Breda Kolff was ejected from the fourth game, his only specific parting instructions to his fill-in, guard Gail Goodrich, were which changes to make when Russell moved Havlicek.

Game five was played in Boston. Boston twice seemed to have the game wrapped up, moving to a 19-point lead in the first quarter behind the shooting of Don Nelson. After squandering that advantage, they led by 18 late in the third quarter. L.A. rallied behind the scoring of Mel Counts to tie the contest at 108 on a layup by West.

Late in overtime, West tied it again at 117 all, but Havlicek scored on a jump shot with 38 seconds left. On offense, Baylor got the ball on the left side of the court. Nelson was guarding him, and Baylor used his patented yo-yo dribble to get by his defender and spun left and shot. Seemingly from out of nowhere, Russell leaped to block the shot. Boston won, 120–117, after a couple foul shots by Nelson.

In Thomas J. Whalen's work *Dynasty's End: Bill Russell and the 1968–69 World Champion Boston Celtics*, Baylor says of Nelson, "I never could understand why we let Don go. We used to play a lot of one-on-one basketball in practice, and Nelson always gave me as much trouble as anybody. I know this: He never had a full opportunity with the Lakers." As they had with Dick Barnett in 1965, the Lakers had let a valuable substitute go—the very type of player who could serve the team well during a combative series against Boston.

Two nights later, in game six at home, Baylor made a memorable move that exhibited some of his mobility. Following his signature head tic, he dribbled the ball on the far right side past half-court, eluded a hopelessly outmatched Larry Siegfried along the sidelines, rose above the waiting Russell, and dunked in Russell's face.

Despite that courageous and crowd-pleasing display, L.A. fell behind by 20, and John Havlicek scored 40, as the visitors took the clincher by 124–109. It was the sixth time Baylor's Lakers had lost in the NBA

Finals to the Celtics. Bostonians celebrated yet another victory over the Californians.

On June 5, the night of the California primary in the U.S. presidential race, the winner, New York senator Robert F. Kennedy, was assassinated while walking through the pantry of L.A.'s Ambassador Hotel. It was in the Ambassador five and a half years earlier, during the NBA All-Star Game festivities, that Red Auerbach had ridiculed a banner proclaiming "Los Angeles, The Basketball Capital of the World" by blurting at a banquet, "Win a couple championships first, then talk about being the basketball capital of the world." Now, one of the scions of Boston's most famous family lay dying within the bowels of the hotel.

A new crop of NBA stars was emerging, among them Walt Frazier, Bill Bradley, and Cazzie Russell of New York; flashy Detroit backcourt tandem Jimmy Walker and Dave Bing; and the most flamboyant of them all, Baltimore's Earl Monroe. Baylor was not merely an old man who had influenced the new breed, however; he was still an offensive force to be reckoned with. Bing, a product of Baylor's Spingarn High School, led the NBA in total points in 1967–1968, with 2,142, but Baylor finished second, with 2,002. Elgin averaged 26 a game, which was better than Monroe's 24.3.

Black players again dominated the All-NBA selections in 1968, including such newcomers as Detroit's Bing. In March 1969, Baylor would tell the *Los Angeles Times* of Washington, D.C.'s reputation for producing basketball players, "I think the success Dave Bing and I have had has been sort of inspiring to the young kids who don't have a chance to get out of the ghetto any other way."

Baylor, Bing, Robertson, and Chamberlain made the first team, along with Jerry Lucas, Hal Greer, and Willis Reed; Russell joined Havlicek and West on the second unit. Each of the 12 NBA cities was awarded one vote for its sportswriters and sportscasters. Chamberlain earned a perfect 12 votes; Baylor was second, with 11.

After the season ended, the Lakers' management team assessed their situation and began thinking about possible changes to their roster. Fred Schaus recalls in *Tall Tales*, "We had been in the market for a big man for years. It was a problem when we faced Boston when I coached." He continually tried to work deals for better centers, but opposing teams always asked for Baylor or West in exchange—a deal breaker. One season, a proposed trade for Walt Bellamy had fallen through. After the 1968 playoffs, Alex Hannum left the 76ers to coach the Oakland Oaks of the ABA (who had signed Rick Barry after a lengthy court battle). Wilt Chamberlain was not satisfied with the numbers Philadelphia was offering him in contract discussions and made it known he wouldn't mind playing on the West Coast again. The expansion Seattle SuperSonics made an offer for 35 percent more than Los Angeles was proposing, and Wilt considered playing in Baylor's college town. The fact that he owned L.A. property and loved beaches and hobnobbing with celebrities gave the Lakers a decided edge. In addition, Chamberlain's father was living in Los Angeles and suffering from cancer. The idea of teaming with Baylor and West was equally attractive. Schaus told van Breda Kolff there was a chance they could acquire "The Big Dipper." The coach was excited.

Sixers owner Ike Richman had recommended a L.A. lawyer, Seymour Goldberg, to Chamberlain. They negotiated with Cooke to match the numbers offered by SuperSonics owner Sam Schulman. During the talks, Bill Sharman, the new coach of the ABA's L.A. Stars, called Chamberlain and told him that although ABA attendance was generally poor, NBA stars like former Warrior Rick Barry were jumping to the upstart league. If Chamberlain followed suit, he alone could make the league a success. Chamberlain shared Sharman's sentiments with Goldberg, who told him to only seriously consider an ABA offer if it involved an extraordinary sum. "Wilt, I'm going to get you a million bucks," the attorney assured him, as noted in *The Rivalry: Bill Russell, Wilt Chamberlain, and the Golden Age of Basketball.*

In July, L.A. sent Archie Clark and Darrall Imhoff, along with their 1966 first-round pick, Jerry Chambers (the 1966 NCAA Tournament MVP, although his Utah team was eliminated in the semifinals), to the 76ers in exchange for Chamberlain. Cooke sweetened the reported $250,000-a-year deal by giving Chamberlain a loan at 4 percent interest to invest $100,000 in Cooke's cable TV company and another loan to sink into tax shelters. Goldberg valued those considerations more than the playing contract.

Pluto's *Tall Tales* recounts that one Lakers vet told van Breda Kolff, "We just broke up a great team. We were in the Finals. Why make a deal like that." Pluto writes that van Breda Kolff assured the player they could build another "great team." He thought, at worst, they would be a stronger rebounding club. "We'll simply have the best basketball team in history," said van Breda Kolff.

For Chamberlain, who, in 1966–1967, had led the 76ers to a 68–13 mark—the best in NBA history—and helped make them NBA champions that year, van Breda Kolff's forecast that the Lakers would now have the best team ever spoke volumes.

In *Dynasty's End*, 76ers forward Billy Cunningham states, "After Wilt was traded, the best the papers could say was we'd be a more exciting team without him. That's like somebody fixing you up with an ugly blind date and then trying to hide what a loser she is by saying she is a great dancer."

Columnist George Kiseda of the *Philadelphia Evening Bulletin* joked, "The Lakers became the first team in the history of the National Basketball Association to clinch the league championship five days after the Fourth of July. With Wilt Chamberlain joining Jerry West and Elgin Baylor, Ronald Reagan and Doris Day could play the other two positions for them."

Jack Kent Cooke staged an elaborate press conference at the Fabulous Forum to announce Chamberlain's enormous five-year contract. While fans and sportswriters speculated that there wouldn't be enough balls for West, Baylor, and Chamberlain to get their shots, van Breda Kolff remained optimistic. In the team's first practice, The Big Dipper shared the ball, blocked every shot, and grabbed each rebound. The coach smelled a NBA title. The second day, however, Chamberlain sulked about. During the third practice, Chamberlain said he wanted to rest his knees but that he'd be ready when time came to play real games. Van Breda Kolff noticed that even when Chamberlain did participate later on, his teammates felt his lackadaisical attitude detracted from their workouts.

There was also the issue of which of the three superstars deserved the most money. Jack Kent Cooke recalls in Robert Cherry's *Wilt: Larger Than Life*,

> From the moment I purchased the Lakers in 1965, it was a continuing battle every year between Jerry West and me as to whether Jerry West got a penny more than Elgin Baylor. Jerry felt the amount of money he got should be greater than Elgin because he did so much more. As far as Wilt Chamberlain was concerned, I never made such a commitment to Jerry. I did, however, make a commitment to him regarding Elgin Baylor. But Wilt Chamberlain was an entirely different story.

Cooke said the annual argument West posed regarding superior pay to Baylor turned him off. West says his disputes with the owner concerned mind games Cooke would play about players' salaries, not his own worries about what teammates earned.

"Not having enough basketballs wasn't the problem at all for us," relates van Breda Kolff in *Tall Tales*. "The trade changed our chemistry. Wilt would set up on the low left block. Elgin's favorite move was the drive from the left wing into the middle. Now when he did that, he ran into Wilt's man. Wilt took that move away from Elgin." Van Breda Kolff wanted Chamberlain in the low post as part of the motion offense that had been the coach's trademark at Princeton. Chamberlain was also reluctant to run screen-and-roll plays with Baylor, as Imhoff had done. When van Breda Kolff discussed defense, Chamberlain protested that he was already blocking more shots than anyone. *Sports Illustrated* reported on February 20, 1984, that van Breda Kolff said, "But I want you to do it like Russell." The coach told the *Los Angeles Times*, "If he wants to he can play defense better than anybody in the league. If he wanted to he could be two Bill Russell's [*sic*] on defense. . . . He doesn't know the word 'work.'" Van Breda Kolff saw Chamberlain's weakness as laziness.

In August, van Breda Kolff traveled to New York for a NBA meeting of coaches and officials to discuss rules changes. It was the weekend of the annual Maurice Stokes charity game, an event star players looked forward to. Van Breda Kolff brought a Lakers jersey to Kutsher's Country Club, where the game was being held, and asked Chamberlain wear it and pose for a photographer. Chamberlain, still fuming from van Breda Kolff's public claim that he was lazy, refused to wear the shirt. The men argued about it but to no avail. The coach had no clue how sensitive the gifted giant was.

Chamberlain's presence with the Lakers also challenged Baylor's chatty leadership and offered an added reminder of Boston Celtics dominance, since Chamberlain was Russell's foil. Longtime pals Baylor and Chamberlain began teasing one another, Baylor telling The Big Dipper he had hands like a blacksmith, and Dipper holding his numerical superiority over Elg.

Training camp opened in late September at Loyola of Los Angeles. After photo day, Coach van Breda Kolff held closed practices, telling the media that the veterans, rookies, and Chamberlain needed time to get acquainted. Rumors arose that the coach was hiding something—perhaps his lack of rapport with the new star. By the third day of camp, Wilt refused to run, insisting on preserving his knees. Since Baylor had famously undergone surgery on both knees, observers found this odd, if characteristic. Maybe Chamberlain didn't want to practice hard because he didn't respect the new coach, with his collegiate and marine-like ways. Chamberlain resented van Breda Kolff's coaching style, which he felt was best suited to college kids. The coach and The Big Dipper even sometimes sniped at one another through the print media. As peacemakers, the rest of the Lakers assured van Breda Kolff they would prefer practicing without Chamberlain, rather than scrimmaging with a reluctant player.

There were also personnel woes, particularly the lack of backcourt depth without Archie Clark (dealt to Philly in the Chamberlain exchange) and Gail Goodrich. *The Rivalry* recounts that Red Auerbach predicted to a friend that, if the guard issue was not addressed, "the glamour boys are going to have trouble." Van Breda Kolff called other teams to inquire about the availability of their guards. He generally floated backup center Mel Counts as trade bait. Yet, when he spoke with Boston coach Bill Russell, he told him Counts was not up for consideration, to which Russell joked that he would rather have Chamberlain.

As a result of van Breda Kolff's talent search, willowy University of Southern California rookie Bill Hewitt made the Lakers ball club. Hewitt was a Boston native whose college-career high mark was 39 points, scored against Lew Alcindor. The Lakers answered the backcourt dilemma by signing UCLA product Keith Erickson from the Bulls and veteran playmaker Johnny Egan from expansion Milwaukee. Erickson, whose forte was volleyball, was a strong defender. With these new players and Chamberlain, Baylor had plenty of adjusting to do.

On the court, the Lakers' offense struggled with Chamberlain occupying Baylor's operating space. In the opener, Wilt's old 76ers ran up a lead of more than 30 points on L.A. No one—least of all Baylor—could make their customary moves to the hoop with Chamberlain down low. Van Breda Kolff benched Wilt, and the team rallied but still lost. After four games, the three superstars recorded one victory. Although he had led Philly to a title in 1967, media copy about Wilt the loser resurfaced. Chamberlain was also moody, especially with his father dying of cancer. That and his lack of a relationship with his coach colored his attitude. In addition, he had never shared the spotlight with players the caliber of Baylor and West.

The fall also brought tension because Chamberlain was publicly campaigning for presidential candidate Richard Nixon, while Baylor, along with most of black America, supported Democrat Hubert Humphrey. In response to the team's political divide, van Breda Kolff took the humorous road: "If Jerry comes out for George Wallace, we'll be in trouble."

In late October, Chamberlain's father died, which sank him deeper into insomnia and depression. On the court, van Breda Kolff and Chamberlain bickered about strategy. The coach asked him to play the high post, to free up the lane for scorers. Chamberlain said that would leave him out of position to make rebounds. And so it went.

Chamberlain was not alone in his low regard for van Breda Kolff. Some of the veterans felt he was a lush, who not only drank with his ballplayers but insisted on buying. On road trips, the coach apparently had an odd habit of making bed checks to ensure the players were in their hotel rooms and then keeping them awake half the night with banter and beer. The guys had to beg him to leave so they could rest.

It was van Breda Kolff's taste in fashion that Baylor found difficult to take. In particular, a gaudy red, black, and gray tweed sports jacket did not meet with Baylor's approval, and the team wondered how their coach braved the coldest NBA cities in nothing more than his collection of sports jackets.

On occasion, Chamberlain displayed some of the old Wilt, scoring 60 against Cincinnati on January 26, 1969, and torching the expansion Phoenix Suns for 66 on February 9. There were signs the trade had worked: in mid-March the Lakers traveled to Boston and whipped the champs, 108–73. *Sports Illustrated* opines that Chamberlain didn't represent the only difference, as Keith Erickson provided athleticism on defense and veteran guard Johnny Egan pressed opposing guards and knew how to run an offense.

In late February, Red Auerbach accompanied the Celtics on a trip to play the Lakers. Boston was in fourth place in the East. Two days before the game, Auerbach hosted a press luncheon at the Forum Club. According to the book *The Rivalry*, he was holding court with his trademark cigar, when Cooke found him. "It's good to see you in your decline," Cooke said.

"No comment," replied Auerbach.

"The declining Celtics are still good for a sellout," beamed Cooke, telling Auerbach and those gathered that the game on Friday was already sold out.

Auerbach couldn't resist any longer. He had the championship rings, and L.A. still had none. The Hollywood boys always tried to one-up him and throw their glitz in his face, dating back to Bob Short's showy All-Star Game luncheon at the Coconut Grove. "We're still magic," Auerbach huffed. "Not even Los Angeles can say that. A few years ago someone said that Los Angeles was the capital of the basketball world. Someone undoubtedly who had been sniffing brandy."

"I wouldn't be guilty of such a redundancy," scoffed Cooke. "I assume that everyone knows it." He went on to chirp, "We're going to win it all."

"You're going to win it all if you don't play us," Auerbach spat back.

"Revenge," said the squirish multimillionaire.

"You'll be an old man before you get that," answered Auerbach. "Russell will be walking around the court on a cane. Chamberlain could never beat Russell."

Short's lofty "basketball capital" claim had been quite a stretch in 1963, but by 1968, when Cooke preened, the city boasted the nation's premier college player and program, Lew Alcindor and UCLA, in addition to two of the most exciting pro stars, Baylor and West, and the game's most glamorous home, the Fabulous Forum. What Los Angeles lacked in longstanding championship tradition, it made up in luster.

Late in the season, Butch van Breda Kolff played Mel Counts more at center, because Counts, a good jump shooter, didn't occupy the left block, from which Elgin Baylor liked to start his moves. During this stretch, the Lakers made up an 18-point deficit to defeat Phoenix and closed a 15-point gap to beat Baltimore. In one game against Boston, Chamberlain, playing with a bandaged left hand, snared 42 rebounds against Russell. In February 1969, John Havlicek told *Boys Life* magazine, "The tougher forwards in the league for me include Elgin Baylor, Dave DeBusschere, Billy Cunningham, and Chet Walker."

* * *

The Lakers finished the season 4–3 against San Francisco, including a triple-overtime loss and another on a basket in the last second. Once they beat the Warriors by more than 30 points. The Warriors' Rick Barry was sitting out a year, awaiting the outcome of a lawsuit barring him from jumping to the American Basketball Association's Oakland Oaks. On March 12, the Lakers blew an eight-point lead on San Francisco to lose at the Cow Palace, 97–85; they were outshot, out-defended, and out-rebounded.

Los Angeles enjoyed their best season in years, winning 10 of their last 13 games. Their 55–27 record placed them seven games in front of Atlanta and 14 ahead of San Francisco—a .500 team. It was their first division title since 1966 and their best record ever. The Lakers sold more than 160,000 playoff tickets for the 10 upcoming postseason games at the Forum, more than 16,000 a game.

The Lakers planned "Elgin Baylor Night" for March 21, 1969. The ceremony would take place at 8 p.m., prior to an 8:40 game against the rival Atlanta Hawks. The event attracted 17,024 fans. Baylor's wife, parents, brothers Kermit and Sal, sisters, nieces, nephews, and other family members attended the event. His teammates presented him with a 100-year-old chair once owned by the president of Mexico. Tom Hawkins said the chair was for "when Elgin's playing days are no more." Baylor, dressed in a gold warm-up suit, sat near the sidelines in the regal-looking chair as teammates, city officials, and some of the Hawks' players paid him tribute. In addition to longtime teammates Jerry West and Hawkins, civic leaders like city councilman Tom Bradley spoke accolades, as did Mayor Sam Yorty and Governor Ronald Reagan through proxies. The ever-dapper John Baylor sported a suit accented by a kerchief in his breast pocket, and mother Uzziel looked on through her framed eyeglasses. Little Alan wore a nifty sport jacket and slacks, and closely cropped curly hair, while his sister, Allison, donned a topcoat and ribbons in her braided hair.

In the April 17, 1969, edition of *JET* magazine, Baylor called it the "most memorable night in my entire basketball career." He was presented with a gold watch, a pool table from the Atlantic Richfield company, and a new Buick GS-400 sports coupe from Jack Kent Cooke. In the printed tribute program fans purchased that night, most of the opposing players and coaches, league officials, and referees who contributed remarks called Elgin Baylor a "gentleman."

Going into the playoff series against San Francisco, Baylor was the all-time NBA leader in playoff points scored, with 3,010, and he held the single-game postseason record of 61. During the 1968–1969 season, he scored his 20,000th point in the NBA.

Laker fans wondered which Wilt, old or new, would show up for the playoffs. In a lackluster first round of the Western Division playoffs, the Lakers beat Nate Thurmond's San Francisco Warriors, four games to two. Chamberlain stepped up to help the Lakers win, going head-to-head with the Warriors' Thurmond. In the first two games, Thurmond outplayed Chamberlain, but in the fifth game, Chamberlain established domination over his opponent. "He outmuscled me," Thurmond says in the April 14, 1969, installment of *Sports Illustrated*, "especially on the offensive boards." Chamberlain had 27 rebounds to only 13 for Thurmond.

Tom Hawkins says in the same issue, "Wilt has been something else. You want to know why he's worth so much money? Because he controls the game, the way he has controlled it in the last three games of this series. He makes the tempo."

Also contributing were Bill Hewitt, the slender 6'7" forward from USC, and Johnny Egan, the little veteran from Providence. Egan animated the offense with his speed and enthusiasm, while Hewitt hit several key shots from outside, firing the ball from off his right ear, with his elbow bent, and fading away on his release. In the clincher, Jerry West poured in 22 before halftime.

The Lakers won the division semifinals series despite a subpar performance from Baylor. He looked tired, and only a few times in the six games did he jump high, hang effortlessly in the air, and bank in his trademark shots.

L.A. advanced to face an Atlanta Hawks, starring Lou Hudson and Joe Caldwell. The first two games were close, but L.A. prevailed. Then Baylor and West slumped, and the Lakers lost game three. West was having migraine headaches and missed the basket completely a couple of times. Chamberlain scored 25 to power a fourth-game victory. Then it was Baylor's turn to shine. In front of 16,273 home fans and a national TV audience on Sunday, April 20, L.A. coasted to a 54–42 halftime advantage over their younger foes. They led, 81–71, going into the final period. Atlanta tied things 88-all with seven minutes to play. Chamberlain blocked 16 shots and scored 29 in what would ultimately be a 104–96 win. But it was Baylor's performance—14-for-18 shooting, 12 assists, and 11 rebounds, for 29 total points—that moved Jim Murray to write the

Los Angeles Times headline, "Elgin Baylor's Alive, Playing at the For-um." The article beneath reads,

> Do you believe in ghosts? Do you believe the dead can walk? . . . Hang
> in the air with a jump shot? . . . People swear they saw the late Elgin
> Baylor haunting the place in broad daylight. . . . Somebody or SOME-
> THING was running around with a basketball, throwing it up through
> a hoop, stealing it from Bill Bridges, dribbling it down the backcourt.

In the victors' locker room, the *Times* reports that teammates teased Baylor about the reporters, shouting, "They're back Elg, they're back." His clutch outburst had come on the heels of countless sports-page "obit-uaries" based on a 12.2 scoring average in his most recent 10 playoff games.

The Lakers won the series, four games to one, to take the Western Division title. Wilt wrote, "Boston, Here We Come" on the locker room blackboard.

In *Dynasty's End*, Fred Schaus is quoted as admitting, "If we can win the championship, I'd rather it be over Boston. It'd be much, much more satisfying."

Boston survived Eastern Division playoff battles with the Sixers and the Knicks. During the Philadelphia series, speaking to *Sports Illustrated* on February 24, 1969, Bill Russell compared young Sixers star forward Billy Cunningham to Elgin Baylor: "You can't really stop him. . . . He likes to go down the middle or across the middle, sort of like Elgin Baylor used to play—hanging up there and making shots under his arm and every which way."

Odds makers favored the Lakers, 9–5, to beat Boston in the finals. Jerry West told the *Times* if L.A. lost again, "it [would] be a crime for the game of basketball."

Wilt Chamberlain also felt the pressure. His father had died during the season, and the media continued to focus its attention on his adjustment to the Lakers offense. "It has been a hard year," says The Big Dipper in *Dynasty's End*. "That's why with all the problems, winning the cham-pionship would mean more than it ever has." He said no one had taken into account the toll of his father's death on his game; instead, he ex-plained, "[E]verybody says, 'Wilt's not doing this,' or 'he's not doing that.' . . . I guess I should be getting used to it."

Elgin Baylor not only felt this was the year L.A. could beat Boston, but he also believed that, although his knees were holding up, he wouldn't have many more chances. He'd be 35 in September. According to *Sports Illustrated*, in a team meeting before the first game, he told the guys they had a big advantage over Boston: Wilt. As important a defensive player as Russell was, Baylor said he also scored a lot of points from offensive rebounds and things that sometimes were enough to grant victories. If The Big Dipper could neutralize Russ there, they could win it all.

For the first time, ABC would broadcast three playoff games in prime time. *SPORT* magazine hired Baylor to write a diary of the finals. Jerry West wore his game face around the house, snapping at his wife, who steered clear of him. A record 17,554 fans turned out to the Finals opener on Friday at the L.A. Forum. *The Rivalry* reports that before the opening tip, Bill Russell asked West how he was feeling. "I feel like I got nothing in me," West allowed. "This season's been two years long." The new coach, the arrival of Wilt Chamberlain, and the annual playoffs pressure were apparently getting to him. "It'll be over soon enough," Russell cryptically assured him.

In the first game, L.A. trailed at halftime and at the end of the third quarter, but West was on fire. In a contest marked by 14 ties and 27 lead changes, Baylor scored 24, and West's 53 points fueled a 120–118 win. At one point in the third period, John Taylor writes in *The Rivalry*, Russell sidled up to the red-hot West. "Empty, huh? I'm getting so I just don't believe you country boys anymore."

"The big story for us the entire game was West," Baylor said afterward. "He was leading us in driving and scoring inside against Russell more than I can ever remember us doing it before. This was our big plan for the night." The Lakers, according to Baylor's magazine diary, realized that Russell couldn't leave Chamberlain alone and offer much defensive help on West. The *Los Angeles Times'* Mal Florence calls it a "game that should be preserved for the ages, one that should be used in future textbooks as a classic example of the way pro basketball should be played."

In game two, Baylor scored 14 points in the first three quarters. He sat out the first five minutes of the fourth quarter and then went on a tear, scoring 18 points in seven minutes. He finished with 32 points on 11-for-15 shooting, and his scoring spurt, which accounted for the last 12 Lakers points, sealed the game. The Lakers had trailed by two baskets with a few minutes to play. Baylor sank a jump shot from the left corner, and his two free throws put them up, 110–108, with 2:30 to go. Boston answered with a Russell hoop over Wilt, followed by a runner from John Havlicek, but Baylor responded with his own timely 17-footer and a pair of made foul shots. With more than a minute on the clock, L.A. held the lead the rest of the way. Fifteen minutes of judicious rest had helped Baylor pace himself for crunch time. "I'd spent enough time on the bench during the game, that I was ready for that all-out assault at the end, but when you end up with a scoring spree like that, and hit for 11-for-15 for the game, you know there's a little luck involved," he comments in *Dynasty's End*. Boston had clearly had more than their share of similar good fortune throughout the years, but that night belonged to the Lakers. Sports announcer Dave Stone, who attended that game, later said, "I was 19 at the time. In the parking lot afterwards, my friends started congratulating me as if it were my father that had played."

Jerry West had scored 41 in the game, but he says of Baylor in *Tall Tales*, "He won it for us. . . . He was the man. Elgin was a super competitor with a great instinct for the game."

Baylor wondered if the Celtics were losing their confidence, as Boston had never trailed two games to none in a playoff series. But the scores were close enough that if West had an average night in remaining games (something he was nearly incapable of in the postseason, if healthy), the Lakers would lose. Celtic John Havlicek notes in *Dynasty's End*, "I'm not discouraged, because both games could have gone either way. We're going home now, and maybe all we need is the home crowd." Championship rings breed optimism.

Chamberlain nursed a sore jaw in the locker room after the second game, the result of a collision with Don Nelson's head. In the visitors' dressing room, in the account in *Dynasty's End*, Nellie joked, "It's too bad my head didn't cut Wilt's chin. Then he would have to shave that beard off." Never mind the fact that the Celtics' player-coach, Bill Russell, had been sporting a goatee for years.

Hollywood came to Boston for the third game, or at least a portion of it. Actress Rhonda Fleming and her producer husband, Hall Bartlett, joined 100 Lakers fans who flew to watch their team try to wrest the title away from their rivals. The big shots sat in the rows behind the Lakers' bench. L.A. went scoreless for the first 3:39 of game three. They trailed, 57–40, at halftime and then rebounded to tie things at 78. Larry Siegfried and John Havlicek, the old Buckeye teammates, shot Boston ahead, and L.A. fell, 111–105.

The next game would either put L.A. ahead, 3–1, or tie the series at two games apiece. Retired Celtics Tommy Heinsohn, K. C. Jones, and Jim Loscutoff sat on the Celtics' bench for moral support.

In game four, the teams went scoreless for 4:05. The game was marred by 50 turnovers, and Boston shot only 31 percent from the floor. Johnny Egan turned the ball over to Em Bryant, who tapped it to Sam Jones. Jones missed the jumper, but Chamberlain fumbled the rebound. Wilt threw a poor pass to Baylor, and referee Joe Gushue ruled that he stepped out of bounds. Baylor insisted he hadn't stepped on the line, but Gushue pointed silently at the baseline. Boston had possession with seven seconds left. In the Celtics' huddle, Havlicek suggested an old Ohio State play—a triple-screen. Sam Jones tripped while receiving the pass but shot the ball with plenty of arc to allow Russell an opportunity for a tap-in— only Russell was on the bench. The ball hit the front rim, then the back rim, and rolled in. There was one second left, and the officials frantically tried to clear the sidelines of excited Boston fans. West threw a long pass for Chamberlain, but Satch Sanders got a hand on it. Boston won, 89–88; West had scored 40 points.

In the locker room, the Lakers cursed fate and claimed Baylor had been fouled or was in bounds. "Kiss the Blarney Stone," writes Mal Florence in the *Los Angeles Times*.

The Lakers took the fifth game at home, 117–104, buoyed by 39 points from West and Chamberlain's 31 rebounds. West left the game due to a hamstring injury with 2:20 to play. Elgin had only scored eight points.

Elgin rebounded with 26 points in game six, to tie for the team lead with a bandaged Jerry West. Chamberlain suffered blurred vision after Boston guard Em Bryant accidentally poked him in the eye, and the Lakers lost in the Boston Garden, 99–90.

After the sixth game, while still under contract to the Lakers, Butch van Breda Kolff secretly signed a contract with Pistons general manager Edwin Coil to coach Detroit.

For game seven at the Forum on May 5, Jack Kent Cooke ordered thousands of balloons to be dropped from the ceiling if the Lakers won and for the USC band to play "Happy Days Are Here Again." When Bill Russell saw the balloons, he motivated the Celtics by telling them, according to the September 26, 2014, *Sports Illustrated*, "There is no way those balloons can be dropped." Jerry West even thought the balloons were a bad idea, because they would give Boston more incentive to win. Boston led by 12 in the first quarter but only by three at halftime, 59–56. The Celtics extended their lead to 15 points going into the final quarter, with Wilt in foul trouble. L.A. had closed to within seven points, when Chamberlain landed after a rebounded and twisted his knee. Mel Counts was substituted for Wilt. Counts's accurate shooting helped the Lakers draw to a 103–102 deficit with two minutes remaining. Wilt told van Breda Kolff he was ready to go back in. According to "NBA Finals Notes," by Dave Smith, the coach reportedly said, "We're doing fine without you." With 1:33 to play and L.A. down a point, Keith Erickson batted the ball away from John Havlicek, but it bounced to Celtic Don Nelson. Nelson hoisted an awkward jump shot from a couple feet beyond the foul line, and the shot bounced on the front of the rim, caromed three feet upward to the top of the backboard, and surprisingly fell in. Boston took the lead, 105–102. The Celtics went on to clinch the title with a 108–106 victory. Elgin was disappointed by another NBA Finals loss to Boston. Approaching the age of 35 in September and playing on two damaged legs, his athletic clock was running out.

Jack Kent Cooke hired Joe Mullaney to replace Butch van Breda Kolff as coach. Like van Breda Kolff, Mullaney was a successful Eastern college coach, having worked with Lenny Wilkens, John Thompson, Jim Hadnot, Jimmy Walker, and Mike Riordan at Providence. Raised on Long Island, Mullaney had played at Holy Cross with Bob Cousy. Following that, he worked for the FBI. His first head coaching gig was at Norwich University in Vermont. He coached at Providence from 1955 to 1969, as the game changed from a deliberate, crafty contest of possessions, dominated by ethnic New Yorkers, to a fast-paced, high-rise show exemplified by Baylor, in which perennially four of the five first team college All-Americans were black.

* * *

Elgin Baylor turned 35 in September 1969. Early in the 1969 preseason, the Lakers enjoyed a 117–100 victory over San Francisco. *Sports Illustrated*'s pro basketball preview of October 1969 reports that before the game, a referee asked Mullaney, "Is Elgin still the captain?" "I believe so," Mullaney smiled. "They haven't told me otherwise." In contrast to van Breda Kolff, Mullaney put Chamberlain back in the low post, telling him that, rather than taking up space there and palming the ball high above his head and faking passes, he wanted quick shots right off Wilt's screens. The new coach also asked Baylor to come hard out of the wing and use Chamberlain's wide picks to get open for midrange shots, as forwards Luke Jackson and Chet Walker had in Philadelphia.

Mullaney installed four new defenses of varying pressures and taught the Lakers that, with Wilt behind them, they could overplay more (as Boston defenders did with Russell in the paint), forcing opponents outside or to the baseline. Mullaney also hoped to work in younger players the likes of Bill Hewitt and rookie Dick Garrett, to make L.A. more of a running club.

The Lakers got in some decent fast breaks in their exhibition against San Francisco. More importantly, the teammates—and even their coach—were communicating much more than under van Breda Kolff.

In an early season game against Phoenix, Chamberlain tore his right patella tendon and was told he'd miss most of the year. His backup, Rick Roberson, was an eccentric in the Ray Felix mold, an unremarkable pivot man out of the University of Cincinnati who chattered to himself, smashed lockers after victories, and even argued for more playing time when Chamberlain was healthy.

On November 23, although Jerry West scored 38, the Lakers lost, 129–97, to Baltimore, in the middle of a seven-game winning streak. The New York Knicks were a hot team en route to the longest winning streak in league history. New York beat L.A., 103–96, despite West's 41 points. In that contest, Mullaney used a controversial play that caused the Knicks to use an illegal zone defense, resulting in technical fouls. Then, on Wednesday, the Alcindor-led Milwaukee Bucks beat the Lakers, 100–81, during which game West sprained his ankle in the first quarter.

Looking to the rest of the season, Mullaney and Schaus brainstormed about players they could acquire to bolster the frontcourt. They also discussed trades in general. Chamberlain was not the only wounded player; Johnny Egan wore a heavy knee brace, and Baylor was fighting a groin injury. What if they could get Goodrich back, in exchange for Mel Counts? Now playing for the Phoenix Suns, Goodrich was a UCLA boy and a jump shooter. Schaus and Suns owner Jerry Colangelo were close, and Colangelo often phoned Schaus about men on other squads he felt could help the Lakers. Phoenix, however, would not part with Goodrich.

Schaus offered Counts to the Hawks for "Jumpin' Joe" Caldwell, another high-riser influenced by Baylor. Atlanta disagreed to the deal.

Sports Illustrated reports that Schaus wondered how Mullaney felt about Detroit forward Hap Hairston. The coach remembered him when he starred at NYU against his Providence teams but had been told some found him difficult to get along with. Fortunately for the Lakers, one of those people was new Pistons coach Butch van Breda Kolff. Hairston had been critical of his new coach in the media, and as with Chamberlain, van Breda Kolff labeled Hairston lazy. Pistons trainer Bud Shacklee declared Hairston fit as a fiddle, although a loner that even his teammates didn't seem to like. Although, when asked by Mullaney, Chamberlain expressed disapproval, the management team decided to offer younger forward Bill Hewitt to Detroit in exchange for Hairston. On November 27, 1969, the Lakers acquired a veteran who would be nearly as instrumental to their fortunes as former Detroit forward Dave DeBusschere was becoming to the Knicks. The 6'7" Hairston proved to be a battler on the boards, a solid defender, and someone who could score a little by virtue of his skill for tap-ins. Chamberlain would complement Hairston well upon his return.

Elgin scored 36 points against the young Atlanta Hawks on December 7, and 37 against Seattle on December 14. His efforts helped supply offensive firepower in Wilt's absence.

Chamberlain gave the media and fans a hard and fast return date: March 13. He was obviously not superstitious—13 was his uniform number. Still, some questioned—as they had with Baylor in 1965—whether Wilt would even walk again. Chamberlain resigned himself to a regimen that progressed from whirlpool baths, to free exercise to regain range of motion, to the stationary bike that trainer Frank O'Neill put him on when the time seemed right. Because no one manufactured a Goliath-size bike, O'Neill instructed Wilt to sit on a table and do leg lifts with seven-pound weights—a nearly impossible task. Before Christmas, O'Neill told the front office that Chamberlain was such a determined therapy patient, he might indeed be back by March 13. Wilt Chamberlain was 33 years old and on a mission.

Hampered by the toll the season was taking on his knees, Elgin only played 54 of the 82 games that season. He was out of action from December 21, when he scored 28 against the Sixers, until January 9. Not long after acquiring Hairston, L.A. was to face four of the NBA's new powers without Wilt Chamberlain, a gimpy Elgin Baylor, or one of their better defenders, Keith Erickson. Against San Francisco—a team weakened by a courtroom decision that ruled the ABA owned Rick Barry and also by injuries—West hit 43 points, but S.F.'s Joe Ellis nailed 14 of 17 shots for 31, and the Lakers lost for the fourth time, 114–108. During the game, Mullaney again baited the Warriors into using an illegal defense, prompting Warriors coach George Lee to call Mullaney a "disgrace to basketball," according to the Associated Press report of December 1, 1969, and later reported in *Sports Illustrated's Basketball Roundup* on December 8, 1969.

In midseason, L.A. beat the league's hottest team, the Knicks, 114–106, sans Baylor and Chamberlain. With the game tied at 85, West went on a tear and scored 17 points. New York coach Red Holzman predicted to *Sports Illustrated*, "If they get Baylor and Chamberlain back, we're really going to have our hands full." On February 1, Elgin scored 33 against Philadelphia to fulfill Holzman's projection.

When the team traveled east in late February 1970, it was a touring emergency ward. Wilt didn't even make the trip; Erickson had two swollen ankles; rookie Willie McCarter had managed to jam his foot off his leg bone; Hairston was nursing a banged-up shoulder as a rebounding badge of honor; and elder statesman Baylor was day-to-day, due to the condition of his fragile knees. Still, Baylor played almost every game. At New York, DeBusschere was able to muscle Baylor around the floor, forcing him into 5-for-15 shooting. L.A. lost, 114–93, as Reed and DeBusschere collared 34 boards between them and little-used sub center Nate Bowman another 13. Even Mullaney was contrite, admitting to *Sports Illustrated*, "The Knicks are too tough. You never get a chance to breathe with them." If both teams advanced to the NBA Finals, Baylor and Chamberlain were going to have to be physically recovered, with Hairston available under the hoop.

In early March, there were whispers that Chamberlain was coming back. Lakers physician Robert Kerlan still insisted The Big Dipper was out for the season, but that contradicted team reports that Chamberlain might practice with them any day. If he did come back and test the knee under game circumstances, a crop of young big men provided a great measuring stick—Lew Alcindor in Milwaukee, Bob Rule of Seattle, wide-body Wes Unseld in Baltimore, and San Diego sensation Elvin Hayes.

On March 18, with three games left in the season, Chamberlain rejoined the Lakers squad. Naturally, the team's offensive patterns had changed with Roberson in the post. No longer did the ball go inside to set each play, with wing players running off screens to receive Chamberlain's deft passes. On defense, they had gone to playing a help-based UCLA type of system, forcing the opposition's offensive flow toward the baseline to accommodate Roberson's shortcomings. In the corners, they hoped to trap ball handlers and force turnovers. With five games to play, everyone would now have to readjust. This was asking a great deal of newcomer forward John Tresvant (who hailed from Baylor's alma mater, Seattle, and his high school, Spingarn, where he never made the varsity team), Happy Hairston, and rookies Dick Garrett and Willie McCarter. They hadn't played with Wilt, nor had Keith Erickson much.

"With Wilt back," Mullaney later mused to *Sports Illustrated*, "[N]othing meshed. We were completely out of sync." Basketball is a sport of rhythms, and a sole presence can alter a finely tuned tempo. Chamberlain was the largest presence—both emotionally and physically—in team sports.

The Lakers finished a respectable 46–36, good for second place in the West, at two games behind the Hawks. If a season can be called "good," even when it's primarily played without a man who had recorded 100 points in one game and 55 rebounds against Bill Russell in another, then L.A.'s good fortunes were aided by San Francisco's bad ones. Nate Thurmond broke his leg, Al Attles and recently acquired Jerry Lucas suffered broken hands, and Rick Barry couldn't play because of his legal squabbles with the ABA.

When the Lakers faced upstart Phoenix and Connie Hawkins in the Western Division playoffs, Chamberlain was not 100 percent, but he'd regained his muscle tone and aura. Because of Chamberlain's limited mobility, Mullaney assigned him to guard power forward Paul Silas, who seldom drove to the basket, and he put Baylor on center Jim Fox, a journeyman from the University of South Carolina. The Lakers won the opener at home, 128–112. The Suns evened the series in L.A. with a 114–101 victory. The series moved to Phoenix, and in a third game, during which the Lakers were outrebounded, 66–47, the younger Suns employed fast breaks led by Hawkins to rout L.A., 112–98, and take a 2–1 series lead at home.

Fans learned in *Sports Illustrated* that the Lakers had begun to argue among themselves. During one possession in game three, Dick Garrett became confused on a play set for Jerry West, and he passed to Chamberlain at the foul line. Wilt, in turn, dished to Baylor, who wasn't expecting the ball. His off-balance shot was far off the mark, and when the players walked to huddle, Baylor and Hap Hairston chewed young Garrett out.

Phoenix took game four, 112–102. Hawkins, the former ABA MVP, had put his expansion franchise on his soaring back for a 3–1 series lead. He not only swooped to score, waving the basketball in one hand as Baylor had done a decade before, but he also snared one-handed rebounds and swatted enemy shots with a vengeance. Hawkins received plenty of support from a trimmed-down Paul Silas and guards Dick Van Arsdale and former Laker Gail Goodrich.

Los Angeles faced elimination as the series returned to the Forum; they could not lose a single game. In game five, Lakers forwards Mel Counts and John Tresvant got more physical with the slender Hawkins, and the home team rode 36 points each from Chamberlain and West, to a 138–121 drubbing.

In the pivotal sixth game, Baylor scored 19, second most on the team, but Mullaney had benched him in favor of Erickson. The Lakers' momentum from game five carried over into a 104–93 win in game six, tying the series.

Mullaney arrived at the Forum early the next day at 4 p.m. before practice. A receptionist greeted him with, "Sir, Mr. Baylor is in your office." Mullaney dreaded the encounter with the fading legend.

In *Sports Illustrated*'s account, the prideful Baylor began, "I just wanted you to know, that lifting me in Phoenix was the worst thing that's ever happened to me as a basketball player. I was humiliated." Coming from a man who had endured NBA Finals disappointments and suffered tragic injuries, this was no light statement. Baylor explained how his son, Alan, had friends over to watch the game when, what should happen, but his dad gets pulled in the second half. "When I got home the next day, he was still crying. No one, no one, has ever done anything to embarrass me the way you did."

Mullaney did not have a comeback for Baylor, because, in that situation, there wasn't one. Coaches are tasked with winning at all costs, monumental egos aside. If the team fell to upstart Phoenix, Mullaney's neck was on the line. In Baylor, Chamberlain, Roberson, and sometimes Hairston, Mullaney had four malcontents whose psyches he had to massage, even on the eve of a seventh and deciding game.

By game seven, Wilt had tired of Hawkins's aerial act, and he served notice he was of sound body and stronger than Hawkins, Silas, or rookie center Neal Walk by scoring 30 points and collecting 27 rebounds. In the deciding game, the veteran Lakers also took advantage of sloppy Phoenix ballhandling and outside shooting from guards Garrett and West to clinch the series, 129–94, making L.A. the second team in NBA history to overcome a 3–1 postseason deficit. Atlanta was up next. The Lakers won their first two games at Atlanta, 119–115 and 105–94, then returned home to sweep with a 115–114 overtime victory and a 133–114 clincher.

Joe Mullaney crows in the March 16, 1970, *Sports Illustrated*, "We expect to do away with the Knicks in seven games." It would not be an easy contest. While the New Yorkers lacked the tradition and intimidation factor of the 1956–1969 Celtics, they had set a league record with an 18-game winning streak. Willis Reed and Walt Frazier emerged as young All-Stars, the team had energized Madison Square Garden fans, and they had benefited from the heady DeBusschere's presence even more than the Lakers had from Hairston's. DeBusschere was, by far, the better shooter of the two and had leadership qualities that carried over from his coaching days. In addition, the confident Knicks had bested the up-and-coming Milwaukee Bucks, who were led by lofty Lew Alcindor. Could the seasoned Chamberlain do what the seven-foot rookie from UCLA had not? Would Baylor finally earn a championship now that Russell was out of the picture?

Willis Reed pondered how to position his considerable 245-pound girth to frustrate Chamberlain, who outweighed him by 55 sinewy pounds. Reed's idol, Bill Russell, liked to keep a hand on The Big Dipper's back, and Russell had enough title rings to cover all his fingers, with one to spare. But Reed thought that strategy gave Chamberlain space to step back, dribble, and stuff the ball. If you played facing him, there was the danger he could twist or pivot. So Reed decided to bump Wilt from behind. That way he might settle for a fall-away jump shot, which was no longer his forte.

Game one was played on April 24, 1970. Reed was playing with cortisone shots in his own knees, yet he planned on running Chamberlain to exhaustion. That was a tall order, given Chamberlain's hallmark—his tremendous stamina. Wilt didn't come out to shadow Reed when he began to sink jumpers. Other Knicks made their open shots, gaining them a 17-point advantage. West drew three quick fouls on Frazier. Mullaney told Chamberlain, Baylor, and Garrett to draw their defenders to the weak side to afford West more operating space. "Mr. Clutch" netted 16 in the third quarter. Frazier was afraid to hand-check him under the circumstances. Baylor and Johnny Egan also got hot, and L.A. soon led, 86–84. New York inserted their instant offense, Cazzie Russell, and his sizzle pushed New York to a 124–112 win. In the dressing room, Reed wisely cut Chamberlain some slack, telling *Sports Illustrated*, "I think he's hampered by his knee. I don't think he reacts as quick." It was an astute stance, because it gave Chamberlain—the king of NBA Finals excuses— an out and didn't run the risk of angering The Big Fella, and if Reed's own stiff knee bothered him later in the series, some would be sympathetic.

Game two was played in the basketball-crazed Garden three days later. Chamberlain blocked Reed's first jumper, and with L.A. up, 105–103, with less than a minute left, he challenged Reed at the foul line, where the Knicks center loved to pop a consistently accurate "jay." Reed passed to Frazier on a give-and-go, but when Reed received the return pass and shot, The Big Dipper also got that one. It was one game apiece.

The series returned to the West Coast for games three and four. Former Laker Dick Barnett missed his first four shots, and the Knicks appeared uncomfortable. He did a good job defending West, which freed up Frazier to focus on offense and playmaking. Barnett's hand-checking frustrated West to the point that he earned the fouls for slapping Barnett's hands away. *Sports Illustrated* notes Mullaney protested to ref Mendy Rudolph, "What is this ---?! If you knock a guy's hand away, it's a foul, but if you jab him in his side, it's okay." L.A. surged to a 14-point halftime edge.

New York shook off the doldrums, and with 1:18 left, the game was tied at 96. A minute later, a Barnett hoop put them up, 100–99. Then Barnett fouled Chamberlain, who sank a free throw. At 100-all, DeBusschere nailed a 17-footer. L.A. was out of time-outs. Chamberlain inbounded the ball to West and then began to run to the sidelines, to reach the lockers before the angry fans hit the court if they lost. Only Reed, in a competitive gesture, came out to contest West as he neared the 10-second mark. He overplayed West to his left hand, but West continued to dribble forward. Two seconds, one . . . West launched a shot that bore the suspicious air of confidence. The heave was a mere extension of his normal from-the-hip jumper. The ball sailed cleanly through the net. Chick Hearn—among 18,000 others—went berserk: "The Lakers tie it! The Lakers tie it! Oh my God!" West had reduced DeBusschere to disbelief, as the swarthy forward sat at half-court trying to relive or make sense of the moment. Chamberlain didn't even see the shot. Yet, despite the miracle for the Lakers, New York regrouped and won game three in overtime, 111–108. For his part, West had badly jammed his left thumb. The teams had the next day off, and Dr. Kerlan speculated that if there was a game that night, West would have been sidelined. The glib *New York Daily News* ran a sports cartoon lampooning West's propensity for heroism while wounded. "Nail Jerry's sneakers to the floor with spikes," it reads. "Put him in chains, like Houdini."

Baylor scored 30 points in game four, calling up his own ghostly magic, and West dished out 14 assists, with 37 points for good measure, en route to a 121–115 overtime win. Now it was two all.

In game five, L.A. jumped to a 25–15 lead eight minutes in at Madison Square Garden. Then Reed drove to the bucket, and Wilt stepped sideways to meet his charge. The big men's feet entangled, and Reed fell on top of the basketball. There was no whistle, but the Knicks' captain and NBA MVP lay writhing. He limped off with the trainer's assistance. The Lakers held their lead, 53–40, at the break.

In the locker room, Bill Bradley suggested that New York employ a one-three-one offense to compensate for Reed's absence. Bradley would play the middle, jump shooters Russell and Barnett the perimeters, and Dave Stallworth and DeBusschere the baseline. It was a strategy that said, "Wilt can't guard all of us." If a man got hot, Chamberlain would be forced to come out on that man, leaving the lane open for players to drive. Coach Red Holzman decided it was worth a shot, this being a tied NBA Finals. When Mullaney observed the set, he cried, "They're in a zone!" to Mendy Rudolph, to no avail. Zone defenses were forbidden in the league, but no one said anything about offensive patterns. The Lakers were so befuddled, West took only two shots, and Frazier hounded his former college backup, Dick Garrett.

The Knicks managed to take game five, 107–100. With New York up, 3–2, the drama returned to Hollywood. Reed was sidelined with what turned out to be a strain from hip to knee. Fans had wondered how sound Chamberlain would be in the series, but now it seemed that Reed's fate might decide the championship. The home team was duly inspired. Garrett did his job for a change, popping in eight consecutive shots. Chamberlain had his way with whomever they threw at him—Nate Bowman, DeBusschere, Stallworth, or all of the above. His 45 points and 27 rebounds powered a 135–113 rout.

Now at a tied series, the teams headed back east to play for the title. The Lakers flew a commercial 707 to New York the day before the game. Every team official, a few select celebrities, and some fortunate boosters made the flight. Onboard, shouting from copies of the *Los Angeles Examiner*, was the headline to a Doug Krikorian column: "Wilt Blasts Emphasis on Winning." There, in black and white, Chamberlain said, when all is said and done, the losing team doesn't earn enough credit. But after dropping 45 points and 27 caroms on his opponents, why even mention or contemplate defeat? His bewildered teammates folded the paper over their knees, avoided one another's stares, and searched their own souls. A disillusioned rookie Garrett frowned in disgust as his veteran teammate offered up the ethos of a runner-up. West, a bundle of nerves on his best day, wished Chamberlain had a muzzle on his big mouth. Baylor, hungry and hoping for the title that had eluded him for so long, wondered what went on in that head seven feet from the realities of earth. In fact, before game six—Wilt's monster performance, with Reed out—Baylor had heard Chamberlain say in the locker room, "Gee, I hope we don't lose it."

For Baylor, it was not a matter of hope and doubt, but rather a matter of forcing one's will upon the opposition. When doctors had told him he would never play again, he proved them wrong and willed himself back into playing condition. When the other knee gave, he barked at doubting sportswriters and retooled the nuances of his game. In the face of segregated accommodations, he took a stand. At the 1964 All-Star Game, when Bob Short had threatened to fire him for not playing, he had given the owner a piece of his mind. As Frank Deford writes in his October 1966 *Sports Illustrated* cover feature on Baylor, he was "A Tiger Who Can Beat Anything."

The seventh game of the 1970 NBA championship was played on May 8 at Madison Square Garden. No one in the stands or the media knew if Willis Reed would play. Neither did Reed. Earlier, backstage, the trainer and docs had observed his movements and mood. Coach Holzman told

Reed he would love to have him out there, but if he couldn't go, the team could win without him.

ABC color analyst Jack Twyman told a national TV audience that Reed had received 200 cc's of cortisone for the torn right thigh. The Knicks center did not join his teammates as they took the Garden floor for warm-ups. The Lakers noticed, and Wilt knew he could have his way with Knicks backup center Nate Bowman.

Out on the court, Mullaney noted that it was five minutes past the scheduled start of the game. He told the Lakers' publicity director to go look for Commissioner Walter Kennedy.

The fans were on their feet. Players from both teams kept peeking at the tunnel that led from the locker rooms to the court. Reed was slowly dragging his sore leg through that tunnel, 14 minutes after the network's 7:30 tip-off time. When he became visible, straining with each stride in his clean, white warm-ups, wave after wave of adulation poured from the crowd. For the Lakers, his presence fired the crowd and his teammates, but the telltale gimp was reassuring. With that leg, surely he could not contest Chamberlain. The way he looked, if he was on the level, he could play only a sequence or two without damaging himself for life.

At the opening center jump, only Chamberlain went airborne. Bradley stole the first Lakers pass, fired the ball to Frazier, and Frazier tossed it to Reed. The fans froze. Millions of TV viewers told themselves he couldn't do it. But Reed dragged his bad leg behind him to a position under the basket, shot, and scored. The place was sheer bedlam.

On the Knicks' next possession, Reed swished a shot from the top of the key. "Oh my," L.A. viewers thought. "How long can this go on? The man can't even walk." When the Lakers had the ball, Reed followed Chamberlain in the laboring movements of a one-legged movie pirate. Step-drag, step-drag. But New York was inspired, and they went up, 9–2. Before the Angelenos knew what hit them, they trailed, 38–24. Reed managed 27 minutes of courage that has become engraved in league history. Yet, the day really belonged to Walt Frazier. In all the anticipation, excitement, and stunned Lakers responses, he swiped basketballs at will, driving for convincing, knife-to-the-throat layups. The visitors were demoralized. Frazier netted 36 points, 19 assists, 7 rebounds, and 5 memorable steals. The Lakers lost, 113–99, proving it was not just about Russell when it came to the Finals. Another lefty center born in Louisiana had gotten their goat.

Baylor had begun to think beyond basketball. By the time Chamberlain joined the Lakers, he had expanded his horizons into other business ventures. He and composer Morty Jacobs, a former nightclub accompanist for Dorothy Dandridge, formed a music publishing company called Main Event, Inc. He also continued to do advertisements as one of the most marketable athletes in the United States and a first-tier celebrity of his race. An opinion piece in a 1968 edition of *Dissent* magazine, examining the ads within *Ebony*, notes, "While the ads in *Ebony* still run heavily toward whiskey and beer and hair and skin preparations . . . [t]here's Elgin Baylor, captain of the Los Angeles Lakers, sinking a shot on behalf of Carnation Milk." Baylor was a role model for young children and a safe product pitchman for their mothers. He epitomized the athlete as wholesome hero.

In July 1970, a new venture for the NBA star, Elgin Baylor Productions, scheduled its first show: a concert at the Forum headlined by the hottest act in the United States, the Jackson 5. Baylor's partner was Carl Dickerson of Symbolic Music. In September, Baylor celebrated his 36th birthday.

Baylor only played two games for the 1970–1971 Lakers before suffering a season-ending tear of an Achilles tendon. He averaged 10 points in the two games. On December 2, he underwent surgical repair of the Achilles. The team finished 48–34 under Mullaney, for first place in the new Pacific Division. The young Milwaukee Bucks, who won 66 games led by Lew Alcindor, took over as the leaders of the NBA West.

In March 1971, 21-year-old forward Spencer Haywood, who had jumped from the ABA's Denver Rockets to the NBA's Seattle SuperSonics, was denied permission to play in the NBA because of an eligibility rule forbidding players to turn pro until their college class graduated. Haywood, who had gone pro as a sophomore instead of waiting, sued the NBA and gained an injunction that kept him with Seattle. Judge Warren Ferguson had ruled that (in language Baylor could appreciate since his boycott of the 1959 game in Charleston, West Virginia, and his role in the threatened boycott of the 1964 All-Star Game) "professional athletes cannot be used and treated as merchandise." After a series of appeals that led to the U.S. Supreme Court, Haywood won a ruling that the NBA's "group boycott" violated antitrust law.

The same month Spencer Haywood earned his right to play in Baylor's old college town, Lakers owner Jack Kent Cooke made headlines for reasons other than basketball or the National Hockey League when he helped put on the biggest showcase in boxing history: the March 8, 1971, championship fight between undefeated heavyweights Muhammad Ali and Joe Frazier. Cooke supplied a record $4.5 million for the extravaganza at Madison Square Garden. Each fighter was guaranteed more than $2 million for his night's work—20 times what basketball's greatest players earned in a year.

On June 4, 1971, the Lakers fired Coach Joe Mullaney and offered him a job in the front office with GM Fred Schaus. No official reason was given for Mullaney's termination, but the general thought in the sports media was that Cooke was frustrated by having come so close to, but not winning, a NBA title. Maybe the best way to become champions was to hire a former champion as coach. In August 13, 1971, Baylor told the AP of the upcoming NBA season, "This is definitely the last. I'd have retired after last season if I'd played a full season. Then maybe I would not play this year. I want to retire healthy, on my own. I don't want injury to force my retirement."

That summer, the Lakers had hired former Boston Celtics star and L.A. Jets American Basketball League coach Bill Sharman to lead the franchise. Sharman was a fitness buff, and he introduced the concept of afternoon shootarounds to NBA practices. Chamberlain initially balked at the idea but eventually came around since the workouts were light.

Sharman ran practices with a personal calm one might expect from a perennial league free-throw leader. He seldom swore and only raised his voice in the locker room after losses. During games, his face and body language gave away nothing.

"I was not hired to win a personality contest," Sharman said to *Sports Illustrated* on December 13, 1971, "I was hired to win basketball games."

Out of respect for Chamberlain's veteran status, Sharman listened to his player. In turn, Chamberlain obeyed Sharman's rules. Although the star center rarely fell asleep until almost dawn and got most of his rest during the day, he never arrived late to or missed any of Sharman's game-day practices.

"I was concerned about my relations with Wilt in that I hoped the things I thought were important and those he thought were important would not clash," Sharman told *Sports Illustrated* for their December 13 issue, adding,

Before the season I met with Wilt, Jerry, and Elgin and got their suggestions. I respect their ideas because they are experienced professionals. The only thing I discussed with Wilt that we didn't see eye to eye on was the morning practices. I told him if I had a choice we wouldn't practice at all, but I didn't know any other way to get things done right. I sincerely would like to make an exception for him, but I can't. I'm aware of his sleeping problem, but we often discuss strategy for the night's game at the meetings, and he has to be in on that. I have told him and the rest of the players that any time they don't want to exercise all they have to do is tell me and they won't have to. But they must still come to the morning meeting.

Training camp began in L.A., then moved to Hawaii. Sharman noticed that reserve forward Jim McMillian, who had averaged eight points a game in 1970–1971, was a strong defender with a steady baseline jump shot. Baylor thought McMillian looked like a chubby version of heavyweight boxer Floyd Patterson and dubbed his backup "Floyd Butterball," or "Butter" for short.

Baylor opened the season as the starting small forward. He only scored 14 in the opener against Detroit, and by the fifth game, he had his season high against Chicago, of only 19 points. Jerry West injured his ankle in the fourth game and missed the next five. Nine games into the season, on Halloween, the Lakers were 6–3. Elgin had back-to-back 17-point games against Cincinnati and Seattle but had yet to score 20. McMillian had scored 28 against his hometown Knicks on the second game of the season on October 16, and 39 against the Hawks four days later. Sharman wanted to play McMillian more at small forward.

On November 4, feeling he wasn't really helping his team and not wanting to take playing time away from Jim McMillian, Elgin announced his retirement. Baylor declared to United Press International, reported in newspapers on November 5, 1971, "I wish to announce my retirement from professional basketball as an active player. I have accepted a position with the Lakers for the next three years." He explained that his new role would include "scouting and public relations activities, and some TV broadcasting." He added to UPI that he had "hoped to end [his] career after one last successful season, continuing, "Out of fairness to the fans, to the Lakers and to myself, I have always wanted to perform on the court up to the level and to the standards that I have established throughout my career. I do not want to prolong my career at a time when I cannot meet these standards." He never played after the ninth game of the season.

Upon Baylor's retirement, Sharman said to UPI, "I say without reservation that Elgin Baylor is the greatest cornerman who ever played pro basketball." He continued, "I have always admired Elgin Baylor and knew him to be a superstar. I have found him to be a super person also." Sharman understood Baylor's decision, noting in Roland Lazenby's *The NBA Finals: A 50-Year Celebration*, "He just wasn't the Elgin Baylor of old. I knew he felt bad, and I wanted him to keep playing."

Sharman named West and Chamberlain co-captains of the Lakers. Baylor's replacement, McMillian, went on to average nearly 19 points per game, and the Lakers won a record 33 consecutive games after Baylor stepped aside. They beat the Knicks in the 1972 NBA Finals, avenging their 1970 defeat. The man who made the franchise a West Coast entity was not part of the equation when glory finally arrived.

Jack Kent Cooke had the franchise retire Elgin Baylor's number-22 uniform. "One of my privileges I have enjoyed as owner of the Lakers," Cooke told the AP in an article released on November 5, "has been my association with the man who deserved the reputation 'superstar' as much as any athlete who has ever lived."

Baylor was not the only figure in the NBA to leave the game early that season. After 10 games, Butch van Breda Kolff resigned as coach of the Detroit Pistons, despite having guided them to a 45–37 mark the year before—their first winning record in 15 years. He was replaced by Baylor's old foe, Earl Lloyd, who became the league's second black coach.

During his retirement in the early 1970s, Baylor had a home in northwest Washington, D.C.'s Takoma Park section on Seventh Street. Neither his community activism nor his athletic participation ended when he stepped aside to give the Lakers a better chance at winning. On May 25, 1972, he coached the NBA All-Stars in a game against the ABA All-Stars, the second such game ever played. He was interviewed before the game on independent TV network TVS by his old pal "Hot Rod" Hundley, and he directed a team that starred Oscar Robertson, Wilt Chamberlain, John Havlicek, and Connie Hawkins. The game was played in front of 14,086 fans at Nassau Coliseum, home to the ABA's New York Nets. The NBA won, 106–104.

On June 11, 1972, Baylor was honored at a black-tie testimonial dinner at Now Lounge at L.A.'s Ambassador Hotel. Tickets for the "Evening with Elgin" went on sale for $17.50, with proceeds slated to assist a scholarship fund for local Jefferson High School. Lakers announcer Chick Hearn served as master of ceremonies, and nearly 800 attended, among them former teammates, coaches, opponents, and journalists, such as Jim Murray. There was Lakers assistant and former foe K. C. Jones; Dr. Robert Kerlan; retired boxing legend Sugar Ray Robinson; New York Yankees co-owner Del Webb; Green Bay Packers great Willie Davis; former Dodgers outfielder Tommy Davis; and city councilman Tom Bradley, who presented a resolution from the city council. Fred Schaus, then coaching at Purdue, was introduced, and former NBA forwards and centers LeRoy Ellis, Tom Hawkins, and Rudy LaRusso—all of whom played both with and against Baylor—attended the gala. Special presentations were made by the United Helms Savings Foundation, which had named Baylor to both its college- and pro-basketball halls of fame, and Jerry West, who gave Baylor a large gold trophy consisting of a life-size basketball on a pedestal. The inscription read, "Elgin Baylor, as Great an Athlete as You Are, You Are an Even Greater Human Being."

Although he had retired, Baylor could still play. On August 4, he laced up his sneakers to play on a team called the Greg Morris All-Stars (after the black costar of the hit TV series *Mission Impossible*), alongside former UCLA guard Mike Warren at the basketball camp of former Compton High School and UCLA star Fred Goss. On the 11th, he played in a benefit game at UCLA's Pauley Pavilion for the Dr. Ralph Bunche Scholarship Fund. This time, his teammates on the Elgin Baylor Pro Stars would be Jim McMillian, Hap Hairston, Pat Riley, and Flynn Robinson of the champion Lakers; Bob Rule and Lee Winfield of the Sonics; and former USC guard Mack Calvin of the ABA Carolina Cougars. They played the UCLA Alumni, a team consisting of Kareem Abdul-Jabbar, Mahdi Abdul-Rahman (formerly Walt Hazzard), Lucius Allen, Sidney Wicks, Curtis Rowe, John Vallely, Henry Bibby, Steve Patterson, and Kenny Booker. The UCLA Alumni won the game, 135–131, in front of 10,000 fans. In the first game of a doubleheader, the Johnny Brown All-Stars—named after the *Laugh-In* and *Good Times* TV comedian/dancer and including Rudy LaRusso; singer-actor Pat Boone, who had co-owned the ABA's Oakland Oaks; and actors Joseph Campanella, Dennis Weaver, and Kent McCord, costar of the TV cop show *Adam-12*—would face a team of real Los Angeles Police Department members.

Later in the month, Baylor teamed with LaRusso, Flynn Robinson, former University of Massachusetts star Bill Tindall, and disc jockeys and staff from urban radio station KGFJ, to defeat a team called the Bank of America Club, 82–73, at Crenshaw High. The game benefited research for sickle-cell disease. A few days later, Baylor appeared at an inner-city Ralph's Market as part of a voter registration drive sponsored by the city's Civic Action Committee, a group in which entertainers Warren Beatty, Sally Field, Goldie Hawn, Eartha Kitt, Tina Sinatra, Jon Voight, and Dennis Weaver participated, as did former athletes LeRoy Ellis and Rafer Johnson. In October, Baylor joined such celebrities as Sammy Davis Jr., Bob Hope, Carroll O'Connor, Danny Thomas, Joey Bishop, Pearl Bailey, Milton Berle, and Don Rickles, as well as sports luminaries Willie Shoemaker, Don Drysdale, Jackie Robinson, Jesse Owens, and Chick Hearn, in a 17-and-a-half-hour KTLA telethon on behalf of the Sugar Ray Robinson Youth Foundation. On January 6, 1973, Baylor appeared on television's *Soul Train*; other guests included singers Tyrone Davis and Lyn Collins. That year, he also worked on a committee to sponsor a performance of the black musical *Don't Bother Me, I Can't Cope*, as a fundraiser for the mayoral campaign of friend Tom Bradley.

In their August 13, 1972, issue, Baylor was asked by *JET* magazine to name his most memorable game. "I really don't think about those games. It was great when it happened, but the next morning you think about the next game," he said. "This is a game where you have to prove yourself every night."

11

JAZZ DUET

But that's a gift. Some guys spend half their lives trying to invent
something like that.—"Fast Eddie" Felson, *The Color of Money*

By Christmas of 1972, rumors had surfaced that Elgin Baylor would
succeed Seattle SuperSonics coach Tom Nissalke. Sportswriters had been
suggesting Baylor as a pro coach ever since the Phoenix Suns were
searching for the proper guide in the summer of 1972. On July 19, 1973,
he coached the Pro All-Stars of the Southern California Summer League
against the UCLA Alumni. Baylor told the *Los Angeles Times* on July 18,
1973, "I am certainly looking forward to . . . coaching against a team
directed by John Wooden."

Baylor had also been dabbling in TV sports announcing, and he hosted
Rap on Sports, a topical show the Chrysler Corporation sponsored on
black radio stations. In the fall of 1973, he signed with CBS to do color
analysis of National Basketball Association games, along with Brent
Musburger and "Hot Rod" Hundley. It was the first season of NBA
telecasts for CBS. On some broadcasts, Baylor teamed with veteran National Football League announcer Pat Summerall, who handled play-by-
play duties. In one game featuring Pistons center Bob Lanier, who wore
size-22 sneakers, Baylor remarked, "Gee, he's got big feet," to which
Summerall replied, "He sure does."

When the Warriors were eliminated from the postseason in 1974, CBS
replaced Baylor with Golden State star Rick Barry. Soon thereafter, Baylor told *JET* magazine, "I was really quite bitter when I first learned that I
had been fired, but it's a cold business. I still haven't heard from anyone

connected with the show. They said they tried to reach me and I was out."
Baylor's attorney, Fred Rosenfeld, had broken the news to him. Baylor
had assumed his job was secure because he signed a one-year contract,
and he said CBS implied that "everything was fine and that they were
pleased with me." He also said the network told him ratings were low,
although he was never shown viewership numbers.

In the 1973–1974 season, Wilt Chamberlain was hired by the
American Basketball Association's San Diego Conquistadors to become
a player-coach for the team, but the Lakers blocked Chamberlain from
playing in the rival ABA, citing contractual obligations with L.A. Chamberlain spent most of the season on the sidelines, not playing and not
really coaching either. That probably didn't surprise Baylor, since in an
October 25, 1973, article for *JET* magazine, he had expressed doubts
about Chamberlain's ability to teach the game:

> I don't think he can coach. What could he possibly help a player with?
> He doesn't have the temperament to be a coach. He never had any
> discipline. He hardly ever came to practice, and when he did, he didn't
> work hard because he didn't think he had to practice. He didn't think
> he needed it.

Baylor turned down some potential head coaching offers that did not
interest him. In September 1974, he became an assistant coach with the
new expansion New Orleans Jazz. He explained to the *Los Angeles
Times*, "I said if I'm going to get into this, I'm going to get into it right. I
wanted to go somewhere other than having a boss who was just an employer." Two of the people influential in convincing Baylor to take the
job were longtime Lakers scout Bill Bertka, who was VP of basketball
operations for the new club, and Fred Rosenfeld, Baylor's attorney and
also the team's president. Baylor added, "I wanted to work with a guy I
know and with people I would know."

Baylor predicted big things for the team. "On paper this is probably
the best expansion team ever," he said. "There's even a possibility of
making the playoffs."

Sam Jones also joined the Jazz as an assistant coach in 1974–1975. He
was uncomfortable with the front-office politics and felt they were a far
cry from his days with the Celtics dynasty, although the situation wasn't
unlike what many other black players had confronted throughout the

1950s and 1960s. "There were some things I didn't like," said Jones to the website Sports by Brooks on November 3, 2009, continuing,

> There was a black kid who we really liked, a good player, a top-15 rebounder, but ownership said we couldn't take him because he was married to a white lady. I thought that was a travesty. It just wasn't in my mode of thinking. We did take a guy from California, Stu Lantz, and he was married to a white girl, too, but the team didn't realize it until it was too late.

Former ABA player Gerald Govan, who played in New Orleans in the late 1960s, says in Mark Kriegel's 2008 book *Pistol: The Life of Pete Maravich*, "It was kind of interesting being a black person there because you couldn't get a place to live. In fact [All-ABA guard] Jimmy Jones was staying in the projects when he first got there." In an anecdote in *Pistol*, Govan told a black teammate, Oregon native Steve "Snapper" Jones, "Man you don't have that accent. You can call and do the talking on the phone, and we might be able to get a place to live."

Scotty Robertson was the Jazz's first head coach. Team management hoped he would employ the principles that brought considerable college success to his team at Louisiana Tech. Robertson told the media, "I give an assistant coach an awful lot of responsibility. Elgin Baylor has the background to handle the job and take care of these responsibilities." The New Orleans Jazz franchise had an auspicious beginning.

Sam Jones told Sports by Brooks that he believed Robertson "had some good ideas," adding, "One of them reminded me of Red [Auerbach], who used to say if you want to be champions, you had to dress like champions, look professional. Scotty fined some guys for not dressing well, and management wouldn't back him up." In the mid-1970s, dress codes were less common among professional sports teams, and Americans in general had become more casual, so Robertson's off-the-court policies were somewhat unusual.

New Orleans didn't quite fulfill its promise during that first season. The expansion team lost 11 games before its first win, a game played in front of only 5,465 fans in New Orleans Municipal Auditorium. After three more losses, management told Jones they were firing Robertson, whose current record with them was 1–14. "I asked who would be the next coach, because Elgin Baylor and I were the only assistants, and was told that 'New Orleans wasn't ready for a black head coach,'" Jones told

Sports by Brooks. At the time the Jazz entered the NBA, the league's black assistant coaches were John Barnhill of the Lakers, Bob Hopkins in Seattle, Jim Davis with the Pistons, Bernie Bickerstaff of the Washington Bullets, and the Knicks' Dick Barnett. Al Attles and Bill Russell were among the few black head coaches, but in that regard, pro basketball was more progressive than Major League Baseball or pro football, which had none.

Baylor was named the team's interim coach. He lost the only game he coached as an interim, when, as a replacement for Robertson, the Jazz brought in Butch van Breda Kolff, who Sam Jones said, "wasn't real professional about some things." New Orleans was an anything-goes party town, and "Butch was right there with the best of them every night," recalled Hot Rod Hundley, who broadcast Jazz games. VBK, as he was called, frequented the popular New Orleans bar Pat O'Brien's, and *Sports Illustrated* reports he celebrated his 54th birthday with a "nine-hour pub crawl." Needless to say, his players did not respect him. Assistant coach Jones felt the same way, and he left soon thereafter, saying, "[O]ne year of that was enough for me."

Van Breda Kolff clashed, in particular, with the team's superstar, Pete Maravich, much as he had with Chamberlain in L.A. "Butch had a big ego," recalls Hundley in the Maravich biography *Pistol*. Maravich's father, Press, who had coached his son at Louisiana State University, felt the Jazz were "only cutting their throats" by thwarting his son's playing style and limiting him to 38 minutes a game.

Under the new coach, throughout the next couple of months their record was 4–26, and at the end of January it was 5–42. The Jazz finally turned things around and, in February, went 10–5, to finish the season at 23–59.

In January 1975, Elgin and Ruby Baylor agreed to a divorce, in which they divided community property valued at $400,000. The court ordered Baylor, age 40, to pay $650 in monthly support to Alan, 14, and Allison, 10. Ruby, who was only 35, was employed with the Los Angeles Department of Urban Development.

That spring, less than 10 years after the Celtics had hired a black coach, Bill Russell, to succeed Red Auerbach, K. C. Jones of the Washington Bullets and Al Attles of the Golden State Warriors coached their respective teams to the 1975 NBA Finals. The national media paid little attention to the milestone in racial progress, as the fiery former defensive guards paced the sidelines in print shirts and leisure suits. The 12-man playoff roster for Golden State featured 10 black players, while Washington had nine black players—and two of Washington's three white players received little playing time.

In 1976, the Lakers hired Jerry West as head coach. Wilt Chamberlain wondered to United Press International, "I'd like to know how Jerry got to be a candidate, considering he's never coached before. . . . Was Elgin Baylor offered the job? I'm just wondering since he and Jerry, both, did so much for the Lakers." In addition, Wilt reminded a UPI reporter, "Elg has coached at the assistant level." This was magnanimous on The Big Dipper's part, given how Baylor had doubted Chamberlain's ability to coach San Diego's NBA team a few years earlier.

Shep Goldberg, the Lakers' PR director, told the *Los Angeles Times*, "I don't even know if Baylor was interested in the job. We couldn't approach him because of his Jazz contract." Goldberg—who acknowledged that Jack Kent Cooke had strongly considered former Lakers assistant K. C. Jones, who was inexplicably fired by the Washington Bullets after leading them to a NBA championship final—added that he was unsure of Baylor's ability to pilot the Lakers: "West was always our floor leader on the court. . . . West was more expressive and outspoken than Baylor. West was better equipped to express his feelings."

As discussed earlier, commonly held impressions of Baylor and West were not true. During their playing days, West was more of a loner, a player who led by example, hustling and playing injured. He didn't enjoy hanging out with the boys (generally a prerequisite for pro basketball coaches in those days), and he was more pensive than expressive. West even admits in his biography, *Mr. Clutch*, and in numerous magazine articles that he could be moody and uncommunicative. By contrast, Baylor was not only gabby and outspoken on every topic known to man, but he was also intellectually inquisitive, a team leader on and off the court, a captain, and an influential labor rep. The man with the nickname "Motormouth" had the last word on team blazers, airplane trivia contests, and current events. Whatever the Lakers' other reasons for not considering Baylor for head coach, neither lack of leadership nor reticence could have been a factor.

Yet, even now, different people continue to offer different impressions of Baylor's demeanor. "I was talking with Scott Ostler of the *L.A. Times* about Elgin a few years ago," said Dave Stone. "He said Elgin has two personalities, a private one, around the public, and another talkative one around teammates. He strikes me as very comfortable in his status as a player, with no need to toot his own horn," continued Stone.

The NBA continued to enhance its profile as a major sports league, the status to which Elgin Baylor had contributed so much. The Bullets had moved to the nation's capital and a new 19,000-seat arena in suburban Maryland. For the 1975–1976 season, the New Orleans Jazz moved into the new Louisiana Superdome, where basketball seating capacity was 19,203 and tickets ranged from $3.50 to $7.50 a seat. Games featured exciting entertainment acts and promotions. A Mardi Gras–style second line processed into the huge arena, led by Elena Tatum, who was known for putting "voodoo" curses on opposing players, so much so that Warrior Rick Barry once asked that she be removed from the Dome. Promotions drew fans by advertising a Rolex watch to be given to someone whose lucky number was selected from the game program or a Subaru to be awarded to anyone who could sink a basket from half-court.

Elgin Baylor finally earned an opportunity to serve as head coach when Jazz leadership had a sudden upset in the middle of the 1976–1977 season. On December 13, 1976, VBK was fired. Baylor was once again hired as interim coach. The team was 14–12 at that time, although guards Maravich and Gail Goodrich had missed games due to injuries. Peter Finney's headline in the *New Orleans States-Item* read, "So Long, Butch," with the subhead "The Amateurs Have Taken over the Jazz." When general manager Barry Mendelson waived a seventh-round draft pick named Andy Walker without consulting van Breda Kolff, the Associated Press reported on December 15, 1976, that the coach said, "Then . . . let him coach them."

The fans loved VBK so much that Mendelson received death threats after the firing and had to have police escorts to the games.

In Baylor's first game as head coach, he played Pete Maravich for 47 minutes—much longer than the 38 minutes he had averaged under van Breda Kolff. "Pistol" Pete hit a career-high 51 points in a 120–117 win over the Kansas City–Omaha Kings. After his second game in the new position, the Jazz hired Baylor for the remainder of 1976–1977. Bill Bertka was named his assistant. Elgin Baylor, Seattle's Bill Russell, and Golden State's Al Attles were now the only black head coaches in the league, although two-thirds of the players were black.

Pete Maravich developed into the NBA's new boy wonder and top showman while with the Jazz with Baylor as coach. (Baylor coached the team from December 1976 until 1979.) Indeed, Maravich had been influenced by his predecessor long before he ever played under him. Sports commentator Billy Packer believed Maravich learned some of his moves while a boy watching the Baylors, Wests, and Robertsons on national TV. As part of basketball's first real television generation, Maravich indirectly picked up elements of the D.C.-area schoolyard game that produced Baylor. The two players even had some of the same moves. Like Baylor's at Seattle and Minneapolis, Maravich's passes were so sudden and deceptive, they often caught his teammates unaware. Between Maravich and Baylor, they had every shot in the book and invented new ones. The two also shared common ground as showmen. Their respective NBA franchises depended on them, and owners banked on their appeal.

Unlike Baylor, however, Pistol Pete had trouble getting along with both teammates and coaches. He had feuded with Atlanta Hawks coaches for four seasons and hadn't gotten along with a superior since his father coached him at LSU. Yet, he and Baylor got along famously. Baylor stated he communicated well with his star guard, saying Maravich was the "best I've ever seen," as Jay Jennings reports in the February 11, 2007, edition of the *New York Times*. Maravich never complained to the media about Baylor, either. The two showy scorers seemed to understand one another; they belonged to a unique fraternity. "Stars know stars," Mendelson is quoted as saying in *Pistol*. But Baylor believed Maravich had the skills to back up his star power. "Oscar Robertson was the best guard I ever played against. Jerry West was the best I ever played with. Pete is the best I've ever seen," relates Baylor in the book *Maravich*.

Maravich would occasionally try to coax Baylor back onto the court. Biographer Kriegel writes in *Pistol* that Maravich would ask Baylor, "How you think you'd do against E. C.?" referring to Jazz forward E. C. Coleman, one of the best defensive forwards in the league. The question turned into a challenge when Baylor, spotting Coleman three inches in height and 16 years in youth, played him one-on-one. Pistol Pete was delighted, since he loved basketball and craved great offense. The men played makers-takers, to 10 baskets. Baylor drove past Coleman for a 1–0 lead. He beat the All-Defensive Team player, 10–0; Coleman never gained possession of the ball.

Maravich did cause problems for Baylor when it came to player relations. His career as a Hawk had been tainted by what Maravich perceived
as jealousy on the part of black players, who resented the big contract
awarded to him when he was an unproven pro. Pistol Pete's professional
teammates continued to resent him and his big contract from then on-
ward.

Maravich, who had been named team captain, was especially disliked
by the team's next best player, Len "Truck" Robinson, the beefy forward
teammates called "The Power." When Robinson said the Jazz didn't employ enough ball movement (perhaps euphemistically claiming that Maravich was a ball hog), Maravich went without shooting until the fourth
quarter in a close game with New York. In *Sports Illustrated*, on December 5, 1977, another teammate said Maravich was "not making sacri-
fices," to which Maravich answered, "If they want me to sacrifice, I'll
sacrifice." He went 4-for-5 shooting, with 15 assists, against Seattle the
next night. A couple of games later he reverted to form, scoring 39,
including a game winner with 15 seconds to play. "I'm the white boy
making the most money," Maravich told *Sports Illustrated*'s Curry Kirk-
patrick for the December 4, 1978, issue, of his feud with Robinson. Robinson's agent insisted the Jazz had "two sets of rules, one for Pete and one
for the rest of the players." Jazz center Rich Kelley termed Baylor a rather
"passive" coach.

Although Coach Baylor acknowledged that the player rivalry caused
the Jazz to play "disgusting basketball," he disagreed about Maravich's
team play. According to *Pistol*, Baylor said, "I don't think it was ever a
question of Pete being selfish. He just felt more confidence in his ability
to get the job done than the others. But I kept talking to him and talking to
him, and finally I got him to play in a way that was beneficial to the
team." Baylor, who had always found a way to get along with fellow star
Jerry West, encouraged Maravich to get his teammates more involved in
the offense, rather than trying to win games by himself. Baylor had been
there—starring on a Seattle University team where opposing defenses
focused on him and then being the Lakers' star before Jerry West blos-
somed as a scorer. Maravich asked to be traded, but there was no movement in that regard.

Maravich was beset by physical challenges in the 1977–1978 season.
On January 31, 1978, he had scored 26 points and was about to pass for
his 15th assist in a game against Buffalo. He threw a fan favorite—a

between-the-legs pass upcourt to a wide-open forward, Aaron James, who easily scored. But Maravich's right knee buckled with what witnesses called a "snapping sound." Of the play on which his star was injured, Baylor reflects in *Pistol*, "Just make the simple basic pass—the guy's wide open. But it cost him. And it cost us. No doubt we would have made the playoffs."

When Maravich returned to the team in March, the *States-Item*'s Ron Brocato wrote that he was "[j]ust a shadow of himself." Pistol wore a knee brace, and when he played the knee swelled with fluid. He played 12 scoreless minutes against the New Jersey Nets, which reminded Baylor of his own comeback attempts a decade earlier. "He wasn't the same player," Baylor comments in *Pistol*. "I guess the knee was more severe than anybody thought." Maravich gave in and had surgery to remove a torn lateral meniscus cartilage.

The next season, he developed tendinitis in his knee after a November 23, 1978, win over Golden State. The problem was reminiscent of Baylor's own playing career; the best remedies for Maravich were rest and exercise—opposite ends of the spectrum. Baylor didn't care for Pete missing practices, but that was the "rest" part of the equation.

The Jazz finished that season 26–56, with the worst record in the NBA in 1978–1979, and Baylor was fired on April 11. He was ready, it seemed, telling UPI, "It will be like getting out of prison."

Managing general partner Larry Hatfield called Baylor a "class guy" and said to UPI on April 12, 1979, "Many of the ball club's problems had nothing to do with Elgin's ability as a coach."

Elgin Baylor once summed up his situation in the *Review of the News*, 1977, saying, "Coaching is easy. Winning is the hard part."

12

CLIPPER COMMAND

Can't anybody here play this game?—Casey Stengel, baseball manager, expansion New York Mets

The Los Angeles Clippers' first incarnation was as the 1970–1971 National Basketball Association expansion franchise the Buffalo Braves. The Braves became a talented young squad relatively quickly, starring such players as Bob Kaufman, Ernie DiGregorio, and three-time NBA scoring king Bob McAdoo. Filmmaker and businessman Irving H. Levin traded the Boston Celtics for ownership of the Braves franchise. Levin moved the team to San Diego in 1978, where they traded away first-round draft rights (which Philadelphia used to acquire Charles Barkley) for guard World B. Free.

Donald Sterling (née Tokowitz) was born to Susan and Mickey Tokowitz in Chicago, Illinois, in Depression era 1934, the same year as Elgin Baylor. When he was a toddler, Sterling's family moved to the Boyle Heights area of L.A. Donald attended Theodore Roosevelt High School in Los Angeles. There, he was on the gymnastics squad and elected president of his class. After high school, he studied at Los Angeles State, where he graduated in 1956. From there, Sterling went to L.A.'s Southwestern University School of Law, where he earned his juris doctor in 1960. In the early 1960s, when the Lakers moved to L.A. with Elgin Baylor, Sterling began to establish himself in his field, first as a divorce attorney, then as an lawyer for those who had suffered injuries in accidents. It was as an adult that he changed his surname to Sterling. In the

1960s, he bought an apartment complex known as Lesser Towers. He later changed the name to Sterling Towers.

Sterling became indirectly involved with the NBA in 1979. Dentist Dr. Jerry Buss used $2.7 million he earned from selling apartment buildings to Sterling to buy the Los Angeles Lakers, the National Hockey League's L.A. Kings, and the L.A. Forum from owner Jack Kent Cooke. Buss suggested that Sterling purchase a NBA team himself. In 1981, Sterling bought the Clippers for more than $12 million. He moved the team to Los Angeles for the 1984–1985 season.

In poorly conceived transactions, the Clippers traded stars Tom Chambers, Ricky Pierce, and former DePaul All-American Terry Cummings. The 1984–1985 team was 31–51. In 1985–1986, Sterling's franchise posted a 32–50 mark. In 1986, the team hired Elgin Baylor as general manager, at a salary of $64,800 a year. Baylor had no agent when negotiating his salary, because, as he later told the *Los Angeles Times* on November 12, 2010, "Donald does not like to talk to agents."

As a result of the unfortunate trades of the aforementioned stars, the 1986–1987 Clippers finished 12–70, at the time the third worst campaign in league history. With the fourth overall pick in the 1987 NBA Draft, Baylor and the Clippers selected Georgetown University forward Reggie Williams. The Bulls took Scottie Pippen of Central Arkansas with the next pick, and North Carolina and Cal-Berkeley guards Kenny Smith and Kevin Johnson went sixth and seventh, respectively. Williams, a 6'7" scorer from a former national championship team, was far better known than Pippen, who played against lesser opponents, and bigger than the two guards selected after him. He averaged only 10 points per game in two seasons with the Clippers, but 18 and 17 a game for Denver in 1991–1992 and 1992–1993, respectively.

The 1987–1988 Clippers won only 17 games in Baylor's second season as GM. Michael Cage was their best player, and Gene Shue replaced Don Chaney as their coach. In the 1988 NBA Draft, the Clippers, selecting first, chose Danny Manning, a versatile 6'11" player who had led an otherwise pedestrian Kansas team to the NCAA basketball championship title. Manning could score, pass, and handle the ball, and was named College Player of the Year in all the major media and coaches polls. As a rookie, he was limited to 26 games, before a torn anterior cruciate ligament required him to undergo arthroscopic knee surgery, a procedure that did not exist when his general manager was a NBA superstar. Manning had averaged 16.7 points, 3 assists, and 6.7 rebounds. Other L.A. starters were burly forward Ken Norman, who averaged 18 points; center Benoit Benjamin, who scored 16 a game and averaged nearly 3 blocked shots; and Pitt product Charles Smith, another forward who averaged 16 points. Former University of San Francisco All-American guard Quintin Dailey averaged 16, and defensive backcourt stopper Gary Grant of Michigan averaged 2 steals, 7 assists, and 11 points for the young squad. The team finished 21–61, 10–28 for Gene Shue, who had coached both Baltimore and Philadelphia to NBA Finals in the 1970s, and 11–33 for his replacement, Don Casey.

The Clippers drafted Duke All-American Danny Ferry in 1989, but rather than negotiate with the hapless Clippers, Ferry chose to play professionally in Italy. Although the Lakers were, by far, the most popular pro team in town, Clippers fans had anticipated a stellar frontcourt featuring multiskilled big men Danny Manning and Danny Ferry. Maybe they would become the Larry Bird and Kevin McHale of the West Coast. And their supporting cast was young and promising. But Ferry remained in Italy, where he shared a house with teammate Brian Shaw, a home paid for by their ball club.

In 1989–1990, Don Casey coached Baylor's Clippers to a 30–52 finish. Manning, although never as mobile after his ACL surgery, missed only 11 games and again averaged 16 points. Charles Smith scored 21 a game, Norman 16 a game, and a new acquisition, leaper Ron Harper, 23 points. Casey was fired in place of Mike Schuler. Schuler had coached the Portland Trail Blazers to a 49–33 record in 1986–1987, when he was named NBA Coach of the Year.

Most fans were unaware that some of the Clippers' misfortunes were a result of their ownership. Baylor recalls in the November 9, 2010, installment of *USA Today* that Sterling said, "Well that's a lot of money for a poor black" during contract negotiations for Manning, who was the son of an American Basketball Association and National Basketball Association player named Ed Manning. Baylor went on to say that Manning got "upset" and "stormed out." Despite Sterling's racist reservations, the Clippers signed Manning to a five-year contract for a total $10.5 million.

Fans thought the Clippers were cursed, especially by nagging injuries to talented big men. Despite one setback after another, the Clippers' GM refused to give in to pessimism. "I'm not a superstitious person, and I don't believe in jinxes," Baylor told the *Los Angeles Times* on December

17, 1991. "Bad things just happen. Unfortunately, they happened to us every year. But I've always felt that our time would come."

The highest-paid Clippers were injury-prone Danny Manning at $2.3 million a year, Ron Harper at $1.65 million, and Doc Rivers at nearly $1.2 million. Seven men were earning at least $1 million in salary. As a player, Baylor had topped out at $150,000 and signed for only $20,000 as a rookie. When asked about the lofty NBA salaries at that time, Baylor reminded the *Times* on December 22, 1991, "In '75 and '76, I said that in the next 10 years, players would be making $5 million a year. I don't resent it, I expected it." Indeed, he and his contemporaries helped pave the way for the gravy train.

Baylor expressed brighter hopes for his 1991–1992 team. "The team has good chemistry," he told the *Times*. "You try to achieve that. You look for talent, but you look for other things—a work ethic, character, motivation. Some players are not self-motivated." The Clippers confirmed Baylor's confidence that season by winning eight in a row in one stretch during November and December, but 15 of their first 24 games were played at home. Unlike past squads, they overcame large deficits to win games, including coming from 19 points behind Utah at halftime on Friday, December 13, and, not long thereafter, winning after trailing the Warriors by 18 in the first half. Doc Rivers was providing floor leadership and defense on the wing, center James Edwards brought championship experience from his days as a Detroit Piston, and former University of Pittsburgh standout Charles Smith was a big man looking to survive the supposed injury curse. Baylor had high praise for Smith. He told the *Los Angeles Times* in a December 17, 1991, article, "Smith can do everything. He can drive, shoot outside, rebound, and defend. He's very quick. Exactly what level he reaches will depend on how badly he wants to become great."

No matter what ups and downs the Clippers experienced, Los Angeles was a Lakers town, in large part due to Baylor's past. Despite the November 1991 retirement of popular Laker Magic Johnson, who had been diagnosed with HIV, the Lakers placed seventh in NBA attendance in 1991–1992.

Clippers coach Mike Schuler lasted only 45 games into the 1991–1992 season, winning just 21 of them. Former University of Southern California guard and ABA All-Star Mack Calvin was 1–1 as a placeholder coach, before Baylor hired proven college and pro winner Larry Brown.

Brown, a product of both Frank McGuire and Dean Smith's highly successful University of North Carolina programs, had played and coached for champions in the ABA. More recently, he had NCAA success at UCLA as one of John Wooden's successors, and Kansas, where his underdog 1988 team won the national championship. Under his guidance, the team won 23 and lost only 12, finishing fifth in the NBA's Pacific Division, with a 45–37 record (29–12 at home) and making the playoffs.

Manning, who had led Brown's Kansas teams, averaged 19 points a game for the Clippers that season, and Harper 18. Manning increased his average to 22 points during the playoff series against Utah, where the Clippers were competitive before bowing to a strong young Utah Jazz team, three games to two. Fans looking toward the future were encouraged that NBA All-Star Manning was only 25 and Smith 26. Former Michigan players Gary Grant and Loy Vaught were also young, although Edwards and Rivers were more than 30.

Brown went on to coach the 1992–1993 team to a lackluster 41–41 mark. Manning played in 79 games and scored almost 23 points a night and was again named an All-Star. Ron Harper contributed another 18 per game. Rivers was gone, and 27-year-old Mark Jackson ran the offense, averaging 14 points and 8.8 assists. At fourth in the talent-rich Pacific Division, the team made the postseason, playing the Houston Rockets to five games (in a best-of-five series) in a first-round loss. The Clippers drew only 532,625 spectators to the old Sports Arena, finishing 23rd among 27 NBA teams in home attendance. The nomadic Larry Brown resigned and took a position coaching the Indiana Pacers.

Former NBA journeyman Bob Weiss took over as coach for 1993–1994, and despite the addition of a few former All-Stars the likes of 34-year-old Mark Aguirre and Dominique Wilkins, the team sank to 27–55. They drew fewer fans than any league club that year—less than 472,000, down some 60,000 from Brown's previous year as coach. The Clippers were again the butt of late-night TV comedians' jokes and a draft lottery team. Manning played only half the season due to injury.

Things grew worse as Baylor brought in former Celtics championship coach Bill Fitch. The 1994–1995 Clippers won only 17 of 82 games, one of the worst records in league history. They were last in attendance again, and their scoring leader, Loy Vaught, tallied less than 18 points per game. Such players as Lamond Murray, former UCLA guard Pooh Richardson, and Malik Sealy occupied starting roles. Gone were the starters from the

1992 playoff team. Yet, mediocre center Stanley Roberts, perennially burdened with weight problems, made nearly $3.5 million of Donald Sterling's money.

Baylor's managerial hands were tied by Sterling. The owner discouraged him from signing players to multiyear contracts, which were standard in the NBA. He also did not pay Baylor as well as the majority of the league's GMs. The most Baylor ever earned in the position was $350,000 a year.

Despite these handicaps, Baylor attempted to stay current with league trends. He attributed the pace of the 1990s game not to Magic Johnson or Michael Jordan: "The game has changed," he told the *Los Angeles Times* for their December 22, 1991, edition. "Nate Archibald was the one who changed it, to my way of thinking," he said. "It's become a fast-break, cheap-basket—what I call the cheap basket—game today. You don't take 22 seconds to get the shot off anymore; you fast break it."

On October 14, 2000, Baylor's 90-year-old mother, Uzziel, died after a prolonged illness. Her last recorded address was Harpers Ferry, West Virginia. The family sold her home at 3616 South Dakota Avenue, Northeast, in Washington, for $145,000 on March 24 of that year. Ruby Baylor has since moved back to the city, where she resides in a quiet neighborhood dominated by Catholic University, only minutes from the former Baylor parents' home on South Dakota Avenue.

In 2003, sports announcer Dave Stone was hospitalized with an abdominal aortic aneurism. After returning home eight days later, his phone rang and his wife answered. "No way!" she giggled into the mouthpiece. "It was Elgin calling me to wish me well," Stone recalled to the author. Baylor did not know Stone but had heard from someone that he was under hospital care. "I had tears in my eyes," said Stone. "I have nothing but the utmost respect for him, and I told him that story about when I was 11, and how my father had called him a mensch."

When Baylor turned 75 in September 2009, WTEM sports radio host and longtime Georgetown basketball coach John Thompson devoted much of his daily program to a discussion of him. During the afternoon show, which aired in greater Washington, D.C., but was heard online nationwide, Thompson told his audience he had called Baylor on his birthday to thank him for inspiring him and so many other Washington-area players. The giant former coach reminded Baylor of a summer pickup game in 1957, when Baylor, then frequenting Washington's toughest courts with Kansas star Wilt Chamberlain, chose a skinny, teenaged Thompson as the last teammate for a schoolyard game. "Elgin remembered it!" exclaimed the man Washingtonians call "Big John." Old-school listeners called in with their own special memories of Baylor, the local hero.

Sterling terminated Baylor right before the 2008–2009 NBA season. Baylor, then 74, sued the owner for age discrimination. In addition, he filed against Sterling on the grounds of "mental and economic distress." The suit was for $2 million. It came 50 years after Baylor had refused to play in a NBA game because of segregated team lodging in Charleston, West Virginia. The *Times* reported that according to the court claim, Sterling told Baylor that he wanted to fill his team with "poor black boys from the South and a white head coach." The suit noted those comments, while alleging the "Caucasian head coach was given a four-year, $22 million contract," but Baylor's salary had been "frozen at a comparatively paltry $350,000 since 2003."

Some considered Sterling a tightwad who publicly berated his players and viewed them as objects. He used to yell insults at Clippers players while they shot free throws. In 2013, ESPN commentator and veteran sportswriter Kevin Blackistone told the author, "If I were a black player in the NBA, I would never play for Donald Sterling. He shouldn't even be in the league." Sterling was approached by parties interested in either purchasing the franchise or moving it from L.A. Instead, he spent his own money to build a headquarters and training facility.

Sterling's negative headlines were not confined to basketball. In November 2005, several years before Baylor sued him, Sterling agreed to pay a fine of $2.73 million to settle claims brought by the Justice Department that he engaged in discriminatory rental practices against Hispanics, blacks, and families with children. He was also ordered to pay attorneys' fees and costs in that action of $4,923,554.75. In the court records, Judge Dale S. Fischer notes "[Sterling's] 'scorched earth' litigation tactics, some of which are described by the Plaintiffs' counsel and some of which were observed by the Court." Fischer adds, "The Court has no difficulty accepting Plaintiffs' counsel's representations that the time required to be spent on this case was increased by defendant's counsel's often unacceptable, and sometimes outrageous, conduct."

In November 2005, the Associated Press reported that Judge Fischer had ordered Sterling to pay the plaintiff tenants $5 million to cover their attorney's fees. On August 8, 2009, Sterling was sued by the U.S. Department of Justice on housing discrimination claims. It was alleged Sterling would not rent to blacks in Beverly Hills or non-Koreans in Los Angeles's Koreatown. There were additional accusations that the Clippers owner said Latino tenants "smoke, drink, and just hang around the building," and "black tenants smell and attract vermin."

In the February 13, 2009, edition of the *Los Angeles Times*, Baylor's attorney, Alvin J. Pittman, says, "I think it is very interesting that this owner has had a history of questionable conduct in his other business ventures. It lends credence and support to many of the allegations we are making in the lawsuit."

According to a June 26, 2006, *Times* article, the Donald T. Sterling Charitable Foundation pledged to spend $50 million on a site in eastern downtown Los Angeles to provide services for the city's homeless. The center was not built. *LA Weekly* reported on February 19, 2008, that some believed the facility would *never* be built. Those skeptics thought Sterling purchased the building solely for its worth. Later in 2008, *LA Weekly* learned the foundation was not yet operating, while Sterling promoted it with full-page *Los Angeles Times* advertisements. Some felt Sterling was not taken to task by the *Los Angeles Times* because he spent so much money advertising such boondoggles in the paper.

According to court documents reported in the *Sporting News* on March 4, 2012, that Sterling sought advice on running his team from a woman named Alexandra Castro, an acquaintance of Sterling's he described as a prostitute. In the Justice Department's 2009 discrimination case against Sterling, there was testimony from Castro from a 2003 case in which Sterling sued Ms. Castro to get back a home he had allegedly given her after they had broken up. The judge in that 2003 case ruled for Castro to keep the home. Part of her affidavit read,

> During our relationship, Mr. Sterling consulted me on issues he was considering almost every day, including, among others, whether he should hire Alvin Gentry to coach the Los Angeles Clippers (although I had no experience in such matters), how he should respond to requests by players for the Los Angeles Clippers for increases in their compensation (Mr. Sterling and I often had dinner at the Arena Club with agents for a number of players).

The March *Sporting News* article adds that Castro's lawyer, Raymond Hersh, stated, "[S]he cooked, drove, cleaned, was consulted on remodeling apartments, who went to dinner with agents, who should be hired— she didn't make the decision, she said, but she was consulted about who to hire in the Clipper organization and what should be done, what he was thinking."

Sterling not only called Castro a prostitute in the 2003 court case, but also called her "a total freak and a piece of trash," continuing, "It was purely sex for money, money for sex, sex for money, money for sex. The girl was providing sex for money. . . . I probably didn't tell my wife . . . maybe I did something morally wrong." He made these accusations under oath.

One player Sterling used to berate from his courtside seat was guard Baron Davis, "Why are you in the game?" the owner would yell, as the *Sporting News* published in March 2012. "Why did you take that shot?" and "You're out of shape!"

Pittman told the *Los Angeles Times* on March 9, 2011, "Whereas the Lakers had ownership showing an interest in winning, Mr. Baylor accepted a position that was challenging, a team that has a tradition of losing and unwilling to pay or resign key players." Pittman further attested, "The Clippers already had a reputation as a horrible franchise" before Baylor was named GM.

According to the November 12, 2010, issue of the *Times*, Baylor's lawyers asked for $11 million in past economic losses, $11 million in future economic losses, $21,000 for stress and emotional therapy, and attorneys' fees of $68,000 before they filed suit against Donald Sterling. On September 16, 2008, his counsel sent their documents to the Clippers' legal counsel and NBA commissioner David Stern. In addition, Baylor sought a two-year, $2 million contract to become a "goodwill ambassador" for the league. The *Times* reported the former GM asked his former employer and the NBA to stage a "fitting (well-budgeted) retirement party for Baylor (not to exceed $300,000)." In response, the Clippers offered Baylor a $120,000 retirement payment on August 18, 2008, for the next year, with an additional monthly sum. Baylor spurned the offer, which he calls "insulting" and "ridiculous" in the November 8, 2010 edition of the *Times*.

Baylor withdrew his discrimination filing on March 3, 2011. The presiding judge, Kenneth R. Freeman, ruled to exclude accusations deemed prejudicial or irrelevant. Baylor's counsel and the team's lawyers did not agree on the excluded claims.

"Based on the court's tentative ruling on the summary judgment motions, the race claim was going to survive. Mr. Baylor voluntarily chose [on Friday] to dismiss the [race] claim," one of Baylor's lawyers, Carl Douglas, reported to the *Los Angeles Times* on March 4, 2011.

The *Times* reported that Clippers attorney Robert Platt said, "We were successful in excluding alleged statements, which gave Mr. Baylor no option but to dismiss the race claim. . . . We anticipated from the day the lawsuit was filed that the issue of race discrimination would never get to a jury."

Baylor said in his deposition he couldn't remember Sterling saying anything racially discriminating to him. He said Sterling and team president Andy Roeser often asked his age.

In an ESPN.com article published on January 6, 2011, and written by J. A. Adande, former Clippers coach Mike Dunleavy referenced similar comments about Baylor's age from the Clippers' upper management, but Dunleavy states, "The entire time that I worked for the Clippers, I never saw any change in Elgin's ability to perform his duties, or that his age had any adverse impact on the performance of his duties and responsibilities as general manager."

Sterling denied any age discrimination. In 2008, when Baylor was fired, he was 74. "He's 6 feet 7," the owner says of Baylor in a *Los Angeles Times* account from March 15, 2011. "If somebody wants to harass him, I'd like to see him do it." Sterling says pro basketball "is like musical chairs, they constantly remove and change owners, general managers, coaches, and agents, but I had a man I protected for 22 years. . . . He kept telling me it would get better. I kept hoping it would get better. It didn't get better. It got worse."

Moreover, Baylor's attorney's presented a memo from team president Andy Roeser that states, "Elgin is 72 and still not getting any younger."

The *Los Angeles Times* reported in March 2011 that for his part, Sterling countered by saying, "The record speaks for itself. Of course, I was disappointed. I'm spending one-third of a billion dollars to win, and who's in charge of winning? Elgin Baylor is a good person, but we lost seven out of 10 games with him. How can anyone feel good about that?"

In truth, Michael Jordan has the worst record as a superstar running a NBA team; his clubs won only 39 percent of their games in Washington and Charlotte as of 2013. Jordan's contemporary, Isiah Thomas, was also a notoriously unproductive GM. Perhaps Jerry West and Larry Bird have been the best of the great players at judging talent and making personnel decisions. But both worked for supportive owners and storied franchises where the game was taken quite seriously.

Baylor's deposition, as quoted in ESPN's article on January 6, also states that Sterling would bring female reporters into the dressing room to watch the players shower: "While ignoring my suggestions and isolating me from decisions customarily reserved for general managers, the Clippers attempted to place the blame for the team's failures on me," Baylor says in the declaration, adding,

> During this same period, players Sam Cassell, Elton Brand, and Corey Maggette complained to me that Donald Sterling would bring women into the locker room after games, while the players were showering, and make comments such as, "Look at those beautiful black bodies." I brought this to Sterling's attention, but he continued to bring women into the locker room.

Despite their closeness in age and Sterling's L.A. upbringing, Sterling testified he did not know about Baylor's basketball career. David Dickerson, who worked for NBA agent David Falk, disagreed and told the author that during the years he worked in L.A., Sterling was known to have hired Baylor because he was a basketball legend who changed the way the game was played. Dickerson compared Sterling's loyalty toward Baylor during those early years to longtime Washington Bullets owner Abe Pollin and Wes Unseld: "As long as I'm alive, you have a job."

In response to a line of questions about Elgin's Hall of Fame playing career from Baylor attorney Carl Douglas, Sterling denied any knowledge of it. "I didn't know [about] that," Sterling said, according to the *Los Angeles Times*. "I hired him for $3,000 a month. I didn't really know what his role was. . . . He was working in a mail-order company back then." If Sterling was genuinely unaware of Lakers legend Elgin Baylor and hired him in 1986, without investigating his background or inquiring about his references, he was not a conscientious owner. Moreover, if Sterling was well aware who Baylor was, he perjured himself in court.

In trial, Douglas asked questions of Sterling to illustrate the hands-off nature of his ownership. The *Times* reported that when Sterling was asked who was the team's general manager before Baylor, the owner said the name Carl Scheer "sounds familiar," adding, "I don't profess to know anything about basketball. I'm a professional lawyer." When asked to what extent he and Baylor discussed the management of the ball club, Sterling said, "[Baylor] . . . ultimately made $500,000 a year. Somewhere in between, he assumed that role." Baylor never earned more than $350,000, a figure the team's attorneys should have known well.

The *Times* reported that, under testimony, Sterling claimed he paid whatever salary Baylor asked and afforded him free reign in signing players and free agents. "Elgin Baylor wouldn't tell me the players he was drafting. He was afraid I'd tell another owner," said Sterling. According to the *Times*, Clippers lawyer Robert Platt blamed Baylor for drafting Joe Wolf, Reggie Williams, Michael Olowokandi, Terry Dehere, and other busts. Platt said such high picks "have gone away in the wind" and also faulted Baylor for not signing Kobe Bryant and Carlos Boozer as free agents.

Baylor also had opportunities to draft Scottie Pippen, Reggie Miller, Shawn Kemp, Sean Elliott, Kevin Garnett, Steve Nash, Dirk Nowitzki, Jason Terry, Jamal Crawford, Vince Carter, and Amar'e Stoudemire, among others. In fairness to Baylor, because of his sense of basketball history and respect for the Lakers legacy, Kobe Bryant would have never signed with the crosstown team. Although many cite Pippen as a prime example of a Baylor draft oversight, Pippen was from small-college Central Arkansas, as previously noted, while Baylor's 1987 first-round choice, Reggie Williams, was a big-time college star at Georgetown.

Baylor claimed, however, that there was an important, largely overlooked reason many players wouldn't have joined the Clippers: "Because of the Clippers' unwillingness to fairly compensate African American players, we lost a lot of good talent, including Danny Manning, Charles Smith, Michael Cage, Ron Harper, Dominique Wilkins, [Corey] Maggette, and others," Baylor says in a January 7, 2011, *Los Angeles Times* article written by Adande.

In closing statements, the team's attorney ridiculed Baylor's claims and urged the panel to deprive him of any financial payoff. In the March 28, 2011, installment of the *Times*, referencing Baylor's complaints against team executives who asked him about his birthday and how he was feeling in the years before the NBA great's split with the team as executive vice president, attorney Platt testified, "You'd have to have police at every workplace saying you can't sing, 'Happy Birthday.'" On

March 30, 2011, two years after Baylor filed his suit, a seven-man, five-woman jury in Los Angeles County Superior Court informed Judge Kenneth R. Freeman by a vote of 12–0 that Elgin Baylor had no claim. Despite the notoriety of the trial in Southern California, Baylor's charges and previous housing discrimination suits against the controversial NBA owner received little or no attention in the national media or from noted civil rights activists or the NBA front office, and there was no civic protest from Clippers fans. Millions of Americans, for whom Lakers Kobe Bryant and Shaquille O'Neal had been household names, did not even realize Los Angeles had a second NBA franchise. Baylor dropped his suit, Sterling kept his franchise.

The legal loss did not silence Baylor from continuing to speak out on race and sport or cause him to retreat from public life. On February 24, 2012, during NBA All-Star Game weekend at the Swan Hotel at Disney World, he participated on a panel to discuss the impact of black leadership in sports and basketball, a panel that included Kareem Abdul-Jabbar, Julius Erving, Earl Lloyd, and Dolph Schayes. Baylor's impact on basketball throughout the generations was evident in the assembled panel members, with Abdul-Jabbar and Erving, who looked up to Baylor during their respective boyhoods, and Lloyd and Schayes, who were two of his rival NBA forwards.

* * *

On December 3, 2012, the *Los Angeles Times* reported that Baylor and his second wife, Elaine, had put their Beverly Crest–area estate on the market for $4.25 million. As the *Times* describes it,

> The contemporary Mediterranean-style home, built in 1981, sits on nearly an acre, with both canyon and city views. Features include a 1,600-square-foot great room that could function as a home theater or game room, multiple decks, six bedrooms, eight bathrooms, and more than 8,000 square feet of living space.

In early 2013, Julien's Auctions, the world's premier sports and entertainment auction house, scheduled the auction of a "collection of memorabilia, awards, and personal property" of Baylor's, including his "1959 NBA All-Star Game MVP trophy, Baylor's 1971–1972 Los Angeles Lakers NBA championship ring, and a number of items from Baylor's professional career, including LA Lakers game-worn warm-ups." In addition, Baylor offered up Adidas game shoes that were taken without his knowledge, bronzed, and presented to him at a talk-show appearance.

The Julien's collection also featured Baylor's 1977 NBA Hall of Fame induction certificate; gold NBA Lifetime Pass; NBA 50 Greatest Players ring; personal 50 Greatest Players jacket; and NBA 50 Greatest Players signed lithograph, featuring the autographs of 49 of the 50 players chosen and numbered "Baylor 1/1." Bidders could also acquire Baylor's 1958 Chuck Taylor All-American Certificate. After first being shown at the Long Beach Expo at the Long Beach Convention Center from February 7 through February 9, the collection went on public exhibition at the Staples Center from February 13 through May 10. It was then slated to be available for viewing at Julien's 10 days before the Memorial Day weekend auction on May 31.

These collectibles would be auctioned only months before Baylor's 80th birthday. The sale temporarily placed him in the local L.A. limelight. Some fans and journalists who reflected on his influence and career wondered why the Lakers had not honored him with a statue outside the Staples Center. Players who were serious students of the game's history were familiar with Baylor. Lakers star Kobe Bryant certainly was. As Bryant was rehabilitating from his 2012 Achilles tendon injury, Baylor sent him the following online message:

> To my friend Kobe . . .
> It's unfortunate and disappointing, especially at this time, to have any injury. I had the same injury when I played, but thank God medicine and rehab today, along with your being in great shape, guarantees your complete recovery. You will come back even stronger. Just be patient and you will be fine. God bless you.

Ironically, it was Baylor's nemesis, Donald Sterling, who inadvertently thrust the forgotten superstar back into the public eye. In the spring of 2014, the Clippers were a playoff franchise. Two of the NBA players most prominently featured in national ad campaigns were Clippers power forward Blake Griffin and their point guard, Chris Paul. With Griffin and Paul as young product spokespeople, their performance highlights featured almost nightly during NBA seasons on ESPN's *SportsCenter*, NBAtv, and YouTube, the Clippers were no longer anonymous. Griffin and Paul were exciting players and perennial All-Stars.

The media had also evolved in recent years, with celebrities' every move caught by paparazzi, fans' cell phone cameras, public cameras, and their own text messages. On April 25, 2014, the celebrity gossip TV show TMZ reported that in a telephone call recorded the previous fall, the still married Donald Sterling complained to a supposed female companion named V. Stiviano about a photo she had posted on the interactive social media platform Instagram, posed with former Lakers star Earvin "Magic" Johnson. On the recording, made without Sterling's knowledge, the Clippers owner allegedly said, "It bothers me a lot that you want to broadcast that you're associating with black people." He told his mistress she could sleep with black people, with the caveat, "[T]he little I ask you is . . . not to bring them to my games." As news of the leaked tape trickled into media and public awareness, Los Angelinos chalked it up to Sterling being Sterling. The national response was very different, as most Americans had no awareness of him. The Clippers began damage control by saying Stiviano was already being sued by Sterling's wife for the return of a $1.8 million home the team owner had bought the girlfriend, as well as several luxury automobiles. The Clippers attempted to discredit Stiviano and the manner in which Sterling's alleged conversation had been recorded. Stiviano, they claimed, was exacting revenge.

Two days after TMZ ran the story, the Clippers, who were predominantly black, held a team meeting about the incident. By that time, reports of Sterling's ill-timed tirade had reached CNN, MSNBC, the major U.S. newspapers, and radio and sports talk shows, and were the subject of discussion for individuals ranging from black activists to basketball fans. In their meeting, some Clippers considered boycotting their April 27 fourth Western Division playoff game against the Warriors. Other NBA players took to social media to express their opinions. Some knew Sterling's reputation because they had colleagues who had played for him. Veteran sports journalists recalled that Elgin Baylor had filed a racial discrimination lawsuit against Sterling. The lawsuit had not garnered national news. The recording was attracting global attention. How, some wondered, could an owner of a team in a league that was 75 percent black believe and say such things? The press satisfied growing public curiosity by hastily cobbling together biographical details of Sterling's life.

During warm-ups before game four against the Warriors, the Clippers wore their uniforms inside out to hide the team logos, in protest of Sterling's biased language. While some sports talk-show hosts and other broadcasters defended not Sterling's words, but his telephone privacy and freedom of speech, others were highly critical. The Los Angeles NAACP canceled a lifetime achievement award they were scheduled to present Sterling in May 2014. On April 29, new NBA commissioner Adam Silver, in his first major act, fined the owner $2.5 million and barred him from the team's offices or having direct operation of the Clippers. No NBA owner had ever been so penalized.

The NBA scheduled a June 3 meeting in which Sterling's fellow owners would vote on the status of his ownership. When he surfaced publicly, Sterling protested that he would not sell. He filed suit against the NBA to block any prospective sale of the Clippers. His estranged wife, Shelly, argued that in their pending divorce, she was entitled to 50 percent of the franchise. Some estimated the team, now successful, was worth $700 or $800 million. The man Baylor had sued was now relevant. Public pressure continued to mount, even after the Clippers were eliminated from the NBA playoffs. On May 29, Shelly Sterling deferred, consenting to sell the ball club to former Microsoft CEO Steve Ballmer. The price tag, more than double the estimates of one NBA owner, was $2 million. A week later, Sterling dropped his lawsuit against the league. Three days later, Elgin Baylor, whose opinion on the events had been sought out by the media for two weeks, appeared on CNN's *Anderson Cooper 360* with his wife Elaine. Of Sterling, Baylor told Cooper, "He's an intelligent man. Great businessman."

As he had in court, Baylor told Cooper that Sterling had never directed a racial slur at him. Cooper asked Baylor if Sterling is a racist. "Of course he is. There's no doubt in my mind now," the Hall of Famer answered. Elaine Baylor said that night on CNN, "He's not running around with a white robe on. . . . He's a very smart man, but he communicates how he feels and what he wants, especially to people who work for him."

Baylor felt his claims against the insensitive owner had finally been confirmed in the public sphere. He told Cooper, "Justice has been served. Now they know what Donald is like, and the things I said before about Donald are absolutely true." Baylor, with a unique opportunity to illuminate Americans about his 81-year-old former employer, shared the story of Sterling bringing women into the team's locker room to marvel at the players' "beautiful black bodies." He also told Cooper he had objected to the practice: "On several occasions I told them not to. You know, players were—you know, they were mad. They were upset about it because I told him on several occasions, and he kept doing it. Eventually it stopped."

Elaine Baylor added (about black players), "Donald thinks if it weren't for him, all of those guys would be playing basketball in the ghetto somewhere. Actually, when Elgin first started, he told Elgin to go out in the inner city and see if he could find some players on the basketball courts."

The details were sickening but, in light of the leaked phone tape, credible. In Sterling's disgrace, Baylor, long the racial pioneer, found vindication. Since losing the discrimination suit, he had not sought this attention, but new media, and a popular team, had converged to bring the Clippers and their owner into a critical glare. For reasons he would never have imagined, even during Sterling's discrimination trial, Elgin Baylor was back in the news. Because of the type of behavior that had led Baylor to sue Sterling, Sterling had become the first NBA owner to be forced by the league's commissioner to give up his franchise. Baylor, four years prior, had told us so.

13

RABBIT REDUX

I have often heard that the word *superstar* was first applied to basketball hero Elgin Baylor.—sportswriter Frank Deford, *New York* magazine, 1972

Elgin Baylor's impact on basketball encompasses playing style, marketing, labor relations, and the professional game's evolution to major-league status. He spearheaded a revolution in scoring, as well as a stylistic change with his one-on-one skills and arsenal of shots. Baylor, complete with no-look passes, was "Showtime" 20 years before Magic Johnson. The 1970–1971 Lakers press guide says, "We sportswriters lost track of the number of nights Elg scored what we all called his 'hat trick,'" leading the team night after night in total points, rebounds, and assists.

Jim Murray writes in the December 22, 1991, issue of the *Los Angeles Times*, "No one ever played the game of basketball better than Elgin Gay Baylor. No one. Not Michael Jordan, Larry Bird, no Knick, Celtic, Piston, Bull, or Rocket in history." Baylor finished third in National Basketball Association MVP balloting as a rookie in 1959, third again in 1961, and second in 1963. "To me, he is the most important player in NBA history—that includes Jordan," says *SLAM* magazine editor Scoop Jackson in the November 2010 edition of the magazine in his article on Baylor, "Original Old School: The Truth, the Whole Truth, and Nothing but the Truth."

In his 1998 autobiography, *For the Love of the Game: My Story*, Michael Jordan himself acknowledges Baylor's importance and influence: "I built my talents on the shoulders of someone else's talent. Without Julius Erving, David Thompson, Walter Davis, and Elgin Baylor, there never would have been a Michael Jordan. I evolved from them." John Castellani said of Baylor, "He was Michael Jordan before Michael Jordan."

During the 2012 NBA Finals, league scoring champion and D.C. native Kevin Durant told the *Washington Post*'s Mike Wise, for an article titled "Is Kevin Durant the Best Washington, D.C., Basketball Player Ever?" on June 13,

> My goal as a kid was to be the best player ever in my area. That was my first goal before even thinking about going to college or the NBA, so that means a lot to me. But I don't think I'm up there with those guys, Elgin Baylor and Dave Bing and Adrian Dantley and guys like that. I've got to keep working and, hopefully, I get there. That's always been a goal of mine, and hopefully I achieve it.

On July 14, 2008, Julius Erving told *USA Today*, "My starting five was, is, and always will be Oscar Robertson, Jerry West, Elgin Baylor, Wilt Chamberlain, and Bill Russell, with Connie Hawkins coming off the bench." Erving exalted him on a level he had not even reserved for Michael Jordan or Kareem Abdul-Jabbar.

In the 1960s, Baylor saved the Lakers. He largely contributed to an increase in the value of the franchise such that Bob Short, who paid less than $100,000 for the team, sold the Lakers for more than $5 million. Within the same period, Baylor, through labor negotiations, marketability, and general leadership, helped his fellow players move from an average salary of $9,500 per year in 1967 to $92,000 a year in the early 1970s (higher than the Major League Baseball average). From 1958, Baylor's rookie year, to 1968, the Lakers went from being the laughingstock of Minneapolis to the team with the best attendance in the NBA, playing in the most glamorous arena in professional sports. When Baylor signed with the Lakers, the UCLA had never won a national championship, and beaches and baseball attracted local boys in the summertime. By his retirement, Southern California was one of the premier recruiting areas for schoolboy players (a development that helped UCLA win seven national championships in eight seasons). At the pro level, the Lakers were able to lure not only players like Wilt Chamberlain, but also the cream of college coaches—Fred Schaus, Butch van Breda Kolff, and Joe Mullaney—rather than relying on the coaching carousel most NBA GMs used as a hiring pool. By the time Baylor stepped aside early in the 1971–1972 season, NBA franchises were located throughout the West—in Los Angeles, San Francisco, Portland, and Seattle.

The place where Baylor originated his game, Washington, D.C., became a basketball hotbed and a prime recruiting area in Baylor's footsteps, its citizenry proud of having produced the game's most exciting player. College coaches started beating a path there looking for the "next Elgin." In 1966, one of Washington's many stellar schoolboy stars was a player at Eastern High School known as "Leapin' Lou" West. Baylor facilitated young West's choice of colleges by leaving a white 1966 Thunderbird automobile in front of his home for the high-flying senior to drive to Seattle University. West is still the seventh leading rebounder in school history, and his Seattle teammate, Tom Little of D.C.'s Mackin Catholic High School, was a 5'11" sparkplug who averaged 20 points a game in three seasons for the Chieftains. Before West and Little, John Tresvant and Ernie Dunston followed Baylor's path from Spingarn High to Seattle U.

When Baylor starred in the NBA, such D.C. talents as Dave Bing and Ollie Johnson (both from Spingarn High), Austin Carr, Collis Jones, Donald Washington, James Brown, and Adrian Dantley extended the list of players whose names followed his in local lore. By the 1990s, the local talent pool was so rich, the area sometimes placed as many as four players on the *Parade* magazine High School All-American basketball team. McDonald's sponsored a prominent schoolboy all-star game, pitting Washington's best against a high school team from the rest of the nation. From 1978 through 1980, and again in 1982 and 1983, Washington's Capital All-Stars defeated the U.S. team. It was Baylor who placed the city on the basketball map. NFL sportscaster James Brown was a high school All-American at DeMatha Catholic in the D.C. suburbs in 1969, and a great leaper at 6'5". When asked about the greatest players the area produced, he said the old-timers all told him how great Baylor was. "He was just a beast," said Brown in a 2010 interview with the author.

Former coach John Castellani told Grantland.com's Dave McKenna, for the August 28, 2012, article "Wilt vs. Elgin: When the World Was Their Playground," Baylor opened his eyes about the quality of hoops talent in the nation's capital. "I didn't know anything or hear anything about D.C. ballplayers before I had Elgin," says Castellani. "But, oh, god, was I sold on D.C. talent after him."

But Baylor seldom comes home to Washington. "I'm just busy, I guess," he explained to McKenna for the March 23, 2011, *Washington City Paper* article "Elgin Baylor, Won't You Please Come Home?" when asked why he almost never visits his hometown. He also avoids accepting too many accolades as a local hero. "Elgin won't talk about himself, he never would," Dunston told McKenna for the *City Paper* feature. "But I hope he knows his name was magic there. He was magic."

Baylor told McKenna for the August 2012 Grantland.com story,

> I know after I left D.C., colleges started going into the city, and players started going to college, and many of them did quite well. And, next thing I know, a lot of players from D.C. were playing in the NBA, including a lot of guys from Spingarn. But to give me credit for that? That's not me. God Almighty gave them the ability.

In a sport that has become synonymous with African Americans, Baylor was the first black athlete encouraged to freely express himself on the professional level. He was, in many ways, a bridge entertainer. Because of his creative offensive game and Lakers owner Bob Short's heightened dependence on his success, Baylor broke barriers. He helped introduce aspects of the urban schoolyard game into the highest level of play. Writes Dr. Gerald Early in the 2000 book *Basketball Jones: America above the Rim*,

> From a DuBoisian perspective, basketball has created a cadre of narrowly talented, extremely wealthy black men who have visibly and unalterably stamped their style—their racial "elegance," to borrow a term from Ralph Ellison, Albert Murray, and Stanley Crouch—on a realm of performance to such a degree that it has changed the entire nature of how the game is played, changed, indeed, the reality and myth of the game, while elevating African American ethos and creativity.

Baylor was at the vanguard of this transition.

Baylor's ballhandling ability, passing savvy, and blind shots echoed the old black touring teams. Where Nathaniel "Sweetwater" Clifton, Dick Barnett, and Cleo Hill felt compelled to tone down their originality for the sake of the team and the palate of their teammates and fan bases, Baylor operated under the sentiment "the more, the merrier." Chuck Cooper, Earl Lloyd, Walter Dukes, Ray Felix, and Bill Russell were drafted or signed to rebound and play defense. Elgin Baylor represented black basketball with the stylistic shackles removed. With this freedom to improvise, he led a new school of one-on-one players—black and white—and his excellence was a prime factor in the eventual association between basketball and black America.

In his game, Baylor used a creative assortment of shots, fadeaway jumpers, runners, flips, reverse lay-ins, and bank shots with his back to the hoop. His was a style often no longer in evidence today. "It's an incongruity. We have better athletes than ever, but they play at a slower pace," says longtime NBA general manager and executive Rod Thorn in the February 13, 2005, issue of *New York Times Magazine*, speaking of today's athletes for a criticism of basketball called "Clang!" Thorn played against Baylor and was the Chicago Bulls' GM when Michael Jordan was drafted. "The reason is they're not as sound fundamentally," he says in the critique.

In his prime, Baylor was a dominant forward, even against such athletic defenders as "Jumpin' Johnny" Green, Tom Hawkins, Gus Johnson, Bill Bridges, and "Pogo" Joe Caldwell. Undersized for his position and hampered by knee injuries after 1964, Baylor's 27.4 lifetime scoring average is still third all-time. And, unlike Baylor, the two players ahead of him, Chamberlain and Jordan, avoided serious injury for the most part.

Baylor spent his heyday in the second-largest city in the United States and the entertainment capital of the world. Where the feats of some other stars, for example, Connie Hawkins and Julius Erving, were often the stuff of rumor, Baylor's best efforts took place on some of basketball's biggest stages: He had his 71-point performance at Madison Square Garden and his 61-point, 25-rebound masterpiece in the 1961 NBA Finals at the hallowed Boston Garden. Baylor's visibility allowed him to wow admirers, breed imitators, and change the way basketball was played. His success made street ball mainstream. By the mid-1960s, the Harlem Globetrotters were an exhibition team skirting the boundaries of racial stereotype, while Baylor was a dignified labor leader who was transforming his sport, while facing the world's best competition. Other than Wilt Chamberlain, no product of America's urban schoolyards has scored like Baylor. Since Baylor, no NBA forward his size—and few at all—has averaged as many rebounds. To this day, perhaps the only forwards who have proven his equal as a passer are Rick Barry and Larry Bird. "I saw a tremendous transition in the game, and I played against many, many great players," relates Baylor's former teammate, Earl Lloyd, in his 2011 auto-biography *Moonfixer: The Basketball Journey of Earl Lloyd*. "Oscar and Elgin—they just epitomize the total package."

Al Attles told the author in an interview, "It was almost a pleasure to play against him. Guys would catch themselves watching him play. It was just a great feeling to be on the same floor with him."

Although Baylor never played on a one-man team and was an unselfish teammate, he earned acclaim for his individual skills. In an age of Mantle, Maris, and Mays, he made basketball a numbers game. American sports fans place great stock in numbers, as both a tool of assessment and a yardstick for folklore. Before Wilt Chamberlain or Pete Maravich, Baylor provided an important standard. In January 1976, Rick Barry said in *Boys Life*, "I'm proud to say that I've also succeeded in doing things the Elgin Baylor way when it comes to scoring." Tom Hawkins, who both guarded and was a teammate of Baylor, says in the 2007 book *The Good, the Bad, and the Ugly Los Angeles Lakers*, "Pound for pound, Elgin Baylor is the best to ever play the game." That is a strong testament from a man who played in Cincinnati with Oscar Robertson and on a Lakers squad with Wilt Chamberlain.

Those who insist that Baylor amassed his Ruthian statistics because the competition was subpar forget that he played against a tiny, talented percentile of the basketball population. Baylor had his best seasons during a golden age in pro ball. In what for most of the 1960s was a nine-team league, the big men against whom he penetrated and spun for his baskets—Bill Russell, Wilt Chamberlain, Walt Bellamy, Willis Reed, Nate Thurmond, and Wes Unseld—were all named among the NBA's 50 Greatest Players in 1996. Baylor's contemporaries from 1959 to 1969 were Dolph Schayes, Bob Pettit, Jerry Lucas, Paul Arizin, Billy Cunningham, John Havlicek, Rick Barry, and Dave DeBusschere, all top-50 honorees. There were no off nights or cream puffs on the Lakers' schedule—or, for that matter, on the schedules of any NBA teams at that time. "Every game was a tough one," states former Hawks and 76ers coach Alex Hannum in Wayne Lynch's book *Season of the 76ers: The Story of Wilt Chamberlain and the 1967 NBA Champion Philadelphia 76ers*, "against Boston, against Cincinnati with Oscar, and L.A. with Baylor and West."

Baylor remains a widely discussed innovator in terms of the evolution of the game. "His legacy lives on," Attles told the author in 2013. "The youngest players talk about Elgin Baylor. The mark of a great one, is they talk about you long after you've stopped playing."

While Baylor's name is legendary among many players, he's not widely remembered by fans at large. "No one mentions Elgin Baylor," Oscar Robertson claims in Dave Hollander's book *52 Weeks: Interviews with Champions.* "I thought he was the best."

One reason Baylor's name and memory have faded in the pantheon of athletic heroism is he never committed his story and thoughts to public record. In 1964, football's Jimmy Brown sounded off in his memoir *Off My Chest.* Bill Russell followed suit in 1966, with *Go Up for Glory*, as racially charged an autobiography as Brown's. Outspoken star pitcher Bob Gibson wrote *From Ghetto to Glory*, and a few years later, fellow Omaha native Gale Sayers published *I Am Third* (the basis for the award-winning made-for-TV movie *Brian's Song*) and Curt Flood expressed himself in *The Way It Is* (1970). There were reams of copy about the paradoxical Muhammad Ali, Chamberlain weighed in with *Wilt: Just Like Any Other 7-Foot Black Millionaire Who Lives Next Door*, and Walt Frazier offered *Rockin' Steady: A Guide to Basketball and Cool*. These books, in some cases, invite fans into training camps and locker rooms and, in others, tear the gilded covers off the American pro athlete and his powerful owner. With Baylor, however, other than the requisite sports-magazine profiles, there is little left for posterity. As early 1970s comedy star Flip Wilson would have said, "What you see is what you get!"

But those who know Baylor primarily for his time with the Clippers are missing the bigger picture. On October 8, 2008, Bill Simmons wrote for ESPN.com,

If you're younger than 40, when you think of Elgin, you probably remember him wearing one of those Bill Cosby sweaters and wincing because the Clippers' lottery number came too soon. That's the wrong memory. You should think about him creating hang time from scratch in 1958. Think of him putting up a 38–19 in his spare time in 1962. Think of him dropping 71 on The Dipper. Think of his eyes narrowing as they passed along his owner's condescending message during that snowy day in Boston. Think of him retiring with dignity because he didn't want to hang on for a ring. Think of him telling Hundley that he couldn't play that exhibition game in West Virginia, not because he was trying to prove a point, but because it would have made him feel like less of a human being.

In June 2011, Oscar Robertson told the *Dan Sileo Show* on WDAE in Tampa, "Let me tell you about what being great is. Ever hear of Elgin Baylor? Never mention his name, do we? Great basketball player."

Although Baylor is best known to basketball fans under the age of 40 for his woes as an NBA executive and his unsuccessful lawsuit, during his playing days he blazed many trails. The NBA moved to the West Coast because of him, which made professional basketball a national, major-league sport. Baylor's stardom and presence did more for basketball in and around Los Angeles than the arrival of Wayne Gretzky nearly three decades later did for hockey.

Baylor's style of play left an indelible imprint on the game, one emulated by the most popular players of each succeeding decade—Erving, Jordan, and more. Sportswriters and announcers often trace Michael Jordan's and even Kobe Bryant's elevated one-on-one moves to a lineage that began with Elgin Baylor. Just as significantly, he was the first player to refuse to suit up for a NBA game on grounds of racial discrimination. He was the NBA's first black team captain. He helped lead the proposed boycott of the 1964 NBA All-Star Game, a landmark event in league labor history. And while he did not win his case against Donald Sterling, the lawsuit helped enlighten the public about Sterling's biases and was the first of its kind in major U.S. sports history. Four years later, Baylor proved prescient, as the NBA forced Sterling to sell his team, a story that dominated national news coverage for two weeks. As an outspoken athlete and for his subsequently emulated moves, Baylor was always years ahead of his time. It is no wonder the term *superstar* was first used in reference to Elgin Gay Baylor.

BIBLIOGRAPHY

CHAPTER 1

"Armstrong Bows, 72–44." *Washington Post*, February 24, 1954.

"Baylor Scores 34 for Spingarn." *Washington Post*, January 30, 1954.

"Eastern Opposes Gonzaga." *Washington Post*, February 9, 1954.

Gross, Milton. "Elgin Baylor and Basketball's Big Explosion." *SPORT*, April 1961.

"Interhigh Stars Play Baylor, Co." *Washington Post*, March 17, 1954.

Kelly, Dave. "Baylor Key to Spingarn Plans." *Washington Post*, January 12, 1954.

———. "Baylor Prize: Area High School Stars Sought by Colleges." *Washington Post*, February 25, 1954.

———. "Tall Center Misses Only Four Shots." *Washington Post*, February 10, 1954.

Lacy, Sam. "From A to Z." *Baltimore Afro-American*, February 13, 1954.

McKenna, Dave. "Elgin Baylor, Absentee Legend." *Washington City Paper*, June 2, 1999.

"Stonewalls Plays Scholastic Stars." *Washington Post*, March 17, 1954.

Watson, Emmett. "Elgin Baylor: Too Good for College Ball." *SPORT*, February 1958.

"Western's Jim Wexler Sets Area Scoring Record, 52 Points." *Washington Post*, February 11, 1953.

Zad, Martie. "Stonewall Wins, Baylor Scores 29." *Washington Post*, March 23, 1954.

CHAPTER 2

Astor, Gerald. "Sammy's Golden Rule." *Sports Illustrated*, March 7, 1955.

Gaines, Clarence, with Clint Johnson. *They Call Me Big House*. New York: John S. Blair, 2004.

Hruby, Patrick. "The Legend of Gary Mays Is No Legend." *ESPN.com*, February 28, 2011, http://sports.espn.go.com/espn/news/story?page=hruby/110228_gary_mays.

Kelly, Dave. "Baylor Prize: Area High School Stars Sought by Colleges." *Washington Post*, February 25, 1954.

"The Long and the Short of It." *Baltimore Afro-American*, April 10, 1954.

McKenna, Dave. "Their Own Private Idaho." *Washington City Paper*, February 25, 2005.

———. "Wilt vs. Elgin: When the World Was Their Playground." *Grantland.com*, August 28, 2012, http://grantland.com/features/the-legendary-pickup-basketball-games-wilt-chamberlain-elgin-baylor-late-1950s-washington-dc/.

Nemitz, Tom. "Number 45: Bob Gibson." *Creighton White & Blue Review*, October 6, 2010.
Raley, Dan. "Baylor, Seattle U Scoring Machine, Was Toast of Town in 1950s." *Seattle Post-Intelligencer*, February 12, 2008.
Shaughnessy, Dan. *Seeing Red*. Cincinnati, OH: Adams Media, 1995.
Sugar, Bert Randolph. *The Sports 100: A Ranking of the Greatest Athletes of All Time*. Charleston, SC: Citadel/Carol, 1997.

CHAPTER 3

Eskenazi, Dave. "Seattle's 1958 Final 4 Run." *SportsPress Northwest*, February 7, 2012.
———. "Wayback Machine: The Two Lives of Elgin Baylor." *SportsPress Northwest*, May 10, 2011.
Raley, Dan. "Baylor, Seattle U Scoring Machine, Was Toast of Town in 1950s." *Seattle Post-Intelligencer*, February 12, 2008.
"Seattle U Opens Elgin Baylor Era in Big Time College Basketball." *Centralia, Washington, Daily Chronicle*, December 20, 1956.
Watson, Emmett. "Elgin Baylor: Too Good for College Ball." *SPORT*, February 1958.

CHAPTER 4

"Bears and Dons Favored." *San Francisco Examiner*, March 1958.
Chamberlain, Wilt, with David Shaw. *Wilt: Just Like Any Other 7-Foot Black Millionaire Who Lives Next Door*. New York: Macmillan, 1973.
Condotta, Bob. "Baylor Returns for Home Opener." *Seattle Times*, November 18, 2009.
Curtin, Dal. "Kentucky Tops Seattle, 86–72, to Win NCAA Basketball Title." *Troy Record* (NY), March 24, 1958.
Eskenazi, Dave. "Wayback Machine: The Two Lives of Elgin Baylor." *SportsPress Northwest*, May 10, 2011.
Koppett, Leonard. *24 Seconds to Shoot*. New York: Macmillan, 1968.
Pluto, Terry. *Tall Tales: The Glory Years of the NBA*. Lincoln, NE: Bison Books, 2000.
Raley, Dan. "33-Day Countdown to New Division I Era." Story 18. *GoSeattleU*, August 2, 2012.
———. "Baylor, Seattle U Scoring Machine, Was Toast of Town in 1950s." *Seattle Post-Intelligencer*, February 12, 2008.
Tax, Jeremiah. "The Fiddlin' Five Make Sweet Music." *Sports Illustrated*, March 31, 1958.
Taylor, John. *The Rivalry: Bill Russell, Wilt Chamberlain, and the Golden Age of Basketball*. New York: Random House, 2006.
Watson, Emmett. "Elgin Baylor: Too Good for College Ball." *SPORT*, February 1958.
Wolff, Tobias. *This Boy's Life: A Memoir*. New York: Perennial Library, 1989.

CHAPTER 5

Cope, Myron. "Elgin Baylor Comes Back." *Ebony*, February 1965.
———. "Life with Elgin Baylor." *SPORT*, March 1963.
Deford, Frank. "A Tiger Who Can Beat Anything." *Sports Illustrated*, October 24, 1966.
Devaney, John. "Pro Basketball's Hidden Fear: Too Many Negroes in the NBA." *SPORT*, February 1966.
Gross, Milton. "Elgin Baylor and Basketball's Big Explosion." *SPORT*, April 1961.

Hardman, A. L. "Baylor's Refusal to Play Here Brings ABC Protest." *Charleston Gazette-Mail*, January 18, 1959.
Lloyd, Earl, and Sean Kirst. *Moonfixer: The Basketball Journey of Earl Lloyd*. Syracuse, NY: Syracuse University Press, 2011.
Olderman, Murray. "Elgin Baylor: One-Man Franchise." *SPORT*, April 1959.
"On NAACP Battlefront: Cage Star Praised for Fighting Back." *Baltimore Afro-American*, January 31, 1959.
Pluto, Terry. *Tall Tales: The Glory Years of the NBA*. Lincoln, NE: Bison Books, 2000.
Reynolds, Bill. *Cousy: His Life, Career, and the Birth of Big-Time Basketball*. New York: Simon & Schuster, 2010.
Tax, Jeremiah. "Bunyan Strides Again." *Sports Illustrated*, April 6, 1959.
———. "Roundball Bounces Back." *Sports Illustrated*, October 27, 1958.
Thomas, Ron. *They Cleared the Lane: The NBA's Black Pioneers*. Lincoln: University of Nebraska Press, 2004.

CHAPTER 6

"Baylor–'Big O' Cage Duel Rewards Overflow Crowd." *Baltimore Afro-American*, February 7, 1961.
"Baylor Scores 47 as Lakers Win, 121–112, L.A. Leads Hawks, 3–2, in Playoffs." *Los Angeles Times*, March 28, 1961.
"Baylor Sinks 71 Points! Lakers Win." *Los Angeles Times*, November 16, 1960.
Brackin, Dennis. "Aging Wonder." *Minneapolis Star-Tribune*, June 2, 2010.
Brockenbury, L. I. *Los Angeles Sentinel*, February 2, 1960.
Cave, Ray. "McGuire Raises a Standard." *Sports Illustrated*, October 30, 1961.
Chamberlain, Wilt. "Pro Basketball Has Ganged Up on Me." *Look*, March 1960.
Cope, Myron. "Life with Elgin Baylor." *SPORT*, March 1963.
Deford, Frank. "A Tiger Who Can Beat Anything." *Sports Illustrated*, October 24, 1966.
Dwyre, Bill. "Elgin Baylor and Jerry West Are Back Together Again." *Los Angeles Times*, February 5, 2009.
Freedman, Lew. *Dynasty: The Rise of the Boston Celtics*. Guilford, CT: Lyons, 2008.
Goudsouzian, Aram. *King of the Court: Bill Russell and the Basketball Revolution*. Berkeley: University of California Press, 2011.
"The Graceful Giants." *Time*, February 17, 1961.
Gross, Milton. "100 Points Next Target for Baylor." *Miami News*, November 22, 1960.
———. "Elgin Baylor and Basketball's Big Explosion." *SPORT*, April 1961.
Hundley, Rod. *Hot Rod Hundley: You Gotta Love It Baby*. Urbana, IL: Sagamore, 1998.
Jackson, Scoop. "Original Old School: The Truth, the Whole Truth, and Nothing but the Truth." *SLAM*, November 2010.
Kahn, Roger. "Success and Ned Irish." *Sports Illustrated*, March 27, 1961.
Koppett, Leonard. *24 Seconds to Shoot*. New York: Macmillan, 1968.
Krebs, Jim. "The Night Their Luck Turned." *Sports Illustrated*, June 23, 1964.
"Lakers Cage Switch Seems Certain." *Minneapolis Star-Tribune*, April 29, 1960.
"Lakers Emphasize, Baylor Is Not for Sale at Any Price." *Ogden, Utah Standard-Examiner*, August 8, 1960.
Lazenby, Roland. *Jerry West: The Life and Legend of a Basketball Icon*. New York: ESPN Books, 2010.
Livingston, Charles J. "Are Court Giants Ruining Basketball?" *Associated Press*, January 1964.
Lloyd, Earl, and Sean Kirst. *Moonfixer: The Basketball Journey of Earl Lloyd*. Syracuse, NY: Syracuse University Press, 2011.
Murray, Jim. "A Trip for Tall Men." *Sports Illustrated*, January 30, 1961.
Pluto, Terry. *Tall Tales: The Glory Years of the NBA*. Lincoln, NE: Bison Books, 2000.

Reynolds, Bill. *Cousy: His Life, Career, and the Birth of Big-Time Basketball*. New York: Simon & Schuster, 2010.

Tax, Jeremiah. "Bunyan Strides Again." *Sports Illustrated*, April 6, 1959.

Taylor, John. *The Rivalry: Bill Russell, Wilt Chamberlain, and the Golden Age of Basketball*. New York: Random House, 2006.

Underwood, John. "A Smashing Hurrah for the Lakers." *Sports Illustrated*, February 8, 1965.

West, Jerry, with Jonathan Coleman. *West by West: My Charmed, Tormented Life*. New York: Little, Brown, 2011.

Whalen, Thomas J. *Dynasty's End: Bill Russell and the 1968–69 World Champion Boston Celtics*. Boston: Northeastern, 2005.

Zikes, Mel. "Baylor, 'Big O' Tie with 45, But Lakers Defeat Royals." *Los Angeles Times*, January 15, 1961.

CHAPTER 7

Abdul-Jabbar, Kareem. *Giant Steps: The Autobiography of Kareem Abdul-Jabbar*. New York: Bantam, 1983.

"Army Confirms Baylor's Notice to Report Already Sent in Mail." *Los Angeles Times*, November 12, 1961.

"Army Defers Elgin Baylor Until Jan. 2: Laker Star to Play Seven Tilts Here." *Los Angeles Times*, November 22, 1961.

"Army Lets Baylor Go." *Los Angeles Sentinel*, August 9, 1962.

Associated Press. "Basketball's Turn-It-Around Man." *Reading, Pennsylvania Eagle*, October 13, 1976.

Banks, Lacy J. "Annual Basketball Roundup: Milwaukee Bucks, an Instant Dynasty?" *Ebony*, January 1971.

"Baylor Faces Army Call in Month." *Los Angeles Times*, November 11, 1961.

"Baylor Sinks 71 Points! Lakers Win." *Los Angeles Times*, November 16, 1960.

Brockenbury, L. I. "Happy New Year." *Los Angeles Sentinel*, January 4, 1962.

Carey, Mike, and Michael D. McClellan. *Boston Celtics: Where Have You Gone?* Champaign, IL: Sports Publishing, 2005.

Cope, Myron. "Elgin Baylor Comes Back." *Ebony*, February 1965.

———. "Life with Elgin Baylor." *SPORT*, March 1963.

Deford, Frank. "Letter to Editor." *New York Magazine*, November 22, 1970.

"Elgin Baylor Soared on the Court through Hard Work." *Hoops Nation*, May 11, 2013, http://hoops-nation.com/community/topic/73103-elgin-baylor-soared-on-the-court-through-hard-work-an-article/.

Farmer, Sam. "He Missed a Shot at Changing History." *Los Angeles Times*, June 20, 2010.

Florence, Mal. "Baylor May Be 'Weekend' Player." *Los Angeles Times*, January, 3, 1962.

Goudsouzian, Aram. *King of the Court: Bill Russell and the Basketball Revolution*. Berkeley: University of California Press, 2011.

Gross, Milton. "Elgin Baylor and Basketball's Big Explosion." *SPORT*, April 1961.

Hafner, Dan. "Baylor Gets 50 as Lakers Win." *Los Angeles Times*, December 13, 1962.

Hundley, Rod. *Hot Rod Hundley: You Gotta Love It Baby*. Urbana, IL: Sagamore, 1998.

Jackson, Scoop. "Original Old School: The Truth, the Whole Truth, and Nothing but the Truth." *SLAM*, November 2010.

Koppett, Leonard. *24 Seconds to Shoot*. New York: Macmillan, 1968.

Lazenby, Roland. *Jerry West: The Life and Legend of a Basketball Icon*. New York: ESPN Books, 2010.

———. *The NBA Finals: A Fifty-Year Celebration*. Indianapolis, IN: Masters Press, 1996.

———. "The Rise of the Lakers." *ESPN.com*, April 4, 2010, http://m.espn.go.com/nba/story?storyId=5049433&wjb=&pg=3.

Leggett, William. "Basketball at Its Toughest." *Sports Illustrated*, February 25, 1963.

Libby, Bill. "Hot Rod Hundley: The Man behind the Clown's Mask." *SPORT*, December 1962.
———. "Jerry West: Case Study of Desire in Pro Basketball." *SPORT*, March 1965.
———. "Who Is the Best of Basketball's Superstars?" *SPORT*, April 1962.
McCarter, Andre. "LeBron 'King James' and Elgin Baylor, 'The Greatest Laker of Them All': A Comparative at Age 28." *International Business Times*, December 21, 2012.
McPhee, John. *A Sense of Where You Are: Bill Bradley at Princeton*. New York: Farrar, Straus and Giroux, 1965.
Mink, Michael. "Elgin Baylor Soared on the Court through Hard Work." *Investor's Business Daily*, April 23, 2013.
Murray, Jim. "This May Be Too Much Even for Elgin Baylor." *Los Angeles Times*, October 9, 1987.
———. "A Trip for Tall Men." *Sports Illustrated*, January 30, 1961.
Ostler, Scott, and Steve Springer. *Winnin' Times: The Magical Journey of the Los Angeles Lakers*. New York: Macmillan, 1986.
Packer, Billy and Roland Lazenby. *The Golden Game: The Hot Shots, Great Moments, and Classic Stories from Basketball's First 100 Years*. Dallas, TX: Taylor, 1991.
Pepe, Phil. *Greatest Stars of the NBA*. New York: Prentice Hall, 1970.
Pluto, Terry. *Tall Tales: The Glory Years of the NBA*. Lincoln, NE: Bison Books, 2000.
Prell, Edward. "Does Basketball Doom the Little Man?" *American Legion Magazine*, January 15, 1962.
"Pro Basketball Roundup." *Ebony*, January 1964.
Reynolds, Bill. *Cousy: His Life, Career, and the Birth of Big-Time Basketball*. New York: Simon & Schuster, 2010.
Robertson, Oscar. *The Big O: My Life, My Times, My Game*. Lincoln, NE: Bison Books, 2010.
Russell, Bill, and William McSweeney. *Go Up for Glory*. New York: Berkley Books, 1966.
Sabin, Lou. "Rick Barry: The Golden Warrior." *Boys Life*, January 1976.
Sachare, Alex. *When Seconds Count*. Champaign, IL: Sports Masters, 1999.
Shaughnessy, Dan. *Seeing Red*. Cincinnati, OH: Adams Media, 1995.
Simmons, Bill. *The Book of Basketball: The NBA According to the Sports Guy*. New York: ESPN Books, 2010.
———. "Elgin Took the Game to New Heights." *ESPN.com*, October 8, 2008, http://sports.espn.go.com/espn/page2/story?page=simmons/081008.
Tax, Jeremiah. "Bunyan Strides Again." *Sports Illustrated*, April 6, 1959.
Taylor, John. *The Rivalry: Bill Russell, Wilt Chamberlain, and the Golden Age of Basketball*. New York: Random House, 2006.
Thomas, Ron. *They Cleared the Lane: The NBA's Black Pioneers*. Lincoln: University of Nebraska Press, 2004.
Underwood, John. "A Smashing Hurrah for the Lakers." *Sports Illustrated*, February 8, 1965.
Whalen, Thomas J. *Dynasty's End: Bill Russell and the 1968–69 World Champion Boston Celtics*. Boston: Northeastern, 2005.
Williams, Roger. "Long Leap Forward of Jerry West." *Sports Illustrated*, November 20, 1961.
"Wyman Rips NBA for Baylor Ban." *Los Angeles Sentinel*, January 11, 1962.
Young, A. S. "Are Today's Athletes Too Dull?" *Negro Digest*, July 1962.
———. "Refreshing World of Sports." *Los Angeles Sentinel*, January 4, 1962.

CHAPTER 8

Araton, Harvey. *When the Garden Was Eden: Clyde, the Captain, Dollar Bill, and the Glory Days of the New York Knicks*. New York: HarperCollins, 2011.
Batchelor, Bob. *Basketball in America: From the Playgrounds to Jordan's Game and Beyond*. New York: Haworth, 2005.
"Baylor Not for Sale, L.A. President Says." United Press International, November 12, 1963.
Boyle, Robert. "Call It Catch as Catch Can." *Sports Illustrated*, November 15, 1971.

Chamberlain, Wilt, with David Shaw. *Wilt: Just Like Any Other 7-Foot Black Millionaire Who Lives Next Door*. New York: Macmillan, 1973.
Cope, Myron. "Life with Elgin Baylor." *SPORT*, March 1963.
Deford, Frank. "A Tiger Who Can Beat Anything." *Sports Illustrated*, October 24, 1966.
Devaney, John. "Pro Basketball's Hidden Fear: Too Many Negroes in the NBA." *SPORT*, February, 1966.
Erving, Julius, with Karl Taro Greenfeld. *Dr. J: The Autobiography*. New York: HarperLuxe, 2013.
Goudsouzian, Aram. *King of the Court: Bill Russell and the Basketball Revolution*. Berkeley: University of California Press, 2011.
Gross, Milton. "Elgin Baylor and Basketball's Big Explosion." *SPORT*, April 1961.
Guralnick, Peter. *Dream Boogie: The Triumph of Sam Cooke*. New York: Hatchette, 2005.
Hundley, Rod. *Hot Rod Hundley: You Gotta Love It Baby*. Urbana, IL: Sagamore, 1998.
"Lakers Get Ultimatum on Rental." *Long Beach Independent*, October 4, 1963.
"Lakers Make Elg Happy." *Los Angeles Sentinel*, September 21, 1967.
Lazenby, Roland. *Jerry West: The Life and Legend of a Basketball Icon*. New York: ESPN Books, 2010.
Leggett, William. "Basketball at Its Toughest." *Sports Illustrated*, February 25, 1963.
———. "A New Knick with a Knack." *Sports Illustrated*, April 17, 1966.
"Letter to the Editor." *Ebony*, March 1964.
Libby, Bill. "The Elgin Baylor Miracle." *SPORT*, November 1967.
———. *Mr. Clutch: The Jerry West Story*. New York: Prentice Hall, 1969.
Lynch, Wayne. *Season of the 76ers: The Story of Wilt Chamberlain and the 1967 NBA Champion Philadelphia 76ers*. New York: Thomas Dunne, 2002.
Pluto, Terry. *Tall Tales: The Glory Years of the NBA*. Lincoln, NE: Bison Books, 2000.
Robertson, Oscar. *The Big O: My Life, My Times, My Game*. Lincoln, NE: Bison Books, 2010.
Russell, Bill. "I Owe the Public Nothing." *Saturday Evening Post*, January 18, 1964.
———. "Success Is a Journey." *Sports Illustrated*, June 8, 1970.
Sammons, Jeffrey T. *Beyond the Ring: The Role of Boxing in American Society*. Champaign: University of Illinois Press, 1990.
Taylor, John. *The Rivalry: Bill Russell, Wilt Chamberlain, and the Golden Age of Basketball*. New York: Random House, 2006.
West, Jerry, with Jonathan Coleman. *West by West: My Charmed, Tormented Life*. New York: Little, Brown, 2011.
Whalen, Thomas J. *Dynasty's End: Bill Russell and the 1968–69 World Champion Boston Celtics*. Boston: Northeastern, 2005.
Wilkens, Lenny, with Terry Pluto. *Unguarded: My Forty Years Surviving in the NBA*. New York: Simon & Schuster, 2010.
"Words of the Week." *JET*, April 4, 1963.
Young, A. S. "Are Today's Athletes Too Dull?" *Negro Digest*, July 1962.
———. "Refreshing World of Sports." *Los Angeles Sentinel*, January 4, 1962.

CHAPTER 9

"Baylor Unhappy, Considers Jumping to ABA." *Los Angeles Times*, June 10, 1967.
"Celtics Win Seventh Straight Finals." *NBA.com*, May 31, 2010, http://www.nba.com/history/finals/19641965.html.
Cope, Myron. "Elgin Baylor Comes Back." *Ebony*, February 1965.
———. "Life with Elgin Baylor." *SPORT*, March 1963.
Deford, Frank. "A Tiger Who Can Beat Anything." *Sports Illustrated*, October 24, 1966.
———. "When the NBA Was Young." *Sports Illustrated*, April 23, 2012.
"Elgin Baylor Irked by Reports He's Washed Up." *Baltimore Afro-American*, March 14, 1964.

"Elgin Baylor Soared on the Court through Hard Work." *Hoops Nation*, May 11, 2013, http://hoops-nation.com/community/topic/73103-elgin-baylor-soared-on-the-court-through-hard-work-an-article/.

"Elgin Returns and Lakers Can Rejoice." *Los Angeles Times*, December 14, 1964.

Freedman, Lew. *Dynasty: The Rise of the Boston Celtics*. Guilford, CT: Lyons, 2008.

Goudsouzian, Aram. *King of the Court: Bill Russell and the Basketball Revolution*. Berkeley: University of California Press, 2011.

Gross, Milton. "Elgin Baylor and Basketball's Big Explosion." *SPORT*, April 1961.

Hafner, Dan. "Baylor Better Than Ever—Ask Him." *Los Angeles Times*, January 22, 1965.

———. "Baylor May Return as Good as Ever." *Los Angeles Times*, June 13, 1965.

———. "Baylor May Test Bad Knee Tonight." *Los Angeles Times*, November 26, 1965.

———. "Baylor to Test Knee in Laker Tussle Tonight." *Los Angeles Times*, September 18, 1965.

———. "Baylor, Wilt Interested in L.A. ABA Franchise." *Los Angeles Times*, June 13, 1967.

———. "When Lakers Are Down, They Look to Baylor for Lift." *Los Angeles Times*, February 15, 1966.

Hundley, Rod. *Hot Rod Hundley: You Gotta Love It Baby*. Urbana, IL: Sagamore, 1998.

"Lakers Romp—Baylor Ailing: Chest Cold Puts Elgin in Hospital." *Los Angeles Times*, December 13, 1963.

Libby, Bill. "The Elgin Baylor Miracle." *SPORT*, November 1967.

Libman, Gary. "No Time-Outs: Dr. Robert Kerlan Stays in the Game Despite Severe Arthritis." *Los Angeles Times*, September 14, 1992.

Murray, Jim. "Call Yourselves the Lakers." *Los Angeles Times*, January 15, 1965.

"Muscle Strain Will Sideline Baylor Tonight." *Los Angeles Times*, December 4, 1964.

Ostler, Scott, and Steve Springer. *Winnin' Times: The Magical Journey of the Los Angeles Lakers*. New York: Macmillan, 1986.

"The Pack Closes in on Boston." *Sports Illustrated*, October 26, 1964.

Pepe, Phil. *Greatest Stars of the NBA*. New York: Prentice Hall, 1970.

Pluto, Terry. *Tall Tales: The Glory Years of the NBA*. Lincoln, NE: Bison Books, 2000.

"Pro Basketball Roundup." *Ebony*, January 1964.

"Rick Barry: Basketball's New Box Office Baby." *Life*, January 6, 1967.

"Schaus Pleased." *Associated Press*, January 4, 1965.

Taylor, John. *The Rivalry: Bill Russell, Wilt Chamberlain, and the Golden Age of Basketball*. New York: Random House, 2006.

Travers, Steven. *The Good, the Bad, and the Ugly Los Angeles Lakers: Heart-Pounding, Jaw-Dropping, and Gut-Wrenching Moments from Los Angeles Lakers History*. Chicago: Triumph, 2007.

Underwood, John. "A Smashing Hurrah for the Lakers." *Sports Illustrated*, February 8, 1965.

CHAPTER 10

Cherry, Robert. *Wilt: Larger Than Life*. Chicago: Triumph, 2004.

Deford, Frank. "A Tiger Who Can Beat Anything." *Sports Illustrated*, October 24, 1966.

Florence, Mal. "Age Factor Doesn't Bug Baylor." *Los Angeles Times*, April 19, 1968.

Freedman, Lew. *Dynasty: The Rise of the Boston Celtics*. Guilford, CT: Lyons, 2008.

Goudsouzian, Aram. *King of the Court: Bill Russell and the Basketball Revolution*. Berkeley: University of California Press, 2011.

Hafner, Dan. "Baylor Credits Fast Start to Wilt's Presence." *Los Angeles Times*, October 29, 1968.

———. "Baylor Sees Several More Years as Laker." *Los Angeles Times*, January 25, 1968.

———. "Baylor Settles Contract Woes with Lakers." *Los Angeles Times*, September 14, 1967.

———. "Wilt's Rebounding Serves to Keep Baylor Youthful." *Los Angeles Times*, November 8, 1968.

"Lakers Make Elg Happy." *Los Angeles Sentinel*, September 21, 1967.
Lazenby, Roland. *Jerry West: The Life and Legend of a Basketball Icon*. New York: ESPN
    Books, 2010.
————. *The NBA Finals: A Fifty-Year Celebration*. Indianapolis, IN: Masters Press, 1996.
Murray, Jim. "Elgin Baylor's Alive, Playing at the Forum." *Los Angeles Times*, April 22, 1969.
"NBA: Goodbye to the Old Balance of Power." *Sports Illustrated*, October 24, 1969.
Pluto, Terry. *Tall Tales: The Glory Years of the NBA*. Lincoln, NE: Bison Books, 2000.
Smith, Dave. "NBA Finals Notes." *TheSportsGod.com*, June 6, 2010, http://thesportsgod.com/
    2010/06/.
Taylor, John. *The Rivalry: Bill Russell, Wilt Chamberlain, and the Golden Age of Basketball*.
    New York: Random House, 2006.
Whalen, Thomas J. *Dynasty's End: Bill Russell and the 1968–69 World Champion Boston
    Celtics*. Boston: Northeastern, 2005.
Wright, Alfred. "For the Lakers, the Season Still Lies Ahead." *Sports Illustrated*, March 16,
    1970.

CHAPTER 11

"Baylor Says Wilt Has a Problem: 'He Can't Coach': Baylor Raps Wilt." *Los Angeles Times*,
    October 5, 1973.
"Baylor Shocked at Firing; Hints at Other NBA Job." *JET*, May 2, 1974.
"Baylor Takes Pro Coaching Job as New Orleans Assistant." *Los Angeles Times*, September
    12, 1974.
Chandler, Rick. "Celtics and Sam Jones: Estranged Relationship?" *Sports by Brooks*, Novem-
    ber 3, 2009, http://www.sportsbybrooks.com/celtics-and-sam-jones-estranged-relationship-
    26798.
"Elgin Baylor Takes the Job." *Los Angeles Times*, December 17, 1976.
Federman, Wayne. *Maravich*. Wilmington, DE: SportsClassic Books, 2006.
Finney, Peter. "So Long, Butch: The Amateurs Have Taken over the Jazz." *New Orleans
    States-Item*, December 14, 1976.
"Jazz Signs Elgin Baylor to 2-Year, $80G Contract." *Baltimore Afro-American*, December 25,
    1976.
Kriegel, Mark. *Pistol: The Life of Pete Maravich*. New York: Free Press, 2008.
Libby, Bill. *Mr. Clutch: The Jerry West Story*. New York: Prentice Hall, 1969.
Review of the News, 1977.

CHAPTER 12

Adande, J. A. "Legal Filings Show Frustration of Clipper GMs." *ESPN.com*, January 6, 2011,
    http://espn.go.com/blog/truehoop/post/_/id/23649/legal-filings-show-frustration-of-clipper-
    gms.
Cherner, Reid. "Elgin Baylor Talks about Donald Sterling's 'Plantation Mentality.'" *USA
    Today*, November 9, 2010.
Dillman, Lisa. "Lawsuit Window into Elgin Baylor, Clippers, and Donald Sterling." *Los An-
    geles Times*, November 12, 2010.
"Donald Sterling to Pay $2.725 Million to Settle Housing Discrimination Lawsuit." *Los An-
    geles Times/LA NOW*, November 2009.
Malamud, Allan. "Notes on a Scorecard." *Los Angeles Times*, December 17, 1991.
Murray, Jim. "Great Moves for Him Easier on the Court." *Los Angeles Times*, December 22,
    1991.

Ostler, Scott. "Elgin Baylor Is Offered a Job in the Clippers' Front Office." *Los Angeles Times*, June 16, 1984.
Pugmire, Lance. "Sterling Testifies He Knew Little of Elgin Baylor's Career When He Hired Him." *Los Angeles Times*, March 15, 2011.

CHAPTER 13

Boyd, Todd, and Kenneth L. Shropshire, eds. *Basketball Jones: America Above the Rim*. New York: New York University Press, 2000.
Chamberlain, Wilt, with David Shaw. *Wilt: Just Like Any Other 7-Foot Black Millionaire Who Lives Next Door*. New York: Macmillan, 1973.
Colston, Chris. "Twenty-Second Time-out: Julius Erving's Starting Five." *USA Today*, July 14, 2008.
Frazier, Walt. *Rockin' Steady: A Guide to Basketball and Cool*. Englewood Cliffs, NJ: Prentice Hall, 1974. Reprint, Triumph. 2010.
Hollander, Dave. *52 Weeks: Interviews with Champions*. Guilford, CT: Lyons, 2006.
Jackson, Scoop. "Original Old School: The Truth, the Whole Truth, and Nothing but the Truth." *SLAM*, November 2010.
Jordan, Michael. *For the Love of the Game: My Story*. New York: Crown, 1998.
Lloyd, Earl, and Sean Kirst. *Moonfixer: The Basketball Journey of Earl Lloyd*. Syracuse, NY: Syracuse University Press, 2011.
Lynch, Wayne. *Season of the 76ers: The Story of Wilt Chamberlain and the 1967 NBA Champion Philadelphia 76ers*. New York: Thomas Dunne, 2002.
McKenna, Dave. "Elgin Baylor, Won't You Please Come Home?" *Washington City Paper*, March 23, 2011.
———. "Wilt vs. Elgin: When the World Was Their Playground." *Grantland.com*, August 28, 2012, http://grantland.com/features/the-legendary-pickup-basketball-games-wilt-chamberlain-elgin-baylor-late-1950s-washington-dc/.
Murray, Jim. "Great Moves for Him Easier on the Court." *Los Angeles Times*, December 22, 1991.
Sabin, Lou. "Rick Barry: The Golden Warrior." *Boys Life*, January 1976.
Simmons, Bill. "Elgin Took the Game to New Heights." *ESPN.com*, October 8, 2008, http://sports.espn.go.com/espn/page2/story?page=simmons/081008.
Sokolove, Michael. "Clang!" *New York Times Magazine*, February 13, 2005.
Travers, Steven. *The Good, the Bad, and the Ugly Los Angeles Lakers: Heart-Pounding, Jaw-Dropping, and Gut-Wrenching Moments from Los Angeles Lakers History*. Chicago: Triumph, 2007.
Wise, Mike. "Is Kevin Durant the Best Washington, D.C., Basketball Player Ever?" *Washington Post*, June 13, 2012.

INDEX

ABOUT THE AUTHOR

Bijan C. Bayne is an award-winning Washington-based freelance columnist and critic and author of *Sky Kings: Black Pioneers of Professional Basketball*, which was named to the Suggested Reading List of the Basketball Hall of Fame in 2004. His work has appeared in *Salon*, the *Washington Post*, *Essence*, the *Boston Herald*, and *SLAM*.